Cyrus Augustus Bartol

Radical Problems

Cyrus Augustus Bartol

Radical Problems

ISBN/EAN: 9783744652803

Printed in Europe, USA, Canada, Australia, Japan

Cover: Foto ©ninafisch / pixelio.de

More available books at **www.hansebooks.com**

Radical Problems.

BY

C. A. BARTOL.

BOSTON:
ROBERTS BROTHERS.
1872.

CAMBRIDGE:

PRESS OF JOHN WILSON AND SON.

CONTENTS.

RADICAL PROBLEMS.

OPEN QUESTIONS.

WHAT legislators sometimes say is true of all questions: they may be divided. Life looks like a page disfigured with interrogation-points; and every answer breeds new curiosity, as if it were a polyp. The child is an incarnate question, posing all his elders; and the widening circle of light subtends such a broader round of darkness as to give color to the old sage's remark, — "One thing I know, that God hates inquisitiveness;" while many, like Lord Bacon, value investigation superficially for its results of utility, despairing of absolute truth. But experience and memory are tests that all inquiry is intrinsically precious. I call to mind a college excursion with the mathematical professor, to measure with instruments, by triangulation, the distance between some towns in Maine. How far it was I have long since forgot, but not the wonderful delight of the experiment, the new dignity of the search for hill-tops of observation, nor the cup of tamarind water a good woman, honoring our errand, gave to the thirsty, foot-sore wanderers by the way. We are glad at every solution of a problem; yet queries are the intellectual miser's hoard, in whose satisfaction by successful study he would not rejoice, but that other queries take their place. I fancy a shade of sadness tinged the exultation of Columbus when the Western hemisphere showed signs of its neighborhood to his vessel, to unbury the mystery of the deep, and give an interpretation to the magnificent dream he had so soon to exchange for ungrateful facts. To guess pleases as to find out the conundrum, riddle, or buried city. Our first conception equals in pleasure any verification. The hen is not happier among the brood she is so anxious about than in her nest; and in the mind's incubation there are no heavy hours, but Time blends with Eternity, so deep and peaceful is its flow.

In all pursuit there is a certain dignity. The money-making we despise is nobler than profuseness, and is often not avarice of acquisition, but activity of worthy powers; so that a sincere Crœsus said, if his children had as much comfort in spending as he in accumulating his fortune, he should be content. It is a pulpit lamentation, as shallow as it is doleful, that we are but getting ready to live, as also that poet line, —

"Man never is, but always to be blest."

Let me join the enterprise, share who will the fruit! To go with Cortes was better than Mexican gold; and my friend's expedition to Alaska is of more worth than any plant or precious fur. You buy your land and build your house, arrange the orchard and trim the garden-grounds, and then expect your reward. Foolish, if you count on any recompense sweeter than you had as you went along! No peach or pear will be more delicious than your thought in setting out the trees. My neighbor grew weary of his perfect situation, and wanted to cross the bay and occupy a lonelier point.

There is a movement-cure for the mind. Of one not established in his views, it is said in pity, "He is all afloat;" as if that were not the best condition, grander and safer than to be ashore, — as if there were a finer spectacle of ships in port than of the yacht-squadron racing along the coast, or the grating of my keel on the beach could be such transport as to be rocked in my boat on the waves. The anchor, said one, is a true emblem: it holds the vessel fast, though it does not hold the vessel still. But the eternal heaving underneath is a signal that the true state is to hoist at the windlass, and away; and no figure of Hope leaning on the fluke is just to its nature of exploration without end. There is provision for further growth in the bones of the skull and organs of the brain after the sutures are closed: let there be space to expand in the hardest understanding.

Freedom is not caprice, but room to enlarge. There is a certain shock from the pavement to whoever returns from roaming among the mountains or by the sea. The city streets, like broad curtains or enormous window-blinds, shut us in; and we feel robbed of the elements — light, air, earth, and water — which make the liberty of our frame, and are better than any physician's medicine-chest for every nervous disease. We want not only so much sun and oxygen as can be got into a chamber, the drink a bottle will hold, and ground enough, like a caged tiger, to pace to and fro in, — but to breathe the whole atmosphere, behold the sky full of radiance, put our lips to the living spring, and have no goal for our feet. Civilization increases liberty, which is not, as jurists say, its price. When institutions become bounds, the soul is cramped. Forms and ordinances multiplied and made essential to salvation feel sepulchral, like some walled town of Quebec whose old defences stand against enemies long since passed away. All creeds and rituals are on the defensive against benefactors who open the question of their truth, and stop them with a challenge for the loyal pass-word. Jesus well prescribed for our communication, *nay*, *nay*, as well as *yea*, *yea*. I admired the little girl who to my questions rolled out a succession of clear *noes* round as a revolver's bullets, — a sign that the footing I should be on with her would never become a swamp of good-nature; and was pleased with the yearling boy who said, plain as he could, "Hands off!" to those who would seize him, issued his declaration of independence that he was no lump of dough to be kneaded, but a block of marble to be turned into beauty by some artist's skill. Establishments must answer for themselves to him by and by!

The dogmatic look is stupid; the inquiring, bright, like that of people eager in the chase. So we can explain the extreme changes in the same countenances. How uninteresting when they are close, with nothing to impart or receive, like the shut bivalve on the tideless flats! People who have made up their minds, and are fixed, as they say, resemble merchants taking account of stock, or householders making an inventory of their goods, instead of venturing bold purchase, exercising hospitality, or driving a brisk trade. Light-houses by day are useless for guides; and your system of theology, which no ever-burning thought illuminates, is an old vase or lantern that lost its lamp long ago. I observe the face of that young woman settling upon the lees of religious reflection, — how plain and ugly the features are! Anon she comes to me, earnest in study, ready to compare notes, and so handsome I cannot believe my own eyes.

We are made for spiritual progress. Our organism hints for its object perpetuation of the race. But the easy propagation of vulgar specimens, and the number of noble members of mankind without posterity; the decease of genius and virtue leaving no issue, though the trustees of those shining glories have descendants also from their loins; or the too much or little of some parental element, giving insanity, eccentricity, or idiocy, instead of the expected soundness, — force us to conclude there are ends beside earthly inheritance and continuance. Jesus and Paul and Washington have no heirs; and to how many might Shakspeare's sonnets to one who was cheating the world with barren singleness be addressed! Without intentions of development outreaching fleshly designs, men would come down to the level of animals and plants. In the unfolding of truth is the honor of our species and the immortality of every soul; and for this all questions of truth must be opened. One thing is sacred, — the sincere thought; and the being of God, character of Jesus, ultimacy of Christianity, reality of heaven, must be discussed. If, in the old Bible hyperbole, the scheme of redemption is so fine the angels desire to look into it, surely we are not forbid.

Doubtless, in the wide charter of freedom, offensive and extravagant things will be said. The remedy is not to mind them. Defy incendiaries not by watchmen and engines, but by building fire-proof! Why be troubled everybody does not think like you of Christ? Tell the defamer of your Master his battery is too weak or your constitution too strong for a shock. Not only children, but childish opinions, are the better for a little wholesome neglect. Irrational rationalists, rootless radicals, and infidels for pride or prominence of unbelief, are to be let severely alone. Only they who have something to say are, with refutation or welcome, to be met. Set your castle-walls and windows too high for the malicious to bombard or break with stones. Are you disturbed by a doctrine? Surely it has ground! There must have been something in the book, or Paine's "Age of Reason" would not have hurt so much or lasted so long. Calvin would not have burnt Servetus could he have otherwise answered his argument. Jonathan Mayhew said the foes of freemen in Church and State, in default of logic, knocked out their brains, and so furnished an effectual reply. That man, you say, is a common scold. Take no notice of him, if you would give him better than he sends. Recrimination of others criminates you, and is the recriminator's proof. Solomon says a fretful wife is like a bitter rain. Let her rain under as it rains on the roof, and heed either storm alike! Oaths and remonstrances in the street are answered every day by not stopping to parley, but simply keeping on. You resist only when wrestled with: the most terrible are the speechless retorts. What an iconoclast! you say. I see not that he breaks any thing. He is impotent who bolts or is schismatic without cause. Outrageous expressions! you declare. I am not outraged. The community is not absorbed in the barking of dogs. Treat the irritable controversialist, who makes a question of every statement, as travellers do the brainless cur who thinks it his duty to run every moment and growl at the gate. I walk right by the guns on the Common bellowing so loud, that have no shot in them for all the noise and blaze, and despised the loud manifesto of a farmer's dog when I learned he had no teeth, though I saw some boys in an English preserve scared by a canine monster alike destitute; and there are critics that mouth and bay, but draw no blood. I suspect the dogs Paul told his friends to beware of had something to say, or could bite.

So God himself sets limits to the objector in the weakness of the objection, and dispenses us from all need to bridle others' tongues, or, like Louis Napoleon with his throne of bayonets, to muzzle the press. Truth cannot be disproved, purity cannot be libelled, nor wisdom overthrown. Repression of free inquiry is not too much ridiculed in the proverb that a cat may look upon a king. I thought, said one, our house in the great September gale would go, till I remembered it was founded on a rock. A basis in the eternal rock who can shake? Pay not folly the compliment of fear. It takes a deep sound to reverberate. What you do not echo, do not dread.

But conservatives distinguish between questions of science and questions of faith: the first are open; not the last, which no theories of nature can affect. To all criticisms of the Scripture history or cosmogony one answer is made: that the Bible does not mean to teach natural knowledge. Doubtless the sentiment of faith lies deeper than the understanding which the peace of God passes. Yet *articles* of faith are amenable to the intellect. We distinguish that, too, as a general power, from any logical conclusions. But it is not true that any feeling is independent of the judgment. Jesus bids us love God with all our mind as well as heart; and the Divine way, not our imperceptiveness, is the basis of our trust. We are learning that horses do not travel better, with more courage or safety, for blinders; and the soul is no swifter for duty or loftier in aspiration for being hoodwinked. Ignorance is not the mother of devotion, but of superstition and obsequious flattery; not of service, but of servility. We worship the King in the world he makes his crystal palace. Has our idea of the building nought to do with our prayer? Had a Ptolemaist as much cause to ascribe glory to God as a Copernican? If to Alphonso creation was on the old notion so misfashioned he thought he could, if present, have given the Creator useful hints, his regard for the Architect must have been lessened by the faults of the house, which Schopenhauer held so enormous he saw nothing to praise, and could not adore at all, leaving us a book not deserving to be opened, and a portrait we should fain turn to the wall, save that the pessimist was so honest and brave. The Deity in Genesis that made such short business of the world, doing it up in six days, — like some master workman, called a driver because he gets through and throws off so many affairs in the twenty-four hours, or a jobber stopping a moment, then off on some other errand, like Jehu with his team, — wins not the reverence we pay to Him who works in spaces no geometry can measure, and through periods no numerals can express.

Faith not touched by sight, taking no guidance or glory from the eye of the mind? The God that commanded Abraham to sacrifice his son, or prompted Jacob to plot with his mother to rob Esau by practising on father Isaac with his anachronism of false hair, — there are people not a few, and ever becoming more, who cannot believe. The old altar-fires are gone out, and we can no more go back to the Hebrew notions than to the lambs and goats of their sacrifice. Science is to be minister in the new temple not completed yet, and will bring abundant fuel to the shrine to feed the flame. The one Jehovah of the Jews, presiding over a narrow province, is expanding to the manifold Pervader of an infinite sphere. His unity is verified by analogies, of whose extent and clearness Moses or Jesus gave no hint, but modern investigation shows the universe kindling and alive with. When from the leafing of plants to the orbits of planets a law of relation is traced, the words, *I am, and there is none beside me*, gather a wider sense than in their first utterance. As the soft aurora and the rending thunder suggest a common electricity, whose spending is followed by cold, we catch a glimpse of threads that stretch through the firmament and sew all parts of

God's live garment together finer than any handiwork or conception of man.

The keeping open of the questions has, more than any closure of them, promoted piety. Religion would have been crushed, if not quenched, by any authority to solve them at whatever Hebrew or Christian time. Could terms of salvation have been written down, and the plenary verbal inspirationists have succeeded in the final settlement they undertook, the Church would have been banished from the circle of light, degraded below the arena of controversy, and dismissed from the region of intelligence as no subject of reason, but a motive to grovel and cringe like abject savages in a fit of terror, too gloomy to be streaked with the twilight of doubt for a reminder and herald of the dawn. If we would be rid of denial, danger, and despair, we must keep every thing open: the conventicle, communion, caucus, hall, and railway track, whose clogging by some untimely train is occasion of ruin and death. The thought of vast assemblies for musical celebrations of peace and international friendship — nobler than that division of the spoils at which the so-called *Internationals*, are, let us trust, falsely understood to aim — has had such fortune as to be accepted now for an inspiration, till we at last invite to wave together amid strains of harmony the flags of all the kingdoms and republics of the earth, type of a Commune worthy to have. Faith must not in its proportions fall below the generosity of amusement and politics, or lag in corners out of sight. Let the Dogmatist give place to the Liberal! When Jesus represents the Judge as setting the goats on the left hand, he may refer not to the lascivious but stubborn nature of the beast, which even in tender years rears on its hinder legs to butt at your kindest approach. If the bigots are so typified, they will turn up in unexpected places. Let them reasonably suffer the love that would emancipate them from their fetters; and not, like the cross cow I saw, hook the benefactor that would untether the bonds from their own feet.

Free inquiry is more than a prerogative of one man against the interference of another. The variety of questions we ask, as of wants we feel, is the length of our scale, and measures the dignity of our being: let us pity the angels if, as we are told, they have found out the secret of Nature and know all. The animals seem to inquire little, and may be classified according to the signs they show, in their several tribes, of wishing to learn. The summer-flies stiffen, curl up, and wither in the autumn wind, without any apparent queries what death is, or any dread of their fate. Their incuriosity marks the degree of their inferiority. Our interest in the subject, our constitution to entertain the problem, Job's desire to understand, *If a man die, shall he live again?* — is the token of immortality; for it is no creation of our will, no fiction of man, but the instigation of God, who hints nothing he will not carry out. Shall not the lower creatures we lord it over, and are so cruel to, have his vindication also? The cook told the complaining duck, "Do not cry: all these things will be explained to you by and by." Of how much we are as ignorant as the bird seized in the barn-yard, or under the doom of the fowler's gun!

Every theological system or sect is an attempt to close questions; and every prophet's word a new eruption through the old crust of conventionality. The denominations are so many extinct craters, only like Ætna or Vesuvius showing signs of activity, and every little while breaking out afresh. What is the deadest conservatism is only a short lull, a temporary sleep. Like the son of Agamemnon, the searching mind comes terrible to purify. Unitarianism, Universalism, Episcopacy, the English Church, and the Romish, are all rumbling with pent-up commotions, and out of the fiery contention in their own bowels ready to throw up, like the *aiguilles* round Mont Blanc, rival summits of belief; and any undertaking to shut up and seal the questions respecting God and man and heaven, Bible or Saviour, prophecy or worship, is like chaining down the safety-valve of the engine or binding too tight the breathing-holes of the globe. Destructive explosions, earthquakes that swallow up cities, ensue.

But is every thing left at loose ends like a feather on the wind? No: questions of doctrine must be open, but questions of conscience closed before the day passes, and the opportunity is lost. No moral problem has many links. Open questions in a house about trivial matters are like open wounds. Of what bits we build our heavy cross! Do not spend the day discussing whether you shall drive or walk, invite a guest or accept an invitation, wear white or black, write a letter, rub out a spot, be on speaking terms with a neighbor, or have honest acquaintance with any woman or man. Time is valuable, nerves are precious. "I cannot," said a man, making thousands every day, "consume my strength in debates with boys whether they shall steal my grapes or run across my shed." Have no open questions to quarrel about and generate in your affections chronic disease. It is better to decide a case wrongly than to get into a wrong state of mind. You are sincere and conscientious in your respective views: do not, therefore, be tyrannical to insist and urge them past all patience, and reopen the topic for bickering without cessation or fruit. Make not your conscience a torment. The worst thing in the world may be a man's conscience, or what, like Launcelot Gobbo, it is his humor to call such. His sting is not that of the bee laden with honey, but the barren wasp. As lief have a hornet buzzing round your ears, or gad-fly searching for the sore spot, as a domestic or social critic falling fatally on your weak side. A duellist may be pardoned for finding out the armor's open joint or inexpert pass of his adversary; but there should be no challenge between friends. Spare in your associate, him or her that leans on your bosom, the tender place. Aggravate not already existing inflammation, but heal and soothe. "Dwelling together in unity is like ointment," says the Psalmist: there is no salve like silence, and no blister of mustard or Spanish flies equal to a fresh plaster of interrogatory words. I do not wonder the poor Malay sailor begged the captain either to whip or scold him, but not do both together; for that, like the multiplication-table to Marjorie Fleming, is what human nature cannot endure. People are prosecuted for assault and battery; but the language they fling is harder than their fists. It is against the law for private persons to carry arms; but what stiletto or pistol is so dangerous as a tongue? It is harder to hold than a bull by the horns. I fancy that excellent actor, Walter Montgomery, followed to England by the woman of ill repute, declaring she would be his wife, who two days after the wedding destroyed himself, whatever she suffered at his hands, suffered something from her lips. Little vexations, more than enormous crimes, lay waste our joy, and turn life from a boon to a ban. They say the Inquisition is abolished: it has an emissary in every house. The mosquito has an open question whether he shall insert his lancet, and take his fill of your blood, which, to settle the matter, you might freely let him do, but for the host of his peers on a like surgical errand behind; and there is a sort of mosquito-mind always alert to consider where most to your disadvantage, and the security of its satisfaction against your comfort, it can make its petty attack. Be not that name for Satan, the *accuser* of your brethren. Put your conscience to private use. Keep it in your closet for a probe, not unsheathe it as a sword. The unhealthy action of the human frame is rightly called disorder: what shall be said of those that disease us with their moral complaints and uncharitable judgments? They are authors of the worst maladies, and most contagious. Our Orthodox friends well bid us beware of the plague of our own heart; for it is catching, whether yellow fever and cholera be so or not. Does anybody in your circle desire to lead? Let him not communicate to you that itch! Ivy or the wild sumach is not poisonous to some vigorous people. But we do not plant the shrub or vine at our door-sill: we give a wide berth to the deadly night-shade, even in the pasture; and we learn to avoid folks who envenom us with their manners and speech, and by their very glance disturb, as some cannot look at or brush by the evil plant but their skin will prick and swell. "This creature worries the life out of me," said one, of a dog biting and scratching only in play. But ill-temper has worse teeth and claws; and, of all the gifts distributed among human beings, the least to be coveted is the positive genius some disputatious persons have for making everybody unhappy, dealing in questions only, and accepting no one's reply.

Questions of action and disposition are somehow, at length, to be closed. I must decide if I am going in the cars or the steamer. If any temper of envy or jealousy enter the lists and contest the prize, it will be master or I shall. To settle moral questions is safe; for no man ever *decided* to be a drunkard or profligate, however sin take advantage of his indecision to make him a slave. Foster's Essay on Decision of *Character* was wise.

But questions of doctrine cannot be wholly closed; because, first, words are inadequate to express all the truth. Some conclusions about finite things abide beyond any power to shake. Kepler's and Newton's laws of attraction hold like theorems in the mathematics. The effects of food and poison on the human system are demonstrable, though it is disputed if alcohol be food or medicine. The physiological and intellectual analogies run further between man and the brute with every day's investigation; and plants disclose similitudes reminding one of the classic Dryads and voices of trees complaining when the limbs were torn. Iron, in the shape of filings about the roots, is given to a pear-tree to prevent or cure a disease appearing as spots on the fruit, — just the tonic the doctor prescribes to his patient; and lime strengthens it as it does our teeth and bones, while it drinks every day, or like an animated creature dies of thirst. But when we come to inquire what God is, or the soul is, or life or death is, or what we are before or after our mortality, our most earnest convictions cannot be precipitated as a solution or projected like a chart. They refuse the confinement of a creed. The longevity of a dog or horse, eagle or elephant, is fixed; but of a spirit there is no report. There are no terms to express it, or our persuasions about it, unless we have made up our mind that this mind is a mode of matter, the phosphorescence of decay, like some vegetable and animal particles ceasing to shine when it ceases to rot. We can compass the definite with ease. What is done in secret or whispered in the ear in closets will come abroad and be published on the house-top; for an occurrence is impossible to hide, or a noise to be unheard. Do not tell anybody, we whisper. It is a vain request! It will be known because it is a fact; and every fact is matter of knowledge. But the celestial realities defy aught but a hint in speech. Because, says the sceptic, they are so vague, have no solidity more than moonshine. But is *moonshine* nothing? Is it less than the stiff and ponderous clod?

"How sweet the moonlight sleeps upon this bank!"

Lorenzo in the play showed Jessica all the orbs of heaven in tune; and the glories of paradise gleam through this same moonshine, as you call it, of the mind, though you can make no medium for this light, and no conductor for this lightning, of a phrase. Is it all in the Bible? As well say the electricity of Nature is collected in a Leyden jar, that coined money has exhausted the mines of Nevada, or some cabinet contains all the jewels of God.

Spiritual questions must be open, secondly, because of honest difference of belief, — open between diverse persons as in every single mind. Attempts to force conformity on the ground of the unity of truth imply our possession of it, delinquency in whoever rejects our results, and the right to inflict penalties for disagreement as a crime. Shall there be for the iniquity of intolerance no punishment? The inquisitor shall come to question at last. Sure as God ordains sincerity of manifold conclusions, the hierarchs will reach a sore pass when the blood of heretics shall call for judgment after long crying. From prisons underground, and tombs they were walled into, above it they shall ascend as shapes of prophets, for sentence not from the oppressor's but the victim's mouth. Sometime I shall exercise the right you deny. Resurrection of the body! A poor boon God grant I may be spared! The rising shall be of the soul in every faculty, and of that best of its parts, free inquiry. The questions choked off and strangled, hushed with the voices that put them, shall return with imperial dignity of divine permission and a prerogative of eternal satisfaction; and "what we know not now we shall know hereafter," though other, greater things to be known, suspected and half seen, tempt and beckon us on. It will appear that Thought did not perish on a cross, and Freedom was not choked on a scaffold, and Humanity was not beheaded with a sword; that of many notes God made the music false pretenders to his confidence branded as discord; and that heaven is no monotony, but, like an earthly performer's, the great Harmonizer's skill is measured by the reach of keys he can command.

The third reason for keeping questions open is room for growth. A small plant is put in a large pot for that spread of the roots which will support the spread of the boughs: and truths are living things that have no fixed or final shape and never get their growth. They stop only when turned to timber and lumber of creeds. If we must have sharply cut opinions to make a house, let us, like tasteful builders, leave green groves of thrifty speculation round our dogmatic precincts. Fell not the whole forest: spare branches of beauty, and boundless woods of mystery. Reduce not this marvellous universe to pure intellectual property, but let wonder and worship have wild and tangled wildernesses to rove in. The Cape-Ann farmer, to win a few more acres of tillage, laid low the pine-trees that girdled his land from the sea, and found too late that the zone of grace was a belt of strength. The north-east winds and waves — avenging furies against making merchandise of Nature — blew the sands in long hillocks for the burial of his whole estate. What but deeper selfishness, exposing to direr retribution, is it to convert truth to a title-deed of salvation and ticket to a celestial seat. Truth is a thing to adore, to live and die for; and, if it will not rescue, rejoice it counts us worthy in its cause to be cast away. But its service is our privilege, and no sacrifice. Nobody ever gave to it so much as it returned. You may survey its field, run the bounds of your persuasions, limit your inquiries, and stereotype your prayers, when you have measured the cords and stakes of the Lord's pavilion. Not an idea but should be ever aggrandized, most of all your idea of the Divinity. An unchangeable God? He should change continually in that greater revelation which is your growing up to him, as Nature changes to the learner, as Niagara to the gazer, as your friend changes to your better appreciation, as you change with all aspiration and culture, as the horizon changes while you mount. "Beauty fled from the eye," writes Rénan of Palestine, "through the gorges of the hills." So of divine beauty we follow the flight.

But some things are sealed. Whether a man shall love his wife, or a woman her husband, is not an open question. Some clergymen will not exact, nor some brides and bridegrooms make the promise to love, on the ground that love is not in a person's own power. The noble religions of all ages are under a mistake! Judaism and Christianity falsely meet in the first *commandment* of the love of God, and the second, to "love our neighbor as ourself," was but an additional mockery from the Master's lips; and as all the law and the prophets hang on these, the whole fabric of worship and morals must give way, and tumble in ruin for the sophistry of sense. This is called affinity.

It is chemistry indeed, above its scope of senseless atoms, in the vital sphere. In Goethe's story of Elective Affinities, with whatever licentious implications, death is preferred to sin. It was left for later teachers to deny that love is a duty,. and baptize inclination with sanctity, on the pretence that the affections suffer no control. Such immorality prepense is worse than yielding to sudden temptation. What libertine wants a better apotheosis! Many a man, not of the Mormons, has any number of free loves in a shifting polygamy, without Solomon's or Brigham Young's responsibility. The foundations of marriage are an open question, but not any husband's or wife's fidelity. It is time for the policeman if it be. Whether I shall love my wife or my wife me a subject of discussion? The man that hesitates is adulterous, the woman that deliberates is lost. Love at my option? Love is a law. Am I at liberty not to love God? I am no more bound to love my Maker than my partner or child. Love is free as a planet not to leave its orbit; and the Free Love that refuses the gravitation of order is a crime and a curse, retain what male or female pleader it will. Alas! that woman should advocate looseness, — woman that has been, more than man, the victim of changing fancy, and would find in larger independence no emancipation for her sex, but the aggravation of its woes. But note the fundamental mistake of this doctrine of easy divorce. It is the delusion that the object of marriage is pleasure, the common-place question being if one party is going to make the other happy; and, if either fails, the missed joy may be sought elsewhere. But the design of no relation of life is gratification, otherwise than by abnegation. Government, religion, society, is discipline as well as comfort: the wedded state is the same; and whosoever seeks in it a paradise of satisfied wishes will be turned out of Eden with a flaming sword, like Adam and Eve. Love cannot be quite housed or fenced in. But true affection without or under the roof is no roving, but a requirement; and he who imagines his regards may be flung round as a prince scatters coin among a crowd makes them a beggarly thing, and squanders the treasury of the King. Every farthing of sentiment in my soul is his property: I am but in trust, and must answer for each item of expenditure and atom of waste. Yet how the flood-gates of indulgence swing! It is time to arouse to an assailant more than robbers threatening the common weal: against the deluge of wild propensity, bulwarks and breakwaters of principle are more important than dykes at the inrush of seas, or props for crumbling hills. Consult the common list of crimes. Whence the murders and suicides that make the daily sheet ghastly, but from inordinate desires? Whence the sympathy for the criminal, which Dr. Wayland said forgets the victim, but from overlooking obligations as essential to progress as the ties of a railway; till murderers, of either sex, are recommended to the mercy they never showed, as if justice were not kindness to all men, and unfair or unadministered laws cruelty. Dreadful as is capital punishment, as yet the shadow of the gallows must remain. Hang a woman? Yes: that is one of the privileges she shares in the new age with man, if she be unsafe alive.

For free preach lawful love! None other in the universe has title. God's love is his law: he has no liberty or right, such as Calvinism would give him, to hate or forsake his children, nor allows their license to leave each other. We are under bonds, and shall have no bail. If you cannot promise to love, do not wed. If I am priest, I give notice I shall exact the vow, which one good woman insisted I should make on her part also to obey. Be married with a ring, if its gold circle be any wise an added link. An absent husband lost his ring, which he said he would rather go home without his finger than not find. Is it on your finger in vain? Love is a good ship, freighted with human welfare: send her not out with sails and streamers only on this stormier than Atlantic sea of our mortal life, but with cables of principle and rudder of a righteous will. Care for the coming race! If married people may, for selfish delight, violate their pledge, what is the lesson to the young, whose warmer passion has no legal block? Hold to your covenant for the sake of your kind. Of liberty we have for the present heard about enough. The dose will last! Tell us of loyalty now. Bismarck to the politicians said, "Is it not well first to ask of our duties?" when they tired him with talking about their rights. We hear the French are strict with the young, but permit the yoked to do as they list. Well, these latitudinarians in America had better emigrate to the city whose majority is said to be of illegitimate birth. Relaxed authority is our ailment. All our relations are lightly worn. Judas, though single and cut off by suicide, has left a numerous tribe; and the circle in Dante's hell for traitors must be enlarged. I have lived through two generations to doubt if that one old sin is less common, — desertion; and to thank those who did not abandon me. Time, that tries all things, is for our friendships what a sieve! There is the marble sculptor, carving epitaphs at the corner of the street; but every one of us has a business large as his in our heart. Well, if an image of the resurrection be formed by the inward chisel! Happy, if the true-hearted exceed those who have failed! Let it be no open question if you are such. Let your constancy outlast any stamp on the document.

Whether to assume the holy estate of matrimony is a question kept open by too many in our land, perhaps by the at present agitated relations of men and women held in abeyance or suspense. But whether to discharge its offices, to meditate an escape from its relations, to have illicit intercourse, or, with what has been called anatomical purity, cleave in imagination to a coveted mate not your own, is not open to any soul.

Confound not open questions with closed. Ecclesiastical or political tyranny, like a retreating host, makes successive stands, as Lee at Gettysburg fought and ran by turns. But the categorical imperative of Duty holds its own. What engagement to enter into is open, but not whether it shall be kept; while to some obligations we are born. It is getting to be settled that mankind is one community, and a man may choose his country with no arm of iron despotism to reach across the sea, impress him into a ship or reclaim him to war for his native soil; but it does not remain for him to say whether he will be a good citizen of the republic in which he stays. The secessionist was doomed already, at Sumter as much as at Richmond, in declaring in Liberty's name his withdrawal. My friend yonder, the monarchist in New England, has but this alternative, — to emigrate, or be a cipher where he lives; while the revolutionist opens the question of government not in orderly debate, but appealing to force. But "the blood-red blossom of war" is a century-plant not considered in regular culture.

The administration, democratic or republican, is open to question and suspicion, if it hide from criticism and hush up abuse. Power tends to corruption, needs watching and calling to account; for party is partiality, to be mistrusted if it cry out when its doings are looked into; and all New York politicians want is secrecy for tracks of fraud whose uncovering astounds the land. Why is politics a name for uncleanness, but because every set of men in place become thieves, if some opposition stand not guard? O official, are you afraid? Then formidable is your foe. Why startled at any raid, but that something in your platform or proceeding — jobs, commissions, corporations, long and costly sessions — will not bear examination, and you cannot, as will every upright man, welcome unfriendly search? One thing pacifies hostility and disarms hate, — a record without spot. Put on the Dread-nought of principle! Flank your enemy by evolution of character: spike with patriotism his guns. But he is a dangerous man! What makes him dangerous, if you are right? Will the people of the commonwealth or nation indorse and exalt a destructive, in hopes at his hands of a division of goods, a confounding of the worth and wages of manual and mental labor, and partition of property like a pie cut into equal pieces for all round the board? Incredible such a ground of popularity in this country. Unjust to the common folk your alarm. Universal suffrage becomes a wiser instrument and safer test every year, with each exercise making us rejoice we are not ruled by sceptre or rank. I fear, says the conservative. Your fear is no argument! I have not learned, said a statesman, to put my hand into the Treasury. You are in it yourself, was the reply; and that man a whole generation of voting has not dislodged.

Conflict means something. Rival partisans use strong words. I know not what that Hebrew statesman, David, had encountered of objection to his reign, when he prayed God to hide him in his pavilion from the strife of tongues; but any one who looks over recent files of the New York and Massachusetts press will understand what a strain for vile epithets the dictionary has endured, and how the English vocabulary has been milked to the strippings for gall. Men balk not to call each other liars, thieves, devils; and the charges are taken quietly, no suits for libel instituted, till one might think the depravity total, virtue quite gone, and all the self-called patriots plunderers and office-seekers alike. But the vilipending must be taken with a grain of salt; and doubtless that proverb, "The devil is not so black as he is painted," arose from extravagant abuse of not wholly base men. But remembering who has by enraged adversaries been called devil and diabolical, from Jesus down, one may query if it be of course so dishonorable a term. Beside, Satan is a useful person: the Old Register informs us, in the case of Job, the Lord put him to excellent purpose to try and sanctify his servant and carry him from the temptations of earthly prosperity through the hell of disgrace and pain into a heaven of purity and peace beyond his first estate. Through a like needed Purgatory, by that particular individual you consider your Beelzebub, you may be led. If any set of men in public life pass muster with such an antagonist, and come out of the mangle with clean hands, and no indelible stains, the agent will deserve something else than utter condemnation and scorn. Will it wash? you ask, of the dry goods. Some things very hard! In Dante's Inferno one class of demons handles for others the penal fires, plunging them with forks into the lake of burning pitch. Set a rogue to catch a rogue. One political hand must wash the other: the Ins and the Outs are the two hands, and purifiers must be respected as well as saints.

Is it an open question whether women shall vote? Not quite, as they already do so in benevolent societies, church-meetings, and educational enterprises, it only remaining to complete their claim in civil affairs; and at every caucus and convention the favor of the growing number asserting it is put up at auction, time only being requisite to decide what party will make the highest bid. Without dogmatism in the case, or prejudgment of the issue, the defenders of woman's right may ask a better argument against it than that of expediency, and alarm that more Irish women than Anglo-Saxon would rush to the polls. Nay, considering how on the ballot our destinies hang, and over what filthy floors we tread with our fate in our grasp, should we not anticipate the plea that women must be dragged in the dirt to the shrine where law and justice are to be sacrificed or saved, by substituting for ward-rooms and dens noble buildings as the suffrage-deposit, making palaces of our polls? If it be a true figure to speak of the temple of our liberties, there is no cathedral more solemn or fit for worship than the place where they are to be maintained.

II.

INDIVIDUALISM.

WHAT curious imputation of human contrivance to God was the old notion of his *scheme* of salvation, in which, like the bits of paper we try to make a rectangle of, all the verses of the Bible were parts of the puzzle. A little larger word is used when liberal believers talk of the Christian *system*. But that, too, implies a fence Jesus never put up. A man does not accomplish much under keepers; and no great thing was ever said or done in sight of limits, or within bounds other than of thought itself. By what prescribed rule did Raphael make that Dresden Madonna, the child in whose arms is King of men? After what photograph did Michael Angelo, in the Sistine Chapel, copy that creation of Eve it takes the breath away to look at, and of which one said he did not see how the Florentine artist could have been descended from that first woman, the mother of all, whom he himself conceived?

There are in art or nature no walls. The autumnal maple I saw all alone in the field, a flame of fire from the bottom to the top, was the very burning-bush Moses saw, and it shone all the way to and from

Egypt while I looked. When the love of God visits me with its glow, there are no longer chambers in my heart, but space for all mankind. I have seen people scowl at finding strangers in their seats in church, and have heard of nails driven in the railing to indicate to the sexton none but members of the proprietor's house should be admitted. But doors are leaving desk and pew, as Father Taylor said his pulpit had none; and the street crowds into the slips of temple and theatre for sermons and prayers, without money or price. Broad Church and Low Church supersede High Church. Faith is genuine as it is generous. Make a dogma or tenet of it, and it is lost. I find, said my friend, the more I reason about immortality, the less I believe it. Throw yourself on your instinct, trust your vision, give your life to your Author and race, and you will not doubt. The sceptics about God and heaven, however polite and complaisant, will be found in the last analysis self-seekers, and no devotees of their kind. Does one withdraw from you and enact the disloyal friend, you will find he lives on the surface, and degrades all realities into problems. Not himself one with God, what wonder his very adhesiveness should be untempered mortar, soft solder for solid support. Say to him, All the distance between us you make: I but keep on the line, trying to reach you if I can. Freedom of thought and freedom of fellowship are the same. What blunder identifies free-thinking with infidelity, when it is the only path by which conviction ever visited the human soul? The time is at hand for those branded as unbelievers to be counted warmer votaries of truth than popes and cardinals and priests.

It is true, in all common interests, from a handful of men to the millions of a nation, we must co-act, and have organizers as well as idealists. Yet all institutions must be mended by the thought they spring from, or abolished by a better thought. But to change an organic habit is hard, and attended with agonies that threaten dissolution. The reformer is always ruiner; though Church and State have by civil and religious doctors been ruined so many times, still to thrive, as do trees once felled, out of their mangled or rotting stumps, that all croaking sounds like that of the ravens sent with food to Elijah. Our Constitution will get aground often, said an old statesman, but there will be always somebody, like the man on the banks of the Mississippi, who pushes the raft from the shore. Cæsar in power may well complain that "Cassius thinks too much;" but the thinker is saviour. What slow and cumbrous processes men use at first! Self-interest of operatives, whose livelihood depends on present methods, resists improvement. But a thought from some brain, mightier than an army, steps softly in, and the old style gives place to a new, though the light of burning mills leads the inventor, showing where past discovery made its way. The announcers of principle give the oil of life to the lamp that illuminates; and, like the captain feeding the boiler with his freight, throw their flesh and bones into the fire that warms and impels mankind. We suspect the seer, and despise visionaries as unpractical. But there is not a comfort in our house, article of food or clothing, harvest of the field or preparation of the kitchen, grain of wheat for the grist or of powder for grinding the foe, but is at first the pure potentiality they perceived and contrived and combined. A man—Erastus B. Bigelow—is still alive, to whose wit the factories in Massachusetts owe a debt exceeding a thousand-fold the sum he received. What is a railway but an embodiment of conceptions, once non-existent outside the solitary heads they visited, putting on a wood and iron dress to walk abroad in. Yankee notions alter the world. All imperfection comes from want of thorough thought. When that stops or lags, and the mind's eye winks at faults or defects in the machinery or manipulation, injury ensues. Intellectual blindness hurts and slays more than any ill intent. Peering into the wreck of the late disaster on the road, what do we see? That a true time-table, making no noise; a telegram, sped in an instant; the silent step of a watchman sent back; an understanding between conductors, — would have kept above the sod a precious score now under it; that if kerosene is not safe in a quiet parlor, it is dangerous in a jolting car; that a good supply of rolling stock for emergencies might hinder the confusion of arrangement, ending in the chaos of destruction. But alas! all these thoughts came too late. Because they were tardy, the trains were! As I looked at the heap of burnt and battered bits of iron near the station, rusting in the rain, all that from the catastrophe the flames had left, I shuddered to think by how little reflection that melancholy monument, lying so still a reminder of anguish untold, might have been spared.

But what application have such illustrations to the working and apparatus of forms and creeds? There is no peril in the running of a denominational establishment. No matter what a man thinks in religion, only how he lives! Men are praised who never attack sects they do not belong to; and if they cannot speak well of others, say nothing at all. We must answer, the spiritual exceeds the utilitarian importance of thought, in proportion as moral culture is of more moment than a patent reaper, mowing-machine, steam-engine, or cotton-gin; for these are all but the mind's servants, serving it ill if it have unworthy aims. Is the telegraph a blessing when fraud or tyranny controls the wires, and they terminate in Napoleon's ante-chamber? Is travelling unmixed good? Half of us were better at home! Where are you in your worship? Whither drawn by the locomotive of will? What sort of engineer is your conscience? What is the latitude and longitude of your course toward the angelic isles? The disciples left all and followed Jesus. It was a splendid speculation. To be shrewd operators, we might be content to part with our lands and bonds, and take neither purse nor scrip, for one degree of progress and character, or surer beholding of our end. There are opinions on these matters we are wronged and put back by.

Take some examples. The Lord's Supper as a line between sinners and saints is no harmless ceremony, but a snare of hypocrisy, a trap of pretence, or a reef which thousands taking for a harbor have been cast away on. A profession of religion hinders practice. A certain prophet foretold that removing the land-mark between church and congregation, and sealing up the book of communicants, would destroy Liberal Christianity, though Paul said eating would not make us better, or abstaining worse. His prediction failed.

Regarding the Bible as so much dried pemmican, a little of which every day is a sufficient ration for the soul, classifies chaff and wheat, with some poison, together. Who reads the Book through now and holds all the parts of Hebrew literature from a hundred pens of equal worth, save such as the old Bibliolatry still besots? Is it pious or blasphemous to put Deuteronomy with the Gospels, David's curses with Christ's beatitudes, or Jewish retaliation with the Sermon on the Mount? A theory which constructs a gilded idol of the whole Scripture, to be multiplied by myriads as the sole condition of salvation, and be a pledge of security because it adorns the table or cumbers the shelf, is a bane. We have against it only the dishonest security of a quiet agreement to let Kings and Chronicles, wrathful prophecies and illogical epistles, go by default while we attend to parables and psalms; or else of an ingenious arguing of truth into the letter and falsehood out. But children and the simple, unable to understand this, are exposed to mischief still. It was said of a certain politician, He is all brass. But the prayer-book betrays a composition so like Nebuchadnezzar's image, no wonder good churchmen can endure the contradiction no longer, but must have a purged liturgy, — as I remember Ephraim Peabody sought in vain to correct the comparatively pure version of the King's chapel, which an Englishman said was the old one watered, but my friend answered was the old one washed; and needs washing a little more.

What so absurd as a prayer for deliverance from

sudden death! The article of death is always sudden; and if the sentence deprecated is of death in the fulness of one's powers, is not that what everybody should crave? What is decline? All that is sad, or casts a shadow into the prospect of old age. How clear an image of blessed departure is Scott's from the set of the tropical sun!

"No pale gradations quench his ray."

How many covet going at once rather than drag to the grave! He that fell by lightning was held by the ancients —

"Favored man by touch ethereal slain."

James Otis wished and had such fate. Job begged not protracted existence, but hunted after the grave and wanted it to open at his feet. If the reader has not, the writer has seen many an hour when death, but that wisdom withheld it, would have been a boon. It pleases God to call many suddenly: why pray against his decree? Of one whose genius years do not dim, it was said, he will fall like a pine-tree, he will dry up and blow away, or creep into some nook; he will not die, nor any man know his sepulchre. What better for Gannett, spinning out his last fibre, turning the wheel when no more wool was on the spindle, than Elijah's chariot of fire? The version of the original form into "death unprepared for" scarce improves it. Not death, but life is the thing to prepare for. Why notice that which Christ abolished? The idea that God changes, turns his face from the sinner who passes unreconciled, takes beyond any profane swearing his name in vain. No repentance or hope beyond the death-bed? As the tree falleth it must lie? The human soul is not a fallen tree! The best repentance for the worst transgressor or most precious saint is after earthly decease, and Watts's line is true of neither, —

"Fixed in an eternal state;"

for it were a fine degradation of the future to annul there the law of progress which is the sole comfort here.

Let such cases suffice to illustrate how thought may act as a solvent on the chronic prejudice of an inveterate phrase. Is not more or better steam welcome? O ye who run the machine of religion, hate not those who supply new motive power; and let organizers suffer search into the basis of organization, as men are employed on the iron road with their clinking hammers to test the wheels. Not what excites, but incites us, is the point. Are you rid of ambitious incentive, of all desire to sound or shine, and sing Monckton Milnes' "Lay of the Humble"? Can you resign leadership and refuse following? Can you hold appetite from lusting and your tongue from reply? Then I care not for your theological name: your connection is with every worthy spirit to which the universe gives breath.

Orthodoxy substitutes legality for love. God cannot remit his law of eternal perdition to the race for their ancestor's first offence; Jesus pays the penalty with his blood, and the ransomed get into heaven on the ground of right in his merit with the Judge to whom he stands bail and pays the fine. Observe the effect on character of this forensic view. Severe deacons and strict members of the church keep the letter at the expense of the spirit of their contract, carrying their divine scheme into human covenants, as Shakspeare makes Shylock quote Jacob's trick about the cattle to excuse his own greed. What signifies my neighbor's heading the list of communicants in good standing, if, as the standard of his proceeding, to the law of equity he prefers the law of the land? Why should he not? Why should he be liberal and humane, or just in the large sense of doing as he would be done by, when the God he worships is so sharp? No: let him encroach, run out his lines against my light and air, return robbery for my bestowment, and, wherever he can, do the legal thing that is immoral and unchristian, and without breaking the statute take the lion's share! He has no higher law. He is as good as a God on whom his own children have no claims he is bound to respect, who forms one vessel to honor and another to dishonor. But, said my friend, God is not a potter.

The critic of what is popular is asked what he proposes instead: it is a malefaction to give nothing, but only to take away. But as a decaying structure is mended piece-meal, as a living organism is perpetual substitution of particle for particle, so no system of opinion comes or goes by human will or at once, but by working through periods of a divine law, one of whose executors is every honest objector, and which Jesus fulfilled for his times not only by positive statement but by finding fault. The trellis a vine clambers on is not torn away; but, if it be not repaired, it will rot and the vine fall. Ever and anon a voice is lifted, We have had criticism enough: construction is in order now. I answer, The two must go together. Unitarianism fancies it is the last landing-place, the pillars of Hercules every voyager must stop at, though seas and continents of truth lie beyond. But the horned bull of Fanaticism is not slain yet. If the Rationalist has been the picador, the Radical must be the matadore in the unfinished fight. It is held dangerous to unsettle a common faith. Not if it is unsettled by thought! Better unsettle your house in season if it rest on the sand. Is it dangerous to disturb a bad style of building, an uneven railway, or any defective machine? We do it that we may be safe. He is the very devil, said one of a Road President who was efficient. Is security of less moment for the soul? What is salvation? Not escape from hell, but entry of bliss. I will not carry my blame of an opinion into my treatment of the man. There is a Public Garden of Humanity where all may meet: there is to be a Museum of Art and an atonement of Beauty. There is another Common than that within the iron fence. As Radical and Reactionist can enjoy a flower, a picture, or prospect together, so the universal Creator opens vistas either way of memory and hope, through which, despite side glances at their respective premises, they can gaze on destiny and glory together.

For all the dogmatism is so stiff, it does not lie very deep. It is a crust, a clod, or hard pan under which, in everybody, we break into fertile soil. With theologic as with social gossips, what an automaton is the tongue! How true the proverb of its being hung on wires! What a perpetual motion is the repetition of a creed, whose articles to the Protestant are like the Catholic beads; and how deceptive the voice they are proclaimed by, which crowds hang on for its resonance and animal heat, three-fourths of the ardor being of the body not the soul, and the speaker being only an additional stove or furnace in the house! When I consider the nature of what my admiration is challenged for, how the famous pulpit-orator may go to his audience with nothing to say, and with what seeming delight it is heard, the fervor seems a kind of insanity, such as populations and nations are touched with in some illusory expectation or aim, — like that French foolishness insisting the downfall of Paris was impossible, which, made into a compound battery for Victor Hugo to handle, did not avail against the German guns, though an English writer calls it the most vital vanity in the world.

The congregation, you tell me, was great. Large it often is, and hundreds have to go away. But to what purpose? There are huge gatherings at concerts and theatres and fire-works and menageries and jugglers' shows, and on the Exchange. Let me celebrate the thin house! It may be a question whether, throughout the world's history, more has not been done with few present than with many. Two or three in sympathy were enough to persuade Christ's attendance. It is a strange fact that the performer's power often reduplicates with the diminution of the throng. He becomes more natural and simple, ambition for effect dies, the inordinate stimulus that sometimes the actor is not inspired but maddened and prematurely killed by is withdrawn: the Spirit comes; and, for a lunatic distracted with conceit of his importance, we have an organ of the Holy Ghost. What joy and upbuilding we remember in small companies, beyond superficial transport of crowds in the laughing gas of ecclesiastical vapor they breathe! We search too much for God in the upper void. He is under foot as well as overhead, in the hell of our privation as in the heaven of bliss, in my conscience and my friend's heart more than among the stars. The earth as well as the air is the Lord's: let us respect the earth in us of which he made us, as well as the soul he blew into our nostrils. O invalid, who hast spun thy brains into the web of thy fancy, the Divinity inhabits the world of fact. Become worldly-minded, a man of the world, as your neighbor is too much and you not enough. Pine no longer among thy theories. Leave thy pillar, touch the earth and arise strong. "Let your parish go," said Abernethy to worn-out Dr. Tuckerman, "and build a barn." Moiling in the dust, striking on the ledge, blasting for a cellar, raising the house, I build up beside my dwelling my nervous system, and learn that the Deity I was soaring after had not left the ground. When I can live close to my mason and carpenter, abide near any human being without jar, I am with Him. Have your own way, you will live the longer, we say. Yes, when it is the King's highway of brotherly love.

But let Freedom be understood. It is no indetermination, but thinking and acting according to law. America borrowed from France her political ideas. But the old French triumvirate — Liberty, Equality, and Fraternity — have fallen out. Say the Communists,

"We do not want liberty, but equality." Equality, like my friend's serpent that ate up the brother he was caged with, has devoured Liberty; Fraternity will be but a side-dish in the same meal. Labor against capital is the form the new strife takes which is to have the next century for its battle-field; and, among the passions that shall thunder, there will be need of thought. We may find no "glittering generality" or "blazing ubiquity," but a half-truth apt to false applications, in the doctrine of all men's equality by birth in any power or for any lot. There is no freedom but in order, harmony, the mutual adjustment of all according to their several ability and worth. "The career open to talents," said Napoleon; exercised, we must add, for the common weal. We learn from M. Coquerel that the late incendiarism in Paris arose from the insane principle of destroying capital, as though it were not a crib at which all men feed. In the Communists pulling down the column in the Place Vendôme to signify the end of war among the peoples of the globe, by self-sacrifice of national glory to the idea of universal peace, there was something sublime; and when they burned the guillotine before the statue of Voltaire, to symbolize the end of its red executions, society seemed growing more humane. But the enterprise of striking a level of human fortunes, Procrustes coming again to dock the long stature and stretch the short, will cause more woe with its brutal average than it will close. The crevice when it is opened, as Dr. Beecher said of the old Revolution, will run blood. Such internationality will be no advance, but another fall of man to the savage state, and, by removing motive to toil, an exchange of riches for general poverty and want. The excess of impulse in the last decade, which has shaken either hemisphere more than earthquakes, needs reason to be its moderator, regulator, and safety-valve.

We want to know not only what to do, but what not to do or say. Socrates says his Demon told him where to stop.

"As fools rush in where angels fear to tread,"

how often impertinent interference and superserviceable suggestion make us wish that Demon might come back! Would the mediums that converse with Socrates be good enough to hint to the old philosopher how we should thank him for sending into the world once more that useful governor of his mental machine? At present, no benefactor could surpass this interior conscience, sitting secret, like Maelzel's automaton, and at every false move in the game of human life saying, *Check*. "In four cases out of five," said a great physician, "we help a patient best by doing nothing, and the chief rule is not to move or prescribe anywise without surety of benefit." The doctors of our sick society might well heed the lesson. Said my medical adviser, "The most I can do is to tell you how to keep out of harm's way." Give nature a chance to rally! He that abounds in political specifics, and meddles most with human nature, is a worse quack than medical societies banish. So-called cure is the main generator of disease.

Our raging publicity overlooks the value of private counsel. From some individual comes the saving word. It is always proscribed as individualism till it becomes the common sense. But the deliverer is the superior soul, communicant with the Supreme to convey its wisdom to half-unwilling recipients; one that shares neither the panic of the multitude nor their zeal, but has a heart beating for his kind, and is in his opponents' citadel the friend of their own secret respect.

"Thy soul was like a star and dwelt apart,"

wrote Wordsworth of Milton, from whom shone the beams of republican liberty brighter than Orion for all men. Of want of leaders, there is much talk; and the leaders, when they come, are often but persons magnetized by some epidemic impression or prevailing superstition, like a certain captain who put himself at the head of an officerless regiment at Bull Run, and simply went with them to Washington in their rout. Our civil and religious commanders are men catching the contagion of any troop that marches by, intent on victory or retreat. The ducal power on the field is not in those who give the loud orders and ride in uniform, but in some unseen Möltke or silent Grant. So in faith and morals, not by the marshals and platform-orators, but thinkers we are led. Such let us cherish as the apple of our eye; and not measure their merit by their power to push and multiply themselves in men's sight. Mr. Pierpont said of Dr. Channing, "Put him into the street to shift for himself and make his living, and he would die." But we knew his quality, and would no more have put him into the street than thrown out our mirror or spy-glass. Is physical strength — to work and lift, hoist or farm, fish or build — the gauge of a man? How with those that poise the telescope in the observatory, watch the currents of air and sea, predict the storms and cyclones, make coast surveys, calculate eclipses, and run the lines of danger and refuge for ships on our maps and charts? "All things in common" was a shallow, transient rule. Equalize tasks or goods when you can equalize gifts. We did not put Channing to the plough-handle, but to the pulpit and the pen. He did braver things than carry a musket to load and fire. It is not always the stalwart whom in the trial we can trust. The woman who, when the Life Boatmen were afraid, and refused to venture out to the wreck on the Irish shore, went alone in her little skiff and rescued the last survivor through the boiling surf, proved that something more than muscle is called for in the dreadful hour, and had a right to vote all those cravens down.

A perfect development is, doubtless, not only the complete beauty of a human creature, but the condition of the highest health of each particular faculty. I fancy my friend's metaphysical glance would not be dulled, but cleared, could he also keenly as an Indian follow the trail. As diamond cuts diamond, and one hone smooths a second, all the parts of intellect are whetstones to each other; and genius, which is but the result of their mutual sharpening, is character too. He who is excellence, and does the heroic thing, will say it with equal however rude expression, as did Luther and John Brown. Said Gangoolly, the Hindoo convert to Christianity, "When I made up my mind, I went into my closet and cast down my idols, to break in fragments on the floor, with fear in one side of my heart, and triumph in the other." How many a pull at windlass and capstan that gesture was worth!

But, if we train not in a Denomination, do not attend the Conference, or subscribe the Compromise, we are charged with individualism. Is it so bad to consider truth or right no creature of a consociation or suffrage of the majority, or level average of differing minds, but an act of duty from a perception of the mind? Sheridan was individual restoring his troops from panic on the Potomac; Grant at Vicksburg, Sherman in Georgia, Washington at Valley Forge, and Butler in Baltimore and New Orleans. It is the fault the synod found with Jesus, the council with Stephen, the Jesuits with Pascal, the Church with Wycliffe and Huss, the Pope with Luther and Döllinger, the Unitarians with Parker; and every sect with whoever presumes to know more than it has laid down. Were these men individual in the low sense? Is number virtue? How easy to outvote God who is only One! If individualism be self-seeking, — like that of the profligate, glutton, miser, and sot, — shall we charge with it those who sacrifice themselves and take up the excommunicating cross? We hear of people on the fence watching the signs of the times, to know which side to jump, to be, as the poor queen tells "Austria" in the play, "ever strong upon the stronger side." There is a theological fence. Popularity is never so sweet as among our associates in an unpopular body. Does it become such as enjoy to indict those who renounce it when conscience bids? The accuser may be target of his own shaft. To be willing to appear on platforms and receive ecclesiastical invitations, and be praised by the religious press, and have one's own books printed by an association, is no demonstration clear as Euclid of philanthropy. The hypocrite is no hermit. The humbug buzzes in a swarm. Your brother's pride of separation may not match yours of communion; and in attempting his portrait you draw your own. "You shall be a major-general," one was told, to tempt him to join the convocation. Did ambition keep him away? If he stood aloof for that luxury of thought, more subtile than of appetite, to be a mental Sybarite, he might be well arraigned. But what if better service were his aim? O brethren, the motives on either side may be deeper than party. At the siege of Paris a wounded Uhlan and Frenchman, both reviving from swoon together, recognized each his antagonist, exchanged smiles and died, with that sign of something more than strife. Pure individuality does not exist, only independent thought.

Such men as Newton and Kepler are said to think God's thoughts after him. But what is the use of thinking? Do not all the churches undertake to do it for us? Does not every creed assume that all the thinking is done; and liberal leaders tell us all we have left us is to go to work, and spin our brains no more. The more you think, said my friend, the more you are puzzled: act on your impressions, or take the current views. Robert Burns says the poet does not find the muse by thinking long; and Shakspeare shows us in Hamlet how over-fine reflection palsies the will. I answer, Thought is deeper than logic, taking for its laboratory both heart and head, and has a use to resolve every mistake. Error is not pure falsehood: it has a mixture of truth. As a man choosing the wrong road is still in the world, and will come by some circuit to his goal; as the ore has in it gold and silver as well as dross, so thought is the process to regain the track we have strayed from, and to smelt the crude mass of opinion. The English Bishop Colenso in Australia, eliminating blunders from the Pentateuch; Father Hyacinthe in France and his colleague in Germany resisting the Pope's infallibility; radical writers in America warning us against Biblical idolatry; and scientific explorers all over the world scouting the superstitions of theology, — are but so many meters. Watch the motions of your own mind in successive years, your varying construction of articles, or emphasis of miracles and prophecies and proof-texts; and you will own how the slow, silent tide of reason sweeps away floating, superficial dogmas, and like the Atlantic surging into some muddy creek hides the old landmarks of belief. It is curious to see how this tenet and that, once made the seal of salvation, passes from the most orthodox pulpit and ceases. One spell upon the minds of men

"Breaks never to unite again."

Why and whence this inevitable disintegration? Because Thought cannot seize the unthinkable: there are things the understanding cannot entertain any longer, more than lungs can respire in a vacuum. That a babe is born totally corrupt, that a favored few are chosen and the rest eternally doomed, that any child of God can be finally lost, that his innocent Son could be punished, — doctrines once unthinkingly proclaimed, — are now impossible propositions; not discarded from among the articles, but suffered to sleep, given the go-by, laid upon the table, because there is no chamber open to them in the human brain. They have gone, with witchcraft and the evil eye, and the power to curse, and demons, and priesthood, and divine right of kings.

Thought also resolves evil into good: this solvent so thorough, this reagent so mighty, that in its extreme application all natural and moral ill disappears. No annoyance or injury, no insult so gross, or harm so unexpected, no treachery of friend, ingratitude of those I forwarded, dislike of those I loved, but under this compound blow-pipe melts. Evil is a snow-flake to swell the current it seemed to resist. Be it great calamity or trifling wrong, its compensation is its food for thought. Riding in the cars through the north-east storm, at a way-station a man coolly takes my umbrella, leaving me to get home in the rain. What do in such a case? Cry, Stop thief! Run after him, as one said he would, though he had lost the train? — sagely adding, It might end in the State-prison. But the man that has made so free with my property must need it more than I, and perhaps he agrees with the Frenchman, Proudhon, that all property is robbery, and he is only getting some of his own back. I can afford to buy a new one better than he: I shall never feel it in any inconvenience to my purse. Going away unmolested may stir in him some generous shame: by and by he may even want to return the utensil he has no right to. That nicely carved handle may tingle in his fingers as he holds it over his head in some pelting shower, as conscience-money has burned in the pocket of many a robber, and been often sent back to this or that private fund or public treasury. Therefore, though I had grown fond of the umbrella, that had shielded me through many a beating storm or scorching sun all the way from Massachusetts to the pine barrens of Florida, did I not get the full worth of it in these reflections; and, though I never should have another, was not my revenge or atonement for its loss complete? Let the thief reading understand I am paid!

Laugh at the trivial instance to illustrate a principle verified on the grandest scale: only try the experiment! Put your trouble into your thought, trace its relations, learn its object, discern its effect, and you get rid of it, — it is no trouble at all: it is transmuted into gold by the true philosopher's stone. So the Mohammedan mystic said, the religious soul is not that which submits or bears patiently, but that which is not afflicted, — does not recognize harm. Perfect love casts out not only fear, but sorrow. No matter how great the grief may appear, — bereavement of nearest companion or dearest child, — thinking of its lesson, you become its master. Said a noble woman: "My anguish is mine: it is my fortune and possession; I own it. You cannot have it: you may make your million of gold on the street; but this is my inalienable treasure." It does not look so, more than a dark rock in the mines of Nevada looks like the silver pouring from it in the furnace heat. Yet you can lose nothing but thought doubles its worth. Yonder is the grave. But there is a deeper grave within. Its walls and fences are the boundaries of your own heart. Nobody knows the way to the gate of it but you. In it are buried no useless corses, but old friendships and associations; sentiments once mutual betwixt you and others, that no longer exist, —

"Fond desires and hopes as vain."

The obsequies were noiseless, without shroud or coffin or funeral procession; yet no crape ever worn, no lament over the dead ever lifted, no hollow sound of the gravel dropping from the sexton's spade, could signify such suffering as went with the interments in that invisible sepulchre. Yet what man or woman whose thought has not from these terrible sacrifices of the seed-corn of human joy reaped a harvest? There are resurrections from this other cemetery as well as from the ashes in God's acre.

"There is nothing either good or bad, but thinking makes it so," says Hamlet. Does not deeper thinking make every thing good? Does one show ill-temper? Do not let your ill-temper match his. The worst sea is where two cross-waves meet. Try to understand it; grapple it with your thought; put it into the refrigerator of your philosophy, not the powder-magazine of your passion, — and you will gather wisdom from it, as the naturalist does, not only from graceful forms, — skin or plumage, of beast or bird; but from wasps and serpents, in his cabinet or museum. If our associates *will* be hard and unreasonable with us, *will* display bad qualities as well as good, while rejoicing in the latter, of the former it is quite just we should, with imperturbable attention, make curious specimens, — as my young friend, traversing from Mount Desert to the Blue Hills, does of hornets and all manner of bugs.

Perhaps our companion cannot wholly help his disposition more than the grovelling worm or stinging insect can: let this thought make us patient. Sin itself this potent element can reduce. Confess our transgressions and cry for mercy, yet we cannot help asking, Why are we constituted so peccable that not a soul escapes? Calvinism makes but one exception, of the Son; Romanism adding the immaculate purity of the Mother. "Shapen in iniquity," as David says, born and begotten so that we cannot avoid excesses and defects, what theory of such a fallible constitution can show the Creator just? Only this, — that sin and remorse enter into his plan of education to make us better and wiser, as Shakspeare says, "Best men are moulded out of faults." What but Peter's denial, Judas's betrayal, all the disciples' cowardice, made them the humble, resolute men they became? The worst of us can turn his vices to account. Sorely as we have offended, we can do nothing fatal. Sheer blasphemy and inhumanity in the old theology is the doctrine of a doom to perdition and eternal woe for personal or our ancestral delinquency. The bottomless pit were a blot on Deity, though but one soul wallowed in it! Every thread of disobedience, every fibre of depravity, God weaves into his whip to scourge us to virtue; and how many find their luck in the offences by which they are lashed out of their indifference and sloth! It was said of a certain hypocrite, fancying he sported all the virtues in his behavior,

It would do him good to be mortified by getting drunk. Damned to all eternity for your wrong-doing? What a monster you make of God with your conceit! He does not reckon up the score of your departures and short-comings to present you with the bill at the judgment-day. He carries no ugly pack of your debts at his back. He has no memory: all is present to him. He has no conscience: that implies violation of law, which he is incapable of. He accepts the purity of your present mood. "Let by-gones be by-gones," he says. He will rake up no old quarrel. "Now is the accepted time; behold, now is the day of salvation." "Though your sins be as scarlet, they shall be like snow; though they be crimson, they shall be whiter than wool." We pray to him: does he not pray to us to turn to him? and may we not well abridge our loud shouts and long liturgies to listen while he so prays? Evil has no existence to him. He to whom the night shineth as the day, and the darkness and the light are both alike, cannot look on sin, and is of purer eyes than to behold iniquity. The measure of a man's character and elevation is his ratio of evil and good. If evil to him is large in proportion to good, he is bad and low; if small, he is good and high; if it vanishes, he is perfect like God.

Thought, once more, resolves deformity into beauty. How much lacks grace! How seldom we see a handsome person, with all the foils of ornament and advantages of dress, at a party or on the street! To the vast majority *plain* is a mild term to apply. In the mental-photograph album, to the question, "What is your finest object in Nature?" one was uncivil enough to write, "A beautiful woman, though I have not seen one for years." But the artist chooses for his canvas not the faces commonly called beautiful, but those in which his keener eye detects expressions of sense and sensibility not revealed to a cursory glance; and pretty people who have learned how pretty they are, and take attitudes and prink and trim before the glass, like the swans in the pond I saw at work on their feathers, he scorns as subjects. An eye which the genius of love makes penetrating will discover a charm in every face. Not a breathing man or woman but to insight will disclose more to attract than to repel. In the scarce-formed frame of the puniest child, what a wonder of fitness beyond the strongest engines and smoothest machines! Physicians talk, not so absurdly as we conceive, of beautiful cases of disease; for what we call the *laws of disorder* manifest the working of supreme wisdom and equity.

Lastly, thought resolves seeming into being. What tries us more than separation or pain is illusion. We cannot grasp the universe. What a kaleidoscope it is of shifting colors, or camera of dissolving views! As I daily reach my door-step, I contemplate the beauty of the Brookline hills across the Back-Bay. I try a hundred times to seize and analyze the spell. It draws me back to gaze and muse, while the children stop their play to survey and smile at me as my hand lingers on the knob, and lifts not the latch of the door. I toil to take up the enchantment, and carry it away with me in my mind. But it baffles me: I cannot hold or tell what it is.

A woman plays to me on her piano. The strings

are so many tongues to tell me more of her experience than she would venture on with her tongue to do. I read or hear between the lines of sounding keys. I spell out trouble and triumph in the tunes. The ivory and ebony under her fingers speak of dark and bright experiences, of struggles with narrow circumstances, mixed with emotions of religious ecstasy. Her state of mind is a problem I cannot solve. Does her condition prove human life the lot of justice, or gibe of fate?

A young girl sees the prospect open before her of all that is meant by wedded joy, and a long line of posterity flowing from her unspotted blood; when, from his covert, the spectre glides in and dashes to the ground the cup just touching her lips. Was this bird of paradise made to be wounded, her bright wings ruffled, and every nerve tortured and torn? We hear of the mirage in the desert cheating the parched traveller's eyes with the empty image of water to slake his thirst. This mirage of human life, tantalizing the soul ready to drink the happiness it craves and is constituted for, is the mockery. Not gall, like that offered to Jesus, is bitter: but the seeming of what we cannot realize; and the old theology is lavish of gloomy fancies to paint the balking of desire: —

> "This world is but a fleeting show,
> For man's illusion given."

> "Each pleasure hath its poison too,
> And every sweet a snare."

So it points to another world for reality, and counts apples of Sodom all the apparent hopes and deceitful satisfactions of this; as if we could trust the note payable at a future time of one giving no evidence he is in funds now. Put aside, postponed, fobbed off in our vain expectations, writes one, with a grim comfort we anticipate death as something that will not dodge. But we want to touch bottom and feel something solid before. If we can catch nothing substantial here, what ground for supposing we shall hereafter? The Oriental writers dilate on this illusory character of all terrestrial experience; and what but this does Solomon the great king intend, when, after describing the bursting of all the magnificent preparations he had blown up for his delight, he puts, like a placard on the rock, this stern brand on the universe: "Vanity of vanities, all is vanity." Who that looks on the dance of blood and death performed by that most gay and wretched of nations, that took for its aim glory, and its name *The beautiful France*, yet tears down the monuments of its own fame, but must read a new commentary on the old text? Shall we look to the men of physical science, the positive philosophers, for the relief from this phantom inspired sages fail to afford? No, they answer: the reality of any thing we cannot reach. Only phenomena, the visible, ever-changing accidents of matter, can we know and arrange in order under law. God is unknowable: we can find nothing but it slips from comprehension, however plain to sense. "Is there no balm in Gilead?" no remedy for this distress of doubt? Yes: not in observation or regulation of facts, but in thought.

"I think, therefore I am." Descartes meant this not for argument, but to say, Being is equivalent to thought, thought the indorsement of being; a proposition we cannot forget to repeat. "I am," said the dying minister, "therefore God, the Infinite Being, is." But *He* is, else how could *I* be? I am because he thought of me. This is the solution of the riddle. What was the beginning of all, said Dr. Channing to me, but a thought? The thought of a family and home like the world is love.

Here is the real, in your mind. You worship no outward object or image, but your thought. He is the thought of your thought. Beyond that you cannot go. Do you shrink from that, as a human measure of Deity? What other measure have you? The seaman might as well throw away his log because it cannot span the Atlantic, or his deep sea line because it can touch bottom only here and there, Cyrus Field refuse to lay the electric cable, or Herschel discard his diagrams because there are stars in the unbounded blue, — as we despise those faculties which are the only gauge we have. They are good far as they go, — counterpart of the creative soul. No illusion is this vision in the breast. Every pure thought is a glimpse of God. We have seen him, though the sight fade the next moment for ever away. One beholding is pledge that to behold him we are made. Somehow the spirit in us, seeing and seen, ours and his, must be everlasting spectator of the eternal spectacle. In a life which has had its share of suffering, for one thing I am grateful, — the power and habit of thought. What a refuge, what an incentive, inspiration, and content! No drug, or ether, or drowsy syrup like it to soothe anguish, lull misfortune like a crying child to sleep, and heal the stabs that are in every heart. Remembrance of your Maker, your Origin and Portion, is oblivion of every wound of earthly affection and all the scars of time.

Such is the plea for individuality. Private sincerity is public welfare. A common Faith is a fortress we agree to defend, and have to desert. How many creeds once alive and swarming with champions resemble the mouldy castles on the Danube and the Rhine! But our thought is an impregnable retreat. No sanctuary or city of refuge, no den or cover for the hunted beast, no tower the fugitive draws up his ladder into, is so safe. Mr. Hawthorne is said to have prevented interruption by a chamber without stairs. But in my mind I am not interruptible. The peace of God not only passes understanding, but also strife. Under censure or insult, or the tiger-spring of hatred and revenge, the thinker, intangible, has meat to eat we know not of, a feast of wine and honey, while mockers hold to his lips the vinegar and gall. Hence his look of rapture you cannot understand. He has another lesson than the lecture you read him. Nobody, said one, ever told me what I tell. Be no gossip of men, but God's tale-bearer of news from heaven, like the prophet who imparts what he overhears; for our breast is God's ante-chamber, and our instinct his door, whose handle we can turn any moment out of care; and to the soul as to the eagle he has furnished an eyrie beyond range of earthly shot.

But thought is practical. Under whatever conditions, it at last must decide. It breeds charity by emancipating from individual bounds. Unreflecting parents expect from children as much love as they give, forgetting that love descends; and they cannot return to us, as we cannot to God, an equal love. When they have children, and we are dead, out of the mists of the grave, over the eternal horizon, will dawn on them the first vision of our old regard. We talk of justice to persons. We owe it to their thought. Are you well disposed to me? — be fair to my thought, greater than I, ruling and using me for its servant and tool, which I stand for to live and die. It has right to be respected, while I have no claim, but as representative of my constituent. I heard of an actor who had an idea of Hamlet by which he was governed on the stage, and of another altering his conception to suit purchasers; and I heard of a preacher who had learned to imitate the New York, Philadelphia, and Boston pronunciation. But a true man never accommodates to a meridian a doctrine that owns the globe. He has not one opinion in his study or club, and another in his desk. He has no policy, but is impolitic for his thought. John Pierpont, being invited to a certain pulpit, if he would consent not to handle exciting themes, said, "No! gentlemen, not if you would give me the salary of the Bishop of Durham!" Unfaithfulness is selfish contrivance. Thought instantly shows its folly; and it detects the quality of evil without respect to the size of the act by which a weak judgment is confused, as if grand had an advantage over petty larceny. A burglar carries off a few silks, utensils, or jewels; a pretended buyer secretes a bit of cloth under her cloak; a pickpocket is found with your currency in his hand; a small counterfeiter is caught; a hungry woman steals meat from a stall, and is hauled before the judge. But millions of money are conveyed away by a Ring, and it is an "operation"! Trust-property sweats, stock-jobbers strike for profits at stock-owners' risk, the bulls and bears toss and pull. Let us ask pardon of the beasts. No creature that scares you in the pasture, or hugs the traveller in California gorges or polar ice, is so cruel. We say the Bank suffers. But it is not alive. Granite walls, brick vaults, mahogany counters, and pigeon-holes have no heart or nerves, back to clothe or stomach to feed. They suffer, whose dividends are daily bread, education of children, cure of invalids. The widow suffers, whose husband can no longer defend his home from land-sharks, or sally forth to check financial moves against his estate; and orphans suffer, who were advised as to the best investment of their little means. Religion suffers when Bible and prayer-book, sacrament and sermon, control human reflection so little they cannot hinder in the cultivated decorous classes transactions that have no advantage but enormity over old plunder on the London-surrounding highways, or Roman brigandage still lurking in the plains of Lombardy or among the Southern spurs of the Alps. Custom and ceremony, civil and ecclesiastical, go on: public sentiment is slow to improve, and the condemners are the committers of crime. But private thought proclaims the need of a sense of God not only in the temple and at the Lord's table, through stately ordinance, sweet incense, and sonorous intonation, — but in the merchant's counting-room and lawyer's office, on the judge's bench and at the brokers' board. When loss and death ensue from mismanagement, and directors are called to account, they feel offended and hurt. But what is the use of them if they do not *direct*, more than does the ship's figure-head or the painted form with the printed *Dirigo* on a shield? Stop your dispute how the wood and velvet shrine shall be illuminated. Take up your candles, carry them forth from every altar, and set them in the courts of Mammon, till all its dusky corners are lighted, and every unrighteous plot exposed. A lamp burning in a store is greater safeguard than a lock. "I want more light about the future," said my friend. We want it in all the purlieus of trade. Certain Italian thieves are said to have their fingers lengthened by the daily habit of searching the persons of their victims. There are long fingers nearer home! Let us trust business is not so rotten, or greed so insane, as to make the revelation of iniquity a nine days' wonder, but that these greater robbers than the Alexander, whom the small thief he would punish claimed fellowship with, may receive their due.

Deeper private thinking alone can heal social dissembling. Reporting some interview, you say, I was on my good behavior and did it nicely. Not on your good behavior when the company went? You could curry favor, and let criticism crouch like a hushed dog, but change your face of compliment as your visitor turned the corner. The man whose tribunal is his thought is on good behavior when he is alone, and as careful of his designs as his words. His courthouse is not the granite building. He stands at a bar whose rail is unseen. He knows nothing of great occasions and small. He cares no more to act than to endure, to speak than to be dumb. Duty has no inequality. The spirit-level varies not for a special effort, more than mountains ruffle the huge sphere they are strewn on like sand. Pulpits and platforms sink; chambers of pain and poverty rise. No rush of events and affairs can unpoise the soul whose collect is conscious truth. In the whirlpool is a centre the mad waters cannot shake.

In an age of corporate agency, whose consolidated wealth challenges comparison with the exchequer of the State, and makes legislatures its tools, of nothing is the need so sore as independent testimony of the moral sense. It is no preposterous fancy, that for lack of vision the people perish. Let Argus with all his eyes come back, and permit no plan or proceeding to escape scrutiny. Away with darkness! If secret societies continue for harmless ceremony, to gratify a love of mystery, or for mutual supply to the impoverished from brotherly hands, let us have no Freemasons or Odd Fellows of another sort to appropriate of the common riches more than their share. Let the manifold Rings that form and contract like anacondas in their destructive strength, to centralize power and wealth in a few, expand by ventilation till they burst! One prerogative dignifies the human race, the freedom of thought, at whose assizes every practice must stand. In much we are excelled by the animals. The crane not only walks like me, but swims and flies as I cannot. But I can dive deeper, wade where it cannot follow, and soar higher. Without moving a muscle, the mind traverses Nature and has ascension without death.

III.

TRANSCENDENTALISM.

THE line of a planet is a compromise between two forces, a resultant which students work out on the slate; and social progress has for its factors the old institution and the new idea, from whose struggle the race shoots ahead, — one represented by the prophet, the other administered by the priest. Mankind depends on what it has hived and what it earns. Moral capital is no metaphor. Knowledge and virtue accumulate as well as silver and gold, and are the highest kind of real and personal estate, without which no business in politics or philanthropy could be done. How sad, said a foreigner, to think all the coined money in the United States could not pay the national debt! Yes, answered a Yankee; and to think, if the harvest failed all over the world for a year, all nations would starve! Labor is the only source of wealth, cries the new party. But manual is not the only, hardest, or best labor. If we grew and applied no fresh ideas, all the words of prophets, biographies of saints, and traditions of Palestine would not stay our hunger, more than the granaries of Egypt or last year's load in store and barn. With all respect to those who run the machine, a dearer honor belongs to such as supply the motive-power. Free and wild speculation, as well as custom and ordinance, has its place. Right as Leroux may be in the doctrine of human solidarity, or the advance of the species in column, the particles change in this huge body, as the ranks of an army in the field are depleted and filled up; and civil or ecclesiastical continuity is no mechanical necessity, but that divine order we must put our own heart and will into, and which the boldest thinker or righteous iconoclast is no less part of than any bishop or sheriff, — nay, is leader of the van. *Nature proceeds not by leaps*, was the old Latin phrase. But closer scrutiny shows she does. There is not only expansion, but eruption, — volcano and earthquake; and, in minuter spaces, signs of sudden action, as though the will of God were no figure of speech. Darwin and Spencer have to modify the doctrines of evolution and development to accommodate facts of rapid change into new orders observed by eyes sharp as their own. There is, said my friend, a track we must keep to in grooves of fate. But there is many a place where Nature switches off, and takes a new departure. The free-thinker long ago was said to have come to where was no more road. But his road has no end; and he has advanced ever since, and still keeps on. The traveller in Switzerland, looking from his carriage, beholds his path blocked at a hillside or plunging into a lake, and for the moment imagines in that direction is no further step. But, arriving at the point, he finds the beaten way winding round the mountain's spur into the rarest beauty of its course; and the mind that goes on without terror comes to the reward of truth. Where will they stop? is the inquiry respecting the critics of established methods; and the answer is, Nowhere. M. Coquerel tells us he was scolded by the French authorities for treating social questions in his paper; and, asking what was meant by social questions, was told, *Things that are!* Yet not a thing but must be unsettled in favor of something better, though the reason of the nickname *Transcendentalist* was, that whoever did this transcended all practical stability. Doubtless he who inhabits the region of pure thought becomes too impatient of existing modes. The air of the church is close and smoky, said one returning from a long sojourn in the country. Yes, I answered: to a person used to the whole atmosphere God makes so big that everybody may have enough, every room, however ventilated, will seem confined. But as we must be content to breathe in houses and temples, and shops and court-rooms, so we must live and morally respire in such establishment of Church and State as the common sense and conscience have been able to secure, enlarging and improving it as we can. The reformer is arraigned as destructive and traitor, accused of breaking the church-windows from the inside, and hewing down the pillars of the pulpit in which he stands. But if the windows are shut too tight to open, or stained with superstitious emblems, and if the sinking pulpit let him down to the level floor where his congregation sits, there may be a blessing from his axe and his stones. There is no church in Christendom where this question, whether some of the keepers are not betrayers of the citadel, does not arise.

What free man in any communion is not charged with having broken his pledge, often unawares, as the excellent Deacon Grant with some horror declared *he* had done, with the first mouthful of brandied mince-pie which his hostess had prepared. To think at all is violation of promise, in principle if not in fact, by marring some actual article of faith. How we queried whether those noble English Essayists ought to stay on the theological premises they took such liberty to alter and extend! The papacy in Rome and every bishopric in America are shaken with the same issue of moral casuistry. Universalism and Unitarianism have expelled from their interior offenders they were griped by, with intolerable pain; and what it is to be a true Radical I have heard the banished discuss with each other, as did the Southern seceders from the Union, albeit they have no home from which to drive the disloyal out. The interpreter and originator must quarrel, and organization be at odds with the unorganized or unorganizable: meantime, for benefit as for peace, it is well to have some estimate of the office of the seer, and the value of his addition to the common stock.

The crisis comes unawares. A new vision reforms all our knowledge, as the astronomer catches a planet in the threads on his glass and the solar system is readjusted. The world of shifting opinion hangs on a hair. How little it was thought, forty years ago, that a Boston clergyman's difficulty with his people about the way to administer the Lord's Supper would be the string let into the loose public sentiment to cause a new crystallization. I remember the horror with which a fellow-student announced to me the unbearable criticism of the ancient rite, and my wonder at anybody's being so much moved. But forms hold fast after the ideas have changed which were their source and support, as shells and husks are no less tough and hard when the kernel and substance are gone. So how to eat the bread and drink the wine, or commune without eating or drinking, was another question added to the many which have made the ordinance a very volcano of controversy, ever ready for fresh overflow; though the Oriental custom seemed not much suited to the Western mind. The young minister was told privately to alter the style of the symbol as he judged right, but he doubted his fitness for such reconstruction; and the discussion sufficed to separate sworn friends and unseat a genius soaring like Phaëton, whose freedom with an outward observance was his mishandling the reins of the Sun. It had come to pass that, when men spoke of the elements, not truth or feeling, but the oven and vintage, were meant. In taking up, later, the line of this ceremony between church and congregation, where by no power it could be restored, we felt the force of this prejudice threatening an equally violent result.

The personal distress of all dislocation doubtless attended that severing of the clerical tie. But the portent was of new growth. There are moral pains of birth and struggle for life. The man was not important to the Church till he left it to become such a figure as to make his judges the world's benefactors. Now he stood for a thought. His divorce from preaching allowed marriage with an idea, till then coyly courted, for an offspring of the best poetry and philosophy of the age. A shrewd suspicion of German inoculation flung at the movement the word *Transcendental*, for a disgrace, which, as of all names of good and odious things, turned to fame.

In truth, the out-break was nothing new under the sun. The fount of the Nile is discovered, but not of this spiritual Arethusa. Whoever was of that club meeting in Concord and Boston must recall the fellowship so dear, the delight as of another revelation, the Quaker peace, with but a dream of seeds of revolution dropping through the quiet air. Edward Everett likened the doctrine to Virgil's thunderbolt, three parts empty air. Was it wind the new husbandmen sowed? The whirlwind that was reaped was a boon. Yet most men did not dread, but laughed at the phenomenon as but moonshine or mirage. As well tell Columbus it was no new world he had reached when heaved in view the outlying island, one of a flock which now beat at our windows in the political storm. Previous explorers had sailed into the same latitudes of thought. The startling doctrine of the soul's sufficiency was no upstart or bastard, but a lawful line of ancient origin, in divers branches, Hebrew and Greek, — going back to Plato and Abraham, Lot and Seth, groves of Academus and Garden of Eden, before Bibles were. It was revived in the best words of Jesus and John and Paul. English translators dipped their buckets for it into the wisdom of the East. The Hindoo found himself a Yankee with no question of caste. The Christian Scriptures were paralleled from books of strange names in other tongues. The spring of wonder burst up in Teutonic soil, the same living water as in Indian bottles or Jewish jars. It filtered into the clear British sense. With astonishing virility the spiritual theory was propagated by Carlyle; and as visionary a mystic as ever wandered on the banks of the Ganges appeared in William Blake. Orthodoxy became ideal with Coleridge's "Aids to Reflection;" Wordsworth put the same meaning into his odes, and Cousin arranged it in philosophic terms. Yet when it was proclaimed in its legitimate conclusions in the sanctuary of Liberal Christianity, it was greeted with a shriek, as though Cudworth or Berkeley or Spinoza had never lived. Religion, under a show of progress, had declined. In too much logic, expression became the ebb of faith, till it reached low-water mark. Sectarian controversy brought down Trinitarian and Unitarian alike to the flats of a dry and barren doctrinality; and the high divine converse with which Puritan and Pilgrim began the Commonwealth gave place to a Babel of words. What splitting of particles, as described by Gibbon in the former age; what ransacking of prophecies, what dispute of the authority of this and that passage, what weighing of jots and tittles in diamond scales; instead of the grand war of ideas, what petty battles of texts! Andover and Cambridge responded to each other with paper popguns, not with the noise of His water-spouts. Into this squabble the angel blew his trumpet to summon to the privilege of direct communication with the Infinite; none so much surprised as the trumpeter at the ague-fit of anger and grief that ensued. He felt in order, without break or fault in the natural evolution. He had occasion to avenge his rejected sentiment in an address to the Graduating Class in the Cambridge Divinity School, which, like the last whirl of sticks of the savage's tinder-box, first struck fire. But what a dish to set before the King, that performance! After the short breathings of the gentle prayer, which had in it no pronouns, and one said was no prayer at all, came the textless discourse, preserved for ever in its sweet pungency, while all the replies to it are forgot. It was no hornet or drone lighting on us, but the sting of a honey-bee guarding for us our own luxury. It was the return of the Holy Ghost with voice, not recognized among manifold opposing echoes so long listened to in its stead. But no rude, unwarrantable assault could have begot such fear as that golden-mouthed speech. It meant business, and laid out a stint of work. The dismissed preacher had not been hushed. If he could not have the pulpit's velvet cushion, he would take the Lyceum's pine desk; and what a power he made the Lecture, is it not to be written in our chronicles?

In his farewell sermon, in Hanover Street, he had said there were functions of the ministerial office he should rejoice to discharge wherever he might exist. For these his change of situation was a help. As the painter stands off from the canvas to mark the accuracy of his drawing, this man's absence from his chosen calling gave distance for a true perspective, while he was doubly impressionable to compare another picture with the ecclesiastical. He had the advantage of a smooth temper. Perfect health stood bondsman for his equanimity, and the cool flesh of a child was type of his unfevered mind. He never rested and was never restless; his figure, the rifleman's statue, — not stirring till the fatal shot. He means something in every sketch, it was said of Hunt; and God filled this word-painter with intention, his own or the Spirit's you could not tell. They were the same. But, called to defend what he had said, he could give no account but his order to think. The responsibility was none of his. *So thought Francis Bacon* was authority enough for that philosopher's page; and this man was under command. His thought was not in his hands: he was in the hands of his thought. Like all who wear not their heart in their sleeve, put on no robe of enthusiasm, and warm their audience with no stove of animal heat, he was charged with being cold. The critics did not look close enough. They could not feel the spiritual flame nor appreciate that baptism of fire the Baptist foretold: which to the senses is a cool combustion. A warm temperament would have disqualified him for his task. Temperance was his star. After so much vapor we wanted dry light. Fondness for persons runs into idolatry of institutions, and checks audacious words. Only his dispassionate, if not unimpassioned disposition could deal purely with his theme. It did not occur to him he was going to hurt anybody's feelings: no vision or prophecy had ever hurt his. A full-grown superstition standing in the way, how but by undervaluation of the past, — as memory, habit, or tradition, — could he throw his whole weight into his axe at the root of the tree? When his friend said, "Here are my facts, I cannot give up them," "Here are my ideas," was his reply. The facts were bad. He wanted them to be better: as Dr. Hedge, being told the facts were against him and were stubborn things, answered, *So much the worse for the facts.* What shall be said to reports of the telescope pointed to sky or sea? We can but repeat them, as the captain below repeats the figures the mate on deck calls out to him from his quadrant lifted to the sun. Here was a finer glass turning to the heaven of truth over the sea of time; and the observer's sentence was translation of his sight. Interrogated, he could but recite what he had already said. When John Marshall's party-friends begged to know why he persisted in refusing to answer Albert Gallatin's speech, he at last said, Because it is unanswerable. So those who complained of and rejected could get no rejoinder to this lesson. He compelled his critics to become his quoters. Out of what root did blossoms of such genuine beauty and fragrance foil the cut-paper flowers of the creeds? The Divine Immediacy with man! One day, before a keen eye, water rising to its own level in a tube made a ruin of the Roman aqueducts. So it was shown the river of God is not confined to Jewish conduits. We must have nearer access to it than that long old file of Hebrew Kings, Judges, and Prophets, magnificent as are their monumental words and refreshing as is the flood they convey.

This seer's originality armed itself with a new style. The surprising fitness of trite terms in his use was a resurrection of the dictionary. The silence of a sage whets our eagerness to hear; and this man's advantage was his superiority to ambition, his willingness to be still, his indifference whether he used his eye or ear, his avoidance of eloquence, — which Dr. Johnson calls exaggeration, — and preference of low to high-sounding words, like the modest artist who gives the whole character of an object in neutral tints or a charcoal sketch. Why be forward or loquacious? Truth will find its own way and organ, and make dumb Moses more persuasive than rhetorical and mellifluous Aaron. It was not the only possible mood, perhaps not the highest manner; but it was his, and apt to the time. There came no prophet's burden or scream, but the voice of one careless of the fate of his person or proposition: trusting truth to the air and allowing it time to sink into the ear, not anxious to multiply himself, but to condense his message. He knew no method could avail but that of his own constitution. Incapable of feeling personal outrage or oppression, in good condition, content with the universe, as well fed as any of the children at the table, delicate in his taste, every pore informing him who was coming, and closing at rude approach, and every nerve an alarm-bell at any catechism, — neither seeking an audience nor itching to hear himself talk, he was quite unfit for an agitator or ecclesiastical demagogue. Yet his individuality kept him out of any class. He stood for humanity, and was one of the people. So his banishment from the Church on a technical ground and punctilio of form was as blessed ostracism as Dante's exile from Florence. Those going without the camp bearing some reproach are always redeemers. Inside the heavens are but half seen. That imagination which is eye and atmosphere is hindered by walls. A fence fences out more than it fences in. I must be free as an Indian, he said; for I want more liberty than that with which Christ has made me free.

These were intrusive allusions but that my topic must be treated with circumstantial illustration. A hero he will not be of his own tale. This story should be told, before all cognizant of the particulars pass from the stage, to vindicate the transcendental position as no affront to history, but protest against a mortgage of the future. It has been described as a transitory affair, like a meteor that shoots and explodes, or a plant without product or healthy root. But, standing guard for progress does not disown the past. Sceptic no more than Orthodox cuts off from his antecedents. Our ancestors had not only their solutions, but their questions too. They had sailed for new discovery, and swung uneasy at their moorings, with doubts suppressed by their situation or unripe for expression, — an inheritance for their sons, and coming to a head in brains born of their own. All our present growth was in their soil. The oak forest, that springs up after the pine is burnt or cleared away, pre-existed as shrubs or germs, for a while overgrown and kept down. Always in generous doubts nobler convictions fasten and thrive. The finest trees on the grounds where I ramble have forced their way through the clefts of the rocks. Paul was all the time in Saul. With his pains to prove his untainted lineage, did it ever occur to him that not the contradiction but cause of his heresy lay in the religious purity of his blood? Gamaliel, be sure, had his queries, however he managed for himself and his pupils, like many a preacher and Sunday-school teacher, to subdue them for the time. Dr. Beecher, accusing some members of the Massachusetts Convention of Congregational Ministers of departing from the faith of the Fathers, was asked by Dr. Lowell if there were any members who adhered to the faith, and could only cough out, Yes, *for substance!* He also in an ordination-sermon hurled Paul's anathema at the Unitarians as preachers of another gospel, and bade them depart and not shoot their poisoned arrows behind. The Unitarians had their pay when Dr. Beecher was arraigned as a heretic before the Presbyterian synod. But were the Unitarians rebellious or degenerate children of their theological sires? No: they maintained the Pilgrim line, were Puritans of the nineteenth century, striking for freedom to worship God.

"Once more unto the breach, dear friends, once more!"

Transcendentalism did not foul its nest, or, as is continually charged, despise its mother; but unfolded the faith implied in every act of the settlers of the land. It cast off naught precious in the old belief; but was a new vessel, a better Mayflower for the Truth's escape from her foes. It set us all afloat; but that may be better than to be all ashore. A church once floated off to Nova Scotia from the British in Boston, and still lives. The essence of faith is advance. Like a political constitution, it provides for its own amendment.

In the moving on of mankind, the way-marks differ

at each turn of the road. It is the general direction we must look at, like a ship that tacks, or carriage winding round the hill. Would we repeat our Fathers' case, the items of their life? That were false imitation, mimicry, a poor copy of those great masters. The living likeness is to apply their principles to our condition. One star differs from another, but they all go one way. One boulder has not its neighbor's weight or size, but every scratch on the primitive rock follows the same line of the compass. The icebergs show every sort of shape and similitude, yet all drift to the South. Our reformers square not their theories to those of any former age, yet steadily with every step near the goal of the same millennium. Like the angel that came down to trouble the pool at certain seasons, this visitation of the Spirit is periodical. One said its return was like that of the seventeen-years locust. But it always betokens conflict. Byron describes the cannon-roar that broke in on the ballroom at Belgium's capital as mistaken for thunder or rattling of a car along the stony street; but volley after volley came to prove its nature: and every stroke of religious genius claims kith and kin with prior ones, though fifty generations lie between. At the gates of hell, Sin convicts Satan as her offspring; and all beneficence is born of goodness. The intellectual regenerator is never heady, but calm as he is warm. He is careful as a surveyor of his spirit-level. Of the re-creator none could tell if his temper were flame or phlegm. He struck no attitude, stood on no stage, had looked in no glass, was no oratoric gymnast, never strained nor sweat, rolled neckerchief in his hand, or wiped emotion from his brow, but had laid the robes aside and sang without singing-garlands. He was poet, but not laureate. His leaves were loose: he found them with difficulty; and his only noticeable gesture was an emphatic look, which a famous lawyer, who thought it worth the entrance-fee, said was directed at nothing. But it indicated that the speaker's subject had in his ecstasy become an object of sight. He was of the family of prophets who first are, then see, and then say, — that being the order. In the old controversy, who were the circumcision and Abraham's children, Jesus decides for the patriarch's spirit against his blood; and what bomb-proof occupant of an accredited church could vie with this teacher of Christianity without its name? It signified execution when into the Spirit's hands was put this imaginative tool, polished with courtesy and taking from good humor the finest edge. The least acidity eats into the steel; but the keenness of rebuke is its tenderness.

Yet this genius was too high and subtile for popular effect. A university of education, doing more for scholars than any college, it needed the supplement of talent to spread its inspiration into the common school; and that came in the stalwart figure — like a second Luther — of Theodore Parker. He made no feast for a few of nightingales' tongues, but a board with bread for millions. He was not a seer, but an officer, — the deputy-sheriff of ideas. Never lived man more strong and faithful to execute the writ. Piety and philanthropy were as the coming and going of his breath. Like an old Hebrew, he turned every piece of paper to see if the name of God were on it;

and all his study went into act. He suffered no volume of truth to rest with uncut leaves on the shelf, no scrap of information to be thrown into the waste-basket. There were those well enough pleased to have the new speculations remain mental exercises, and let institutions alone. Parker tore down the partition of esoteric and exoteric as the veil of the temple was rent in twain. He could not conceive of a scholar keeping a bit of his learning from the people to himself. He bitterly denounced the policy of doling out wisdom as the folk were thought able to bear it. All the poetry he undertook to turn into prose, as Wendell Phillips wanted Lincoln's proclamation, in Georgia, in spurs and boots. Whatever could be truly said or sung, with him must be done. Radical doctrine, says my Orthodox friend, is not practical: it goes to pieces in North Street. In Parker's hands every thing the doctrine was opposed to went to pieces, — as Schiller says of the cannon-ball shattering all in its way that it may shatter its mark. Call the new views mist? He condensed them into a thunder-bolt. Call them nebulous? He showed they were world-stuff. Slavery, intemperance, vice, criminal classes, perishing classes, no cause or human condition but he took for his province. Overladen with social work in Boston, he carried his crusade against superstition and iniquity into every corner of the land. Soft-hearted, he made his sensibilities the furnace in which to forge his weapons, beside the transcendental writings which were his Springfield armory. Many friendly ties broke under his heresy. He seemed to have gone to the funeral of his affections, till he lost all bias of sentiment, and dealt justice without extraneous considerations. He disowned the maxim that scorn and anger were instruments unfit to be used. Only bad men had no right to them! Whose contempt should be so great, whose wrath so terrible, as that of the good against the ungodly and all their works? He had no private malice, bore no grudge against the individuals he publicly scored; but he carried his antipathies of principle so far as to be styled an intellectual ruffian. Calling of names in meeting, where the assailed cannot answer, appears to them an unfair advantage, and stirs ill blood. To impeach the motives serves less than to argue the case. But though his sarcasm was resented and complained of, it was the base custom or false doctrine the holders had identified themselves with which felt his severity. In that his arrows stuck. Dr. Channing said the slaveholder was to him an abstraction: it was the system of slavery he discussed. Mr. Garrison answered, Is the slaveholder an abstraction to the slave? To Parker, sin was a man. Living in Luther's time, he would have believed in and thrown his inkstand at the devil. Incarnate evil he condemned, and would make way with that Dagon, planting his shoulders like another Samson at the pillars of Gaza. "Stick or stone, whatever comes to hand," says Virgil, "the mob will throw." His only choice among means of offence was of the most effective, thinking no such rights of war as Grotius describes belonged to wrong-doers, in the conflict of words. For the tyrant or traitor he had wrath, and freely drew for his portrait a copy of Herod or Iscariot; for the bibliolater, ridicule, — but his anger or irony; like the Indian bullet that cleaves the buffalo and pursues its way, went through the embodiment to the essence of mischief in society and the soul. Had the Calvinist some artificial condition of redemption? He laughed at it as like a red string tied round the little finger for an amulet or charm. He was not revealer, but administrator, of a new testament; and Cobden or Cobbett, Webster or Lincoln, did not use a more resistless plainness of speech. He had occasion. Religion had deceased into tenet, like the coral insect into the coral bed. Men were at ease in Zion: liturgy had become lethargy. As the keeper stirs the sleepy lion with his pole, or the electrician passes a spark through the torpid frame, or the guide shakes and rouses the traveller sinking to deathly slumber in the snow, he made no scruple of roughly disturbing the more fatal repose of the elect in their assurance of heaven, while leaving their brethren to perish of oppression on earth. When the fugitive was in his house, this new Templar added cocked pistols on his pillow to his grandfather's rusty gun at the door, and was ready with word or blow. He had a relish for irony and enjoyed the fray. When one said to him, "You have not your ancestor's military bent," "Have I not?" he grimly replied. His brain was a masked battery ever ready to be unlimbered. As public questions degenerate into private disputes, he sometimes descended into personalities and details which he should have looked down on from the sun. But truth took a step forward in his word.

Yet Liberal Christians, already persecuted as extremists, not only refused to follow, but hesitated to own his freedom of thought. They had gone far enough. It was time to stop. Channing was the last result of reason. An inch more was the jumping-off place. Parker had assailed what Channing stoutly defended, — the supernatural; and the miracles of the New if not of the Old Testament were now the citadel whose defence alone prevented the surrender of Christianity. Belief in them was made the test. Norton maintained the miraculous as the essence of religion. Channing was disappointed in Parker because he declared it unessential, if not untrue; but Parker has prevailed, if not in refuting or setting aside, yet in displacing it as the touchstone. Moreover, he questioned any verbal gospel. The leading scholars had with much trouble purged the text. He denied the authority of the text, however pure. He removed every outward landmark, and planted the boundaries in the soul. What we shrank from was the logical conclusion. Yet the basis the Unitarian majority still repose in is the history, the prophet, not the human mind. That is not trusted as a final organ of truth. Channing is leaned on as the pillar of this Scripture position, and it will by many be held sacrilege to doubt his claims as a seer. His writings, however, hold not with thinkers their place. They defy not the tooth of time. His genius was for reflection and sentiment rather than insight. Eloquence was his peculiar mark. Who that was young when he was in his prime can forget the matchless simplicity and fervor of his speech, — that voice of melody so singular, and resonance one could not credit from the slender chest, audible to the vast congregation because of the might of interior whispers it reverberated; not a syllable lost because every one was saturated with spirit, and carrying the hearer to heaven on that unique rising inflection which, though a generation has passed, must still ring in every ear on which it once fell? Yet, in the record on the cold page, eloquence takes up too much room. We tire, if we read for information or new direction, of the long climacteric roll. As the world quickens its speed, we dislike preface: we want pith, and praise orators like the English who give us figures of arithmetic rather than rhetoric, and come to the point. Emerson, in the region of intellect, meets this demand. He sees too clearly and too much to dilate with emotion or expand his phrase. If his style for a moment takes on a fine sound, he resists temptation, checks the impulse. Immensity of meaning constrains him to study economy of words. Channing called him poet, but no philosopher. But there is no distinction of poetry from truth. Only verse-wrights deal with the unreal. Shakspeare is as prudent as Bacon, as judicious as Hooker, as metaphysical as Kant. Emerson reaches the supreme height, if not of Mont Blanc, yet one of the *aiguilles*.

As a philanthropist, Channing was sublime; but truth is the highest philanthropy, and whoever describes a circle about yours exceeds you as benefactor. To behold and declare how things stand in the universe, — to widen a man's horizon, — is a greater mercy than to feed or clothe. A good feeling, a humane theory, does not suffice. Conscious benevolence is a lower motive than Christ's martyrdom for the truth. Channing's feeble health and solitary life separated him from the race his ideal goodness would bless. He spoke as an apostle, hardly of the same blood with those who heard, discoursed downward from his desk, distanced the laboring men he talked to, held at arm's length the masses for whom he professed his interest and in whom he felt a serious concern. He was not in direct fellowship. He had views rather than vision. He used a reflecting telescope, not the naked eye. Conversing with him, one felt not so much like a fellow-creature as part of the instrument he was at work with to find and catalogue the celestial facts. He respected another's mind as an explorer does his companion for his help in the expedition. Something not organic, but derivative, characterizes his instructions. "A potted Plato" one called him. Unsurpassably lofty in feeling and aim, his page is so deficient in close reason or imagination one-half the sentences can be omitted with no disturbance of the method or loss of sense. Not for the sake of odious comparison, but of a true leadership, I would lift the standard on which testimony is blazoned in larger letters than any scheme even of charity. To one whose sermons had disturbed his audience it was said, "Why not suit and time your matter better to those in your charge? I suppose you preach to do good?" "No," he answered: "I do not. I preach to testify. Let me be true. God will see to the good, which he alone is and does." The great modern character is the reporter, who keeps the world of society and politics in motion. But he is tool and servant of another head-reporter of thought, of an interviewer of conscience, of a watcher of that sky Coleridge looked at when he said, "Only after celestial observations can terrestrial charts be constructed." *It will make you see stars*, says the coarse worldly proverb, of any sudden shock. But these spiritual stars are no unsubstantial sparkles of a stunned brain. The eye that saw them can turn the other way, and in "English Traits" and "Representative Men" prove as keen in the earthly direction as in the heavenly. *It is all in the eye*, whose lenses no surveyor's theodolite can match. He who has sight need not attack another or defend himself. This ocular or binocular arm makes a new style of warfare, like that introduced into the field. Cæsar led his troops. Napoleon figures in a cocked hat, and Jackson on his horse. In the holy bard's imagery, the Most High is made to copy human warriors, gird his sword on his thigh, and ride prosperously to battle. But here is a war most wonderful in history, fought by an invisible man called Möltke, without musket, spear, or coat of mail, — only map and pencil; and a million of men stand ready to follow where he draws. It is a ghostly conflict, rehearsed on the stage of fancy: the awful engines play harmless as a little model in the secret chambers of the brain, before hosts fall dead and fortresses capitulate, and civil populations, a hundred-fold more than the beleaguering army, surrender and sue for peace, and the old boundaries of nations are changed. Not by unreasoning passion are social victories won. Said Ichabod Nichols, when one talked of using strong words, "Put your strength into your reasons." Poisoning of wells, Southern proposals to import plague into the North, assassination, and starvation do not carry the day. The Communist throws petroleum to fire the city, pulls down the Column, tears up coffins and murders priests; but brings not in the free, equal, and fraternal reign. In America or France such methods make the gentler sex the worse. Light is better than lightning; and lightning is the best social and civil help when tamed to run soft and obedient on an errand. The great reformer is the discerner, —

> "Who revolutions works without a murmur,
> Or rustling of a leaf beneath the skies."

Transcendentalism relies on those ideas in the mind which are laws in the life. Pantheism is said to sink man and nature in God, Materialism to sink God and man in nature, and Transcendentalism to sink God and nature in man. But the Transcendentalist, at least, is belied and put in jail by the definition, which is so neat at the expense of truth. He made consciousness, not sense, the ground of truth; and, in the present devotion to physical science and turn of philosophy to build the universe on foundations of matter, we need to vindicate and reassert his premise. Is the soul reared on the primitive rock? or is no rock primitive, but the deposit of spirit, therefore in its lowest form alive, and ever rising into organism to reach the top of the eternal circle again, — as in the well one bucket goes down empty and the other rises full? The mistake is to make the everlasting things subjects of argument instead of sight. No logic can compass them. The more we reason about them in the terms of the understanding, the farther we are away. Wait awhile, says the investigator, and we may tell you if God exists and you are immortal. But God is no conclusion. A Deity deduced from phenomena were finite as they, and nothing worth. God is the commencement, if he be at all; and to expect, by breaking open some atom, to see him come out like the smoke into a giant from the fisherman's box is atheism at the start.

The Transcendentalist sought a basis of knowledge beyond the senses, and of religion beyond ecclesiastical services. His religious feelings were hurt by going to church, and he encountered the odium of going into the woods and fields, or on to the sea instead. He affronted the procession of Sabbath-keepers with the needless insult of secular avocations, or sports in plain sight. Because it was Sunday, in a meeting-house and a pulpit, and with a Scripture text and ordained minister, bigotry and bad scholarship were not sanctified. He heard not only the truckman and porter swear, but the name of God taken in vain in the worst profanity of the lifeless repetition of liturgical forms. In rocky resounding clefts, he could worship better than in the house made with hands. Standing outside the church-door, the music of praise pleased him better that he could not hear the sectarian sermon. On the reeling steamer's deck, with ecstasy through the cabin-windows came to him the anthem accompanied with a part, described in no musical notation, by the winds and waves. He disowned the temple's peculiar claim; and a band of play-actors with the sacrifice of their talent and time to help some poor and aged member, or promote a worthy cause, made the stage a pulpit, and the theatre a church. Holy day or place? There is no such thing. A holy man or woman, and a Holy Spirit, but no holy time or spot save that hallowed by a righteous act. Sacred office or exercise? An innocent child teaches more than a sensual priest, politic cardinal, or bad pope; and we scout the notion that any base officials are in trust with the waters of salvation, or have a lock on the river of life as one commands a valve or faucet with his hand. A face with the beauty of that shadow cast by the first consciousness of a parentage beyond earthly father or mother communicates wisdom which canonical books and apostolic succession cannot match. As in old time some people worshipped in churches and cloisters outside city walls, these Transcendentalists defied the conventional adoration with a piety of their own.

The Transcendental school must, however, encounter one criticism. Part of it led into the doctrine of Divine Impersonality. Emerson followed Cousin. The objection to Personality was its supposed limitation. It lowered the Infinite. But you say a great deal about God when you say he is *impersonal*. You lower him negatively, and deny his chief attribute, if not his being. The guilt of presumption is not avoided, but incurred. Does piety decline to imprison him in human measures? We had thought humanity not his prison, but his image. What other larger measure of him do you propose? The sky were a prison. Besides, we do not measure God: he measures himself with countless graduations in all his creatures, and without this self-measurement on an endless scale we could not know him at all. We conceive ill of him in outward dimensions like a giant. He can fill the firmament, and dole himself out in the wing of a fly, brain of an ant, or burnish and buzz of a bee. He is spirit; and that we cannot imagine as impersonal. Spirit is intelligence and intent. If you hesitate to ascribe to him purpose, you resist the instinct of mankind in all ages, which from the Hottentot to the Hindoo, the Chinaman to the North-American Indian, the Greek to the Turk, and the Christian to the Mahometan, finds the staple and fundamental article of its devotion in the will of God. In teaching that he is spirit, and that birth from the Spirit is like the *sound* of the wind, Jesus curiously identifies spirit and *person* as synonyms of speech. Spirit or Person: neither implies finiteness more than the other.

The world affirms Personality. Is *world* or *whirled* its proper name? What is it but motion from centres of force, in mighty balls or imponderable particles: in the stone that resolves itself into orbits of atoms, and the drop that is a sea for living things to swim, nor, more than leviathan, lack room? All this action, and no will? Nothing too heavy to lift, or too light and little to get hold of; yet no agent, meaning, energy, or behest? If no divine, then no human personality, which were a causeless effect. In scholastic phrase God is not *personated*, but *personating* Person. If this human quality is no gauge of him, he is lost altogether, as we are lost; for with our personality goes immortality, and we are photograph-plates taking pictures to-day, broken to-morrow; and then no more impressions. A strange way to dignify and exalt the

Divinity to make him and his work such a shallow fading surface! To say he is an idea of the human mind, and comes to consciousness, or is conscious of himself in it, does not belittle him. Ideas are substantial and eternal; and where or how else he is conscious who shall say? You have several homes, — in city, country, at the Springs, or by the sea. His houses who shall number?

Person signifies the unfathomable. Who shall say where the whisper of the wind begins? A man's voice or sound is from his inmost self, like the character an actor performed through his mask; and what is the material universe but the pipe Omnipotence shapes, as a boy his whistle, to play what tunes he likes. God is the word: what speaks in the beginning was with him and was he. Personality is no degradation. As the sparkle of a dewdrop implies the sun, and that is a spark to the light that feeds it; as a trickling drop balances the sea, and nothing less could be its parent; as the running of the drops together between the shrunken boards of a barn first brought to my mind the mystery of the world; as a breath were not without boundless ether; as a pebble dropped in the water or as a blow or gesture of the hand goes to the confines of Nature and is co-extensive with gravitation, — so the faintest emotion implies the Most High; and God takes up his abode in the lowly and contrite heart.

Doubtless we bely him, as we do every thing, in our speech. But it is greater untruth to him not to speak. Some word we cannot help. Those most stout like Goethe to say all words are inadequate go on to use them, though every word, used or emphasized alone, cleaves from our thought and breaks down. But if we discard the *Infinite Self* we lose the *Universe*, which is *Version* of One, or Person translated; and what does Person mean but that the world is not senseless surface, but stands for something, was made in earnest, and not by accident or for sport? Personality is not part of it, but the whole, — top and bottom of things, sum and substance of philosophy; and the impersonality the sage imputes as an honor is poor, cheap, and finite. We argue what are called the Carlyle and Buckle theories of history. Are events determined by persons, or by laws? If history relates what is done by inspiration or design, the question disappears. Personality is nothing, or it is all. It is not the pound we put God in, but essence of the freedom which is his necessity, and to share which is man's glory. If we are personal, we have a destiny; if impersonal, only a doom. But this personal persistence was by some Transcendentalists treated with slight; and all curiosity about it flouted as impertinent peeping into what we had no business with. Such scorn is affront to the aspiration of mankind. Forceythe Willson, after listening to a lecture that brought immortality into doubt, said, "Philosophy is good; but if philosophy contradicts my instincts, I throw it overboard."

Personality alone vindicates prayer. If Deity be Immeasurable Consciousness in which I have part and lot, then prayer is no gymnastic self-excitation beginning and ending with my own will, but some stir of the Divinity it comes from and goes to. It constrains God so far as his liberty can be constrained; for there is that he cannot help. How can he help seeing and hearing his child whose voice is part of his soliloquy? Can he say, I will not listen or look? He is bound in his own nature to hear and answer prayer; for he is not one Individual and you another, he sitting up there with ready-made laws to apply to you as a foreign substance; but you and he, even as Jesus and he, are One. He cannot get along without you, or avoid blessing you. Your inmost desire is his interpreter. Were prayer an arbitrary whim, across the track of his predestination it were crushed like a pin on the iron rail. But request or answer is foreordained and insured against possible failure or loss.

To one Transcendental philosopher — Mr. Alcott — we are in debt for his vital conception of Personality. A pure mystic, subsisting on the thin sweet grass of the mount of vision, in the full sweep of the pervading theory that blew like a trade-wind against the conception of a conscious and willing Deity, he kept his footing and saw God keeping his. In all his Conversations East and West expounding matters, so singular to charm and hard to penetrate, he has held by selfhood as the sheet-anchor of creation, and rendered a service for which his memory will be honorable and dear. He was true Transcendentalist, teaching that the soul is no ephemeral thing, but lives beyond the momentary impression, in the past, the distant, the future, and in that eternity where time disappears or all times are alike. True philosophy is no peculiarity of dainty speculation, but staple of practical life. It is an idea becoming flesh, or common sense exalted by sentiment. Not only a poet, like Wordsworth, can address his ideal child, —

> "Thou whose exterior semblance doth bely
> Thy soul's immensity,"

not only Shakspeare can make Lady Macbeth say to her husband, —

> "Thy letters have transported me beyond
> *This ignorant present*, and I feel now
> The future in the instant,"

but the negro pilot could tell the captain in Charleston harbor, "Wind and tide against you, it is ten miles to the city; but, weather favoring, you are there now." We are not blind to what we see through. The Transcendentalist leaps out of routine, shakes off the weight of custom, most are fettered by and drag as a ball and chain. He detaches every thing from himself, to make it an object of contemplation and enchanting marvel. His own personality he wonders at, and tries half vainly to explore. "I want to know more of myself, — this very Jonathan: I have lived seventy years with him, and he is a great mystery to me." His theory enters into character as well as thought. While dogmatism makes out its exhaustive schemes of the universe, and ambitious conceit and desire to shine babble their presumptuous judgments, he sits and smiles at the depth their lines dangle in; and, when they correct or contradict him, learns not to answer again. He asks nothing for himself but to be allowed still to think, and put his observations in words which passion may reject till reason receives. He takes all injury and wrong, from foes or friends, out of his sensibility and into the alembic of his reflections, whence the crude ore and rough fragments run pure gold. No Caliban or Shylock but enriches the poet's drama; no people so bad and hard the thinker cannot enjoy. Said my friend, I like that "Great Misery" island: it is like so many folks I have seen, barren and unpromising at a distance and first sight; but when you are there, the green fields are all around you. His forecast lights up the darkest hour. Said my friend, walking among the cliffs, Reasoning is like the rock ahead you hope to mount and see further from; and faith has foretaste of paradise.

We shall discover that our glory is not pure passivity, to be the sport of impressions, like feathers in every wandering breeze, but personality. We shall be convinced that conscious selfhood rooted in the self of Nature, and spreading into man or angel, is no selfishness, but the only possible generosity. A certain dissolute sympathy may survive self-reliance; but all genuine love and sacrifice die with it. No earthly good a noble person will not sooner decline or impart than demand. Personality has no measure: it is measure of every thing else. It is the golden rod with which the angel takes the length and breadth of the New Jerusalem. In the present rage of physical science the *particles* are contending with it for victory. But they are its servants, and usurpers when they snatch at its rightful sway. The thinker goes with his thought, which can reach nothing beyond itself. No God is cognizable above my inmost being, which he is. Where my imagination goes, I go; and it goes to him and heaven.

The objection to personality in God is its likening him to man's which is limited. But this objection assumes its own fact. Who has laid down or reported the metes and bounds of *human* personality? It is unlimited. Person in the sense of appearance is finite. The body which the soul is in, or rather which is in the soul, has limits, but not that in which the body is contained. Man's eyes, says Herbert, "dismount the highest star." David's description of trying to leave the Lord by ascending to heaven, or making his bed in hell, or flying on the wings of the morning to the uttermost parts of the sea, not only shows where God was, but where David was! Is our imagination the compass of Nature? But our imagination is the carriage we sit in. Paul knew a man who was in the seventh heaven. Rise high and float far as the balloon will, the gazer from beleaguered Paris walls, or a Fourth of July muster-field, outstrips it standing on the ground.

> "One morn is in the mighty heaven,
> And one in our desire!"

But the last outshines the first.

> "And those eyes, the break of day,
> Lights that do mislead the morn."

Shakspeare knew space was not the holder, but the accident and servant of the mind. We, like God, possess it; not it us. "I own part of Boston Common," said Father Taylor; "and I will tell nobody which part it is." We cannot tell where our property in Nature ends.

Nor is human personality limited in time more than in space. Doubtless the almanac or family register will tell us when we were born. But our soul is older than our organism. It precedes its clothing. It is the cause, not the consequence, of its material elements; else, as materialists understand, it does not properly exist. Jesus asserted the truth of all men when he said, "Before Abraham was, I am." Who can tell where he began? It is a wise child that knows his own father. Grandparents reappear in the babes they play with. The Jews thought older prophets returned in later ones; and it might be Elias that had come back in Jesus. Naturalism traces man farther than to Eden, and finds his progenitor in some fossil fish or reptile that lived measureless cycles ago. Napoleon said he was the founder of his own family. We were our own ancestors, and shall find it quite impossible to decide our commencement in time, though we point to our cradle in the garret. We all lay in one crib, if we knew where it was; and Plato's doctrine of pre-existence we have laughed at only to see it recur under the flag of the straitest orthodoxy of our day.

Human personality has no intrinsic limitation in itself. It is sometimes said, men or particular races of men, as the Negro or Chinese, stop growing like an animal or plant. But they are only by adverse circumstance or their fellow-creature's oppression tethered for a time. None can predict or set any goal to the progress of science. Yet that is only one of the lines: art, society, government, are others in the progress of man. This shock of conventional horror at supposing any likeness of God with man is as profane as it is inhuman. God and man must rise or fall together. We have been afraid and ashamed to think nobly of ourselves. But he is like us! He made us in his image; and, laugh at it who will, we do and must somehow make him in ours; for were the parent unlike his child, it were absurd to speak of parent or child.

Nothing in us lasts like faith. Richter calls it the night-flower blooming into the hour when sense and memory fade. I learned the fact in an involuntary experiment of being thrown to the ground by a train of cars. It was "a vision of sudden death." For a moment it was all of death that can be known, only that in returning consciousness came resurrection to myself and my friends. But in that moment of decease was no fear. Had I been riding above, not with a crushed limb underneath, I could have felt no more sure of the wise regularity, in whose chariot without falling I was borne.

Orthodoxy and Physical Science are considered foes. But they build on the same foundation. In their method they meet. The last asserts we get all knowledge, and the first that we get religious knowledge, through the senses, — the Book, the Prophecy, the Miracle being the foundations of faith, as if there were less piety in Plato than in Locke. Transcendental Thought is the only communion with God, save by some proxy that casts our vote for us, like a master for his slaves, or patron for everybody under the roof of his mill. What wonder the believer should conclude in the scepticism with which the scientist begins, and doubt be the Land's End for them both. With neither is any option. The structures they put up are different, but the site of both alike is the sand; only the believer sees not how he is logically shut up to the scientist's frank expectation that the rain and the wind will beat and blow till the edifice fall, according to the Latin proverb that we owe our possessions and ourselves alike to death. The consistent physicist, like Mill, carries his point to the denial of all necessary truth. The figures of the multiplication-table and the properties of a triangle, all the axioms of the mathematician and geometer, a square, cube, line, or circle, may be such only to us and not in some other world, there being no such thing as ascertainable truth. The contemptuous proverb, "He does not know much, and what he does know he does not know for certain," hits the whole race with its vulgar fling. The Christian solace so many millions have hugged to their breast, "What thou knowest not now thou shalt know hereafter," is refused; for death is no solution, but only the last dodge.

So truth is not what is, but what one troweth; a name for everybody's notion and all contradictory beliefs! It is the honor of the Transcendentalist — every great soul from Hebrew Moses to Hebraic John Brown — to affirm truth otherwise as eternal vision of what suffers no change, the consonance of reality in Nature and the mind. Apart from perception truth is not. The Greek tongue excels the English in having a verb for truth corresponding to the noun, and the apostle speaks of "*truthing* in love." No canonical book has a nobler verse than that in the Apocrypha,—"Wisdom is a loving spirit:"

for love is not born of wisdom, but wisdom of love; and neither is born of matter or the flesh. To rest our case in miracle is to rest it in the letter that killeth; for all phenomena, like the letters in the Primer, are but an alphabet making sense only as arranged by some intelligence. It matters not what shape matter may take: it is an unmeaning syllable till adopted by the intellect. If the water became wine, or a few loaves and fishes a ton of food, it was a cipher still of no significance before it was chosen to convey the spirit's despatch. It is not the wire stretching from England to America for which we care; but the messages sent over it beneath the deep, unquenched by all its billows, unsilenced by its mighty roar.

Preoccupied with ideas, God's true mediators, we look upon marvels with an incurious eye. I confess I am not moved when the table tips. The wonder is just as great when it reposes firmly on its legs. Stones thrown through the windows by freakish elfs hold not my reflections like the glass made from the flux of their crumbled grains. All is in discrimination; nothing in the gross fact. The delicate odor of a tea-rose, said one, transports me: but at one smell of the pond-lily I say, No more I thank you! The Divinity gives us facts enough. We cannot manage one of a thousand. I rather ask him to stay his hand than from his horn of plenty continue to pour. He has led me into the Gallery; and I have no fear of his hurrying me out before it is half seen. The Transfiguration by Raphael, or Wedding-feast in Cana by Paul Veronese, or Conception by Corregio, is not a subject that holds or concentres my regards more than any simply human theme, — a ship in port by Turner, landscape by Corot, or the "Sower" by Millet; for God is as near in the field or on the sea as by any mountain, in any marriage or origin of life, with whatever unusual signs. Sinai made no better thunder and lightning than the Jura, or the wood-crowned hill whence in my boyhood the flaming cloud made its rush, and the red bolt leaped as a sword from the scabbard. I am grateful to antecedents and ancestors; but why explore the processes by which they earned what I inherit, instead of for my posterity earning more? I value the Bible; but shall I prefer it to what it records? It were to prize the family-register before the domestic joy. The Scriptures are not authority, but notes and memorandum book for experience, which has no Heretofore or Hereafter or Elsewhere, but interminable omnipresent Now.

IV.

RADICALISM.

WE learn how much there is in a name to love or hate. The apostles, forbid to speak in the name of Jesus, rejoiced to be counted worthy to suffer shame for it. It is not the word that is detested, but the thought, the dearest part of a man. He that loveth father or mother more than that is not worthy of it. "I do not like the word Radical" is the last phrase in thousand-fold repetition. But is it well to quarrel with the dictionary, like Don Quixote with the windmill? Words do not exist by our permission or any governor's proclamation. God makes them. They are born out of the air. Democrat, Republican, Copperhead, Communist,— it were easier to reduce a fort than silence any such epithet. Chartist, Fenian, International,— William or Victoria might be glad to expunge those titles. But they will not down at the bidding of count or king. No arrival so important as that of a new denomination, a name in the mouth, an organic power on the earth. Dr. Channing said he belonged to no sect, but willingly bore the name Unitarian on account of its odium. I do not choose to be called Radical; but, if it be an unpopular designation, label me with it. It must mean something good. Let us be what respectability and conservatism have an instinct to scorn! Out of some corruption is forged every new thunder-bolt of speech which people deprecate and dread. Yet a bad name loses its repulsiveness by degrees. As the tortoise shell is cut and scraped, dropping some roughness with each process, at every touch of the saw and file and sand, to get its last polish from the human palm, so a distasteful term, Whig or Abolitionist, under the critical knife and after much handling, shows signs of preciousness, becomes bright and smooth. Print it, roll it under your tongue, and it will come out right.

Everybody takes his turn at reform. The Tory Eldon said with an oath, if he could begin again it would be as an agitator. We know the ethics of *compromise* and *temporize*. Men have made Christ's tenderness in withholding some things from his disciples a warrant for treachery. An eminent preacher says he has thoughts it were premature to publish. What is the time to tell a thought but when you have it? The inspiration is your commission.

Radicalism is *rootedness*, the quality of the root, which Paul says we are borne by and do not bear, the stability of plant or man. Is it tearing up by the roots? Jesus announces that operation for what his Father had not set out. But the gardener knows how the good tree is made thrifty by going down to its roots to stir them. Scraping my old myrtle makes it quick and green.

There are two kinds of radicalism. The one boasts: the other prays, and joins the great communion of human dependence. Faith is no manufacture or article of private consumption, but a tradition of the human race. The mark, not to be counterfeited, of the genuine Radical is humility, — confessing God in history, that we are lifted to our vantage-ground by all foregoing action as mountains rise by successive throes. My dear friend professes to put himself squarely outside of Christianity, and thinks so he does; but he can no more do it than eliminate from his veins his ancestral blood. Do we disdain to inherit civilization, government, art, material benefit from our sires? Let us then raze the old houses and shops, despise the custom of the ancient stand, pry up the rails we ride over, and, as the Irishman said, to decry asking my neighbor's help, not be under a compliment to anybody! Is there no moral capital? Can we dispense with customs and institutions more than with the wharf and street, reservoir and sidewalk, town-house and bridge? Jacob's well stood for more than water. Better unlimber your organ of destructiveness on outward improvements, than those within. Continuation, not origination, is our part. Build on the old basis, stand and walk a step forward in the old path. If God be father, the Past is mother, of our mind. I heard of a man preferring his immortality to his source, his own existence to his Maker's. He was logical, on the supposition that he was made by himself and for himself, and, like the Pharisee, to pray thus with himself. But if there be such a thing as Humanity, that I am part of, then there is Divinity. A disinherited man we pity; a disinherited race were extinct.

Step by step: that title of the story is the tale of

mankind. We are to rear an Art Museum. On what ground? First, a wilderness; then a battle-field with savage nature and more savage man; then a harvest-field; then a mart of commerce; lastly, the hall of knowledge and delight. Contempt of the rudest aboriginal ways knocks out the underpinning.

But we must go on. "There are in Boston," said one to an old citizen, "no ancient families to justify pride of birth." The citizen replied, "We have their descendants." "Point me," was the rejoinder, "to one case of the blue blood." "I do not like to be egotistical," answered again the long-descended man. Doubtless we need the grace of self-criticism to temper self-complacency. Our individuality runs not only into variety, but oddity. In avoiding monotony and uniformity, we lose unity in our architecture. Let the new Museum be an academy to reclaim us from our riot of independence to some standard of beauty and criterion of taste, not only in our edifices but our manners and thoughts, to grow from that root without which there can neither be a great community nor a California pine.

But let us have the branch as well as the root. No conceit of progress is so gross as that of eschewing all change. What absurdity is this circular and printed sketch of doctrine, sent us to sign, as if words could be bonds or bounds! We must be atomically united, like the parts of a tree, with the Spirit for our enlivening sap. At a meeting for church union I heard a speech informing the company how Unitarians were to be killed off, by preparation of books of moral science suited to establish the Trinitarian truth. Harness a horse of high spirit into your chaise, he travels with alacrity and joy. But he would resent being tackled into a truck; and the Holy Ghost, set to drawing the old cart which passes for the Church, will tear it to pieces. If you would be safe, hitch a donkey into your dray. Science a means, and your establishment the end? Every thing outward must serve the soul. Every creed is an arrested development. We think of the Bible as a structure solid and eternal. It is the record of alteration without ceasing,—patriarchs giving way to judges, judges to kings, kings to priests, priests to prophets, and prophets to Jesus their head, and Jesus to the Spirit. Vital power sloughs off old formulas. Some Northern churches had negro galleries a quarter of a century ago. It was suggested, in one case, to evacuate or remove the wooden box from which, as one said, the colored folk looked down on the congregation like crows. The fierce and almost universal opposition to this it is difficult now to conceive. But at length the high enclosure went; and not by all the king's horses and all the king's men could it be restored. So pass the stiffest ceremonials beyond recovery. Who could be at charges or shave the head to conciliate bigots, as Paul and his companions did? Yet, such is the superstition for Scripture examples, a friend says on the strength of that old instance he could cross himself among the Catholics. Does then an apostle's act of course indicate the law of perfect conduct? If the Trinitarian Doxology be sung, I can join in the tune, but not in the words. When one declined a true believer's asking for alms, saying, "I am a heretic," "Oh, sir, your money is orthodox," was the reply. Of the orthodoxy of good music there is no doubt.

True Radicalism is also of a loving spirit. There is a sour sort of it, the fruit being still green; but the ripe and sweet variety we shall have to adopt. We fix on a creed as final, as the farmer calls his choice apple *Seek-no-further;* but the new growth outstrips and leaves it behind. Progress is the law. When the Eastern Railway was built, ample room was left at the crossings for the cars. But forty bridges have to be raised to let the Pullman palace cars pass through. Narrow terms of Christian communion have at great expense of good feeling to be pulled down; else the Church becomes one of those corporations that have no soul. Like University graduation, like organic evolution, Free Religion is an unfolding of previous forms, and is not that bolting from them affected by some, ending like the side path I took in the woods, — in a swamp and a squirrel track. A good man humorously expressed the development in his case by saying, "I spell my God with two *o*'s, and my devil without a *d*." In an old anti-slavery Quaker family I served at the funeral of a young man who had never heard a dozen sermons, yet was a pattern of all good works. His wedding-day had been set, the bride's wedding-dress made, the wedding-house nearly done; yet he welcomed death. The Eastern mists were the mourning robes; but the bereaved had clad themselves in cheerful attire. As it pleases God the beautiful flowers should grow not only in gardens and enclosures, fenced from the cold and the wind, but on wild hill-sides, along uncultured meadows and plains, and up near the snow-line of Alpine peaks, so, not in any revival hot-house or paradise of a sectarian conventicle, the finest human excellence springs. Virtue within and without the ritual must be compared. The lists are set in this noble tournament; a fair field is open; the Judge throws down his warder: leap, holy knights, to the conflict, and God defend the right!

Not what we profess, but produce, is the test. Dissenters from Calvinism were told, Yours is a good religion to live by, but not to die by. That is all we want. We do not expect to *die*, yet are willing the case should be settled by what are called death-beds.

We must have, theologians tell us, a revelation of God; as though he were hid in his works. Are Shakspeare, Raphael, Beethoven so hid? Creation is God's transparency, not screen. Goethe's earth-spirit weaves the garment we see Him by. This veiled Deity reminds one of the coarse preacher's figure: God is like a squirrel in the wall; he can see you though you cannot see him. So says not that man of no Christian birth or breeding, the Hindoo, Chunder Sen, — a pearl of Orient piety welcomed by the leaders of a dozen religious sects, from Martineau the Rationalist to Dean Stanley of the Established Church. The wisdom has been queried of letting into our pulpits this illuminated heathen, whom Jesus would have taken to his arms. Well if our liturgies, or prayers without book, could touch the rapture of this latest of the Magi from the East!

What a Radical is Nature! See the plants, from a mixture of sun and rain, start in a thousand stretches of greenness to make a garden of the globe, their clinging to the root not hindering their airy ascent. Abide as it will in the ground, no dead past for the tree. It scatters in autumn the leaves it will not reclaim in spring. What cares the orchard for last year's apples and pears, forgotten in preparation of the new crop? No merit made of the heaps of twenty seasons falling ruddy and yellow from the boughs; no expectation of being saved by the old works, but only by grace of the new: the yield on the branches a transformation of the vital juice from beneath the soil. What a Conservative that barren fig-tree, occupying the room of its betters! But blasting or burning is the doom of what does not bear.

Development not allowed, revolt, revolution, will come. The workman's proverb, "Steady by jerks," is illustrated by how many a crisis in the world. Causes, says Björnson, have to be repeated many times ere the explosion we call an effect. Witness the downfall of France from its long diet, not of duty, but of glory. Grown-up pre-occupants insist we shall act on their conscience and will. We cannot abide our own children contradicting us, as, with a mite of spirit, they will. Things degenerate till, as Goethe says, the gods will not recognize the sire's features in the faces of the sons. But the true Conservative will thank Goth or German who restores the type of a religion run down.

As all conception is covered, and none can tell just where Anti-Slavery, Woman's Rights, the Sanitary Commission, Etherization, Steam, or the Telegraph, began, it is hard to trace the genesis of Radicalism. Its germ, dot or double-dot, is as obscure as that origin of man which mortgages another century for its decision. As the new planet may have several simultaneous discoverers, so with the dawn of an idea. Real originators resign in favor of the Spirit. Always there is engineer and brakeman: always driving-wheel of the thinker, the safest of men; the danger being from some stone of ultra-conservatism on the track.

But what occasion, in the little band of Liberal Christians, had any but to keep the peace, instead of showing teeth to bite their cherry in two? Paul blames Peter for conforming. Yet in a signal instance how Paul himself conformed! Why could not we conform?

The first radical motive was the law of truth. When, six years ago, the churches were invited to send to the first Unitarian Convention, in New York, delegates authorized to represent their convictions, and pledged to pay great respect to the decisions of that body, we protested against such putting of personal and congregational freedom under threat. It seemed insincere to confound diverse opinions in the one stripe, which chosen messengers might hold out for a banner. We were told, You will stand alone and wear motley. We said, Better Joseph's coat of many colors than the prison-uniform. We prefer citizens' or soldiers' to policemen's dress. An officer of the steamer *Lexington*, escaping on a cotton-bale, told the court when the fire covered the deck he thought it a *case*. So did we, when a synod appeared as the precipitate from the solution of independent thought. It was time to be a martyr or witness-bearer.

But another motive was the law of faith. We wanted to believe. We were accused of weakening the ranks. But the fellowship of honest dissent anticipates wider sympathies, and enlarges the Church. When once, in Faneuil Hall, the constables tried to close the door against the crowd, the president cried out, Faneuil Hall is open! However, for convenient concert, one end of Liberal Christianity might be shut, we meant the other end should swing; and, at whatever cost of house-warming, to keep open doors. Doubtless the articles assumed made a trig marching costume. The reports say that the number of believers and churches has been multiplied by the platform and working plans of leaders so busy and brave. But what census shall give, beside the poll, the weight of those saved by the defended rights of reason! How serious the secession, but for the victory of thinker over priest! Would not our ship have been dismasted, or unmanned and abandoned, or, amid waves of controversy, lacked seamanship to reach port, but for that modifying of the first stringency, which the new Protestants compelled? The rebels against human leadership did good service; the appellants to the higher law promoted justice; the heretics preserved unity, and schismatics kept the faith.

A third motive was the law of growth, erroneously supposed to come from hushing up differences. Stifling private judgment may yield mechanical increase. A thoughtless huddling together in the rabbit-warrens of conformity makes the denominational count large and easy. Self-interest and gross social instinct furnish a conglomerate or pudding-stone of assent. But the articulation of limbs or branching of a tree figures vital spread. Largeness is not greatness. An artist was asked what should be the proper price of a certain picture measuring six by nine, — the amount of putty being the standard, not the painter's art. It is said all the boughs brought together would make a uniform bole; but where then the green expanse, the lungs of leaves, the sap, blossom, and fruit? The tree were timber, without axe or saw; and any sect that forbids outgrowth is a stick. Liberty reproached as dissolving ties? It alone knits them.

Mark now some illustrations. Cutting the old Hebraism to graft in the Gentiles was as painful as to King George the Colonial Declaration. But it was good for Jewish as for English blood. Luther's attack on the Romish corruptions saved Rome, and gave the papacy a new lease, as uncapping the central fire keeps the earth from splitting; beside that the volcanic upheaval gathers the vapor into springs, laces the valley with streams, slopes the rocks to grind into intervals, and produces corn and wheat below, to laugh to the wind-flowers and nodding vines above. Another sort of rending makes the grandeur of history. Was Methodism in England the ruin of religion, or its extension into new realms? Did Puritanism, driven from home or fleeing from the halter, waste one drop from the vials that hold the tears of the saints? Compare its commonwealth with the establishment that fears it can no longer wring revenue of *royalty* from the poor, but must stand on a footing with other orders, or come to the ground! Did our doctrinal Fathers, forsaking Pilgrim Orthodoxy, destroy Congregationalism? These cases history vindicates. But, one radical step more, we are among the breakers; and Put about ship! is the cry. Hard aport! sang the captain from the upper deck to the man at the wheel, as he steered in the fog, upon Cape Race, so near I saw the brown rocks bare with each retiring wave. In our theological ship, is the Free-thinker, advising a new course, going to cast us away? What pilot within hail but the candid student, who keeps abreast with science and does not stay behind to be petrified at any Salt Lake with Mormon leader or Mistress Lot? Our guides with their verbal basis broke the harmony they would bind. With but a touch, light as that at which the Touch-me-not bursts, scores of clergy and others met in private rooms, in Boston, to consult lest the ecclesiastical republic might receive harm. The press launched gibes at the improperly advertised movement as still-born. But it was a new and living generation, which the newspaper — sometimes generous, but servant too much, not of man, but of the majority — has come to respect. We always repent of going with the multitude. People are sorry for their senseless shouts and stupid throwing-up of caps. The denouncers become the accepters of ideas. Their assertors and martyrs behold the scoffer creeping into their ranks, and pretending he was always there.

> "The astonished Muse finds thousands at her side."

The servile print grows polite, and begs to be reporter of that it had visited as abortionist. It is the old story. What to-day crucifies, to-morrow crowns. That first meeting, to which the parlors were open for fair play, became parent of the Free Religious Association and the Radical Club. In their formation some of the

Radicals took no part, having no talent nor relish for machinery to act on the popular mind, deprecating a new sect, or dreading a hard concrete of their precious ideas. They loved free thought as an element, resented the appearance of a curb, coveted no personal publicity, and would not put their principles in any conventional gear. Religion is not only an institution, it is an inspiration; and, in the necessary division of labor, some serve best where the electricity is generated, leaving others to apply it to the fine or useful arts. Radical doctrine is needed less as a weapon or tool than a leaven in the yet heavy lump of this world's dough.

But what is the Radical position? It is against any final wording. Unitarians still hold that in the Bible, the New Testament as supplement of the Old, the Divine mind is fully expressed, though they quote Robinson that "more light is to break out of God's Word." But we say there is more *Word!* As a sailing-master gives new directions every day, we must have fresh orders from the Navigator of our humanity, at each degree of the voyage. The old chart alone will not suffice. Can we find all we need, every coast and island laid down, on the sacred map? What specific rules does the volume hold for Liberty, Republicanism, Temperance, Prohibition, Woman's Rights, Free Trade or Protection, War and Peace, Labor and Capital, Poverty and Wealth? For every live question we do and must take counsel of the Spirit, as did Isaac or David, Noah or Lot. Which is the blasphemy,— to find their instructions insufficient, or to declare there are none for us? "Honor the king," says Peter.

What king do we honor? God is no linguist. He does not talk Syriac or Greek. At Pentecost, he was understood in every tongue because he used none, and no translation was needed of his speech. You give your dog the meat you have made him speak for, rising on his legs. In the heavenly air our food is hung high for us to aspire.

The Radical position is next against individual authority. Truth is God's note, needing no indorser. Jesus its authority? It is his. Inspiration is not its warrant, but effect. Of all eloquence of pen or tongue it is cause. Christ's impersonation of it was his power. But it was not exhausted in him, more than the atmosphere in one wind instrument. If in Scripture, the splendid score of the old masters, we read aught that does not chime with the string under God's finger in our breast, sweet as it sounded once, it is discord now. Corrupt birth, arbitrary choice, bloody atonement, hopeless woe, — is it between the sacred lids? It grates on me no less, and I will reject it as quick as the last crudeness vented with impunity in this rash-speaking day. In any creature, son of God or son of man, no authority but the response of the spirit that rises to the Spirit that comes.

The Radical protest is, once more, against any contradiction of science. To the constitution of Nature your religion must give way. This has got through the hair of our head in regard to Galileo, who, once alone against the Church, now has a unanimous vote. Lyell and Darwin may get such a verdict some day. To give man or the world a date of but six thousand years would, but for theologic imperception, appear as absurd as to make the sun a satellite of the earth. The doctors tell us, never was a man like Ruloff for thickness of skull. Suitable callipers might match it in many an ecclesiastic head. Sydney Smith told the dignitaries they had but to put their heads together to make the new wooden pavement for St. Paul's. The men, be they able as Agassiz, who assert, will have to scout a creation of man apart from other tribes. Religion above science is the eagle scorning the fowler, in the sky; religion against science is the earthen pot clashing with the iron in the stream.

But has Radicalism no principles? Yes: it denies to affirm, clears the way to travel, vetoes less than it signs, and tears down but to build. Its affirmation is, Spirit takes in all. My friend says, The Spirit is born of Christianity. I answer, Christianity of the Spirit. He says, Spirit is an abstraction. I say, A reality. He says, The gospel covers the ground. I reply, Neither actual nor ideal. I stand within the Christian lines, the lowest private in those ranks. But I look out to the origin and end of the march. There are greater words than Christian, — the Divine Humanity, the image of God in the soul of man.

The second principle is, forward character. Respect the past, we are told. Yes, and the present too! The past is no bed to lie down on. Ancestral achievements are abused for a lounge and easy-chair. Foregoing legislation had its place; but, in this parliament of the world, what is the motion in order now? Lay the next course. Better not have begun than stop. To bless is not to bolt, but tug at the load that tries our united strength. Not revolution, but evolution, is benediction. Would that lesson were learned in France!

The third Radical principle is the perpetuity of the Church. Never was falser maxim than that religion is a thing between a man and his Maker. It is a bond betwixt men, as well as with God. Jesus prescribed no form; and a generation passed without any binding outward order. The Church, like the world, is over-governed by base love of power. When one tries to rule me, I have a vision of thrones on which his progenitor was king or queen. Tyranny is the heritage of every sect. But the check of that great Italian water-wheel is felt in every denominational cog. The Church will survive, because it does not consist in any mode of discipline, but sympathy through every varying statement and style. Uniformity is not unity, which liberty and law constitute, and law without liberty prevents. Centralization, with dominant will, passes before the dawn of local privilege with universal light. Architecture is one shadow of this on the dial. The cathedral, that overshadowed the town and nestled the population around its walls, as the fountain draws them in a Tyrolese village, dwindles. Though New York and Boston put up large edifices, these are but on a reduced scale, copies in pale ink of the ancient magnificence. No more structures like St. Peter's and Strasbourg, and the Duomo at Milan, long for such as Ruskin may! Cologne, since most of us were born, remains, save on paper, unfinished, with some builder's crane on its tower for a sign. Palaces of shingles our bishops have to put up with. What is the temple to the traveller's road? Theatres and railway-stations, warehouse-blocks, dwellings of granite and marble, costly stones, gray and ruddy, in parks and reservoirs, outshine the modest audience-rooms mostly reared for Christian assemblies. What meeting-house can vie with river or ocean-steamer, or the hotels where we eat and sleep? David might repeat his complaint to Nathan: "I dwell in an house of cedar, but the ark of God dwelleth within curtains." Is it all a mark of decay? Rather that, in time to come, less ritual and more life shall compose the Church. Like its Head, it will triumph by going away. It will become Christian society. It will not, like the papacy, absorb, but be absorbed in the commonwealth. Conference and communion will take the place of throngs, excited or amused by some fine organ or famous voice. Whatever reaction entice the unthinking multitude to popish mimicry for a while, conversation will come, instead of that gallop of words called eloquence. But the Church will survive. Without her the reformer, who reproves her backwardness, would not have been. From the altar, where she too much kept the coals to warm her own hands, he has seized the brands to kindle every holy fire. Her insulter may behold his own blood in five generations of her priests.

But she is not to stay a place for ceremony, empty and apart save once a week. Household affection, loyal friendship, honesty in affairs, justice to the laborer, fellowship with the poor, and example of temperance for a law, are the transformation wherein Zion's latter-day glory shall appear. From her Liturgy shall not the name, with the fact, of slavery drop? No grain of humanity can she leave out. Those diggers in the trench, along the dark wet tunnel, amid flaring lamps, her light must include. Employés, conductors, switch-men, brake-men, signal-men, ticket-sellers, draw-tenders, machinists, ought, as much as sailors, to have public sympathy, vacations from their task, and a Bethel of their own. How will their lack of science, religion, and sound morals, react on us! Their eyes were wet when they were told, nothing but antique phrase kept their coming, with car and engine, as much as the tents of the patriarchs and ships and camels, into our prayers. This will be communion, and no longer protest.

Radicalism means room. The old barns in the country were not built large enough to let the modern breed of horses in; and my friend visiting me had to feed his team out of doors. The old churches were not built big enough to let the new men in. There is space for the body to sit down or lie prostrate, but not for the soul to stand up. The science, scholarship, culture, character, cannot be accommodated in the temple. I remember how the animals, that drew the families to church, used to graze on the juicy herbs round the sheds; and it still seems to me a chaffy nutriment parent and child tried to masticate within. Large-hearted, high-minded men and women, with their towering heads, have yet to resort to fodder in the field, not being able to get at the hay on the mow. What food we furnish is the test. What is their commissariat? asked General Scott, when told the rebels were marching to Washington. Whether we touch the shadows of bread and wine in the supper or not, we must be communicant with God, to supply men.

We flatter, brace, and backen ourselves on compliment, with mutual quotation and commendation, keeping a market of praise and running an exchange of vanity, instead of treating one another with verity and right.

For Radicalism one virtue we may claim, sincerity. These men are not pretenders. To honesty they add ability, and often aptness to teach, which can ill be spared by the Church. We may have an equal wonder at what the pulpit welcomes, and what it excludes. We can think of one with a genius for piety like that of the Hebrew David, whose line he stands in, and a voice of electric speech, yet under the ban because miracle is to him mythology, and he cannot believe a troop of angels sang over Bethlehem. He writes a book of "American Religion," humorously by a critic called an *asteroid* in comparison with the "Ten Great Religions" from another hand, which are related to it rather as mammoth and mastodon are to man. Another, under the ecclesiastic taboo, is an author, of national fame, soldier and leader of a black regiment in the civil war, advocate of every philanthropic reform, treating every question with alarming candor and wit. A third, a master of every liberal art, poet and philosopher, on all subjects a catholic, comprehensive, unpartisan judge, may be found like Levi, sitting at the receipt of custom. A fourth, too true to trim, and as unable to purchase place with sacrificing a grain of frankness as an old martyr with a pinch of frankincense in the fire of Jupiter, shall be content to read the proofs when he might furnish better matter for the press. But the inward panorama is lighted with a score of such in the social circle, respected by no organized power, yet drawing looks of reverence and love. Two appear in singular contrast: one accepting Jesus, and rejecting Christ; the other a devotee of Christianity, and indicting its reputed author. The free thinker, of however different shade, is scared with being told he will be classed with them; as if he were looking after his classification, not the truth.

But shall we allow such men to be heard, or put them down? If Jesus were the man I take him for, he would permit the sharpest interrogation of his claims. I honor my Master too much to defend him with any ostracism. He that with equal patience and plainness confronted hypocrites, and wanted Thomas the sceptic to put his hand into the wound, is no example for muzzling inquiry, or thrusting it from our side. The empire which professed to be *peace*, with its censorship of the pen, ended in war; and the tongue we bridle in others we shall ourselves be run away with. Do we give dignity to the pulpit by covering it with restrictions removed from the press? It is unsound flesh that shrinks from being touched. There is something rotten in the Denmark that fears. Courage to pursue every study, with hospitality to the results of investigation, is the flag of faith. Until it appears that church-men or creed-men make the best *men*, are more gracious neighbors, live by a higher law than legality, or bring up their children to be more modest and respectful than those of other parents, we may believe it possible still, as with Saul, to be bred after the most straitest sect of our religion a *Pharisee*. While so many use form as a Sunday cushion for their mind, or put dogma instead of fidelity into contracts, and the old rule lasts of knowing a man by his fruits, let us give Liberal and Radical a fair chance at the tribunal of worth. We cannot let the candidates be umpires too; but, as we choose arbitrators of national claims, leave it to mankind, God's representative, to judge of all men. The verdict at last is just.

V.

THEISM.

IT is a fact, meriting reflection, that the word which has been most hateful to religious people is Deism, or a belief in God, so direct through his instant care as to make small account of special revelation. Was it from a kindly wish not to irritate this sore of old prejudice, that by the name Theism, of equivalent sense, the same sentiment returning after generations is now baptized? Who was, of theists, the chief but Jesus? Who but Christians should be deists above all believers beside? That a synonym for infidelity should be found in either term may imply in those who gave or bore it some share of a common fault. If one party underrated the written gospel, the other too much disparaged the universal light. It is possible to blaspheme not only a visible rite, but the interior soul, that temple without which is no sanctity in all the gold of prophetic wonders and words. Shall we brand as a sceptic the man who wishes no particular mediator, he confides in his own Author so immediately and much? For what comes any seer but to revive the sense of Deity, and work the miracle of resurrection on no dead body,' but our buried faith in that Being so indwelling and surrounding, nothing and nobody can come betwixt him and us — as the old story tells us none did betwixt Enoch and him? We hear of atheists. But atheism is impossible. Without God, man were not. There are only atheistic theories which we touch, by summoning the witnesses.

The first is Nature, by which we mean a certain whole, or unity. The world is not all in pieces, but all together. For convenience, we talk of this thing or that as distinct; but separate or separable nothing is. There is no such thing as a *thing*, but every thing is part of something and of every thing else. This relatedness makes all one, hard as it is to define the relationship. We are taught in childhood boundaries on maps, and so fix in mind an artificial notion of dividing-lines which God never made.

"Line in Nature is not found."

There are no exactly measurable degrees of space or time, latitude or longitude. We name for practical purposes gross quantities which do not square with the fineness of the facts. But in their faith or unfaith men are fooled with words. One says, If the truth should turn out there is no God, we must abide manfully the result. But God is the Truth you imagine requiring you to deny him. He is the Truth you set out from, as he is that you reach. God and Truth are both dictionary words. What right to define them differently, or make Truth the larger of the two? The atheist says, No God distinct from Nature. I answer, No Nature distinct from God. What beside Deity is this entire and infinite simplicity we mean when Nature is pronounced? It is alive. A dead unity we cannot conceive. Death is dissolution into disconnected particles or parts. But, as no such absolute disconnection can be, death but seems, and is not. You say matter, I spirit; you, that spirit is finer matter; I, that matter is coarser spirit. It remains for us both to find what substance is, since two substances cannot coexist. That all phenomena blend in unity is the point science arrives at more clearly every day.

> "The world 's mine oyster
> Which with knife I 'll open;"

but the point of cleavage neither Positivist nor Metaphysician finds. In Nature's armor is no joint a spear can pierce. Is God *super*natural? Then he is limited; for here is something called Nature no eyes ever saw the end of, and no terms of human conception can exhaust, from which he is cleaned out and confined to quarters, like a monk in a convent, nun in a cloister, or student ordered not to go off the college-grounds. Shall we tell him, as we do a child, to make himself small, or lie on his own side? "God is a definite idea," said that great scholar and masterly writer, Andrews Norton, in reply to the supposed pantheism of Schleiermacher represented by George Ripley. But, open the box of your logic, he has escaped; as well set a trap for the light. "Lo! God is here," we sing in the temple; and many think of him as an unseen priest haunting the church, or huge anchorite, like Simon the pillar saint. Yet, outside at the corner of the village meeting-house, or on deck when the Sunday praise gushed through the cabin-windows with organ accompaniment of the winds and waves, I have worshipped him as devoutly as any that sat and sang within. My friend, who went with me to the mighty sea-beat rocks, whistled some light tune. I could no more have done it than in the cathedral-choir, where, in Dresden as in Boston, I heard the operatic airs intrude.

God is held holy and apart: that is finite. He is holy in the sense of *wholeness* and health. The loss of wholeness, any nerve or organ acting on its own account and setting up for itself, is disease. All secession is sickness in the body politic or animal frame. When one said *Beauty of Holiness* in a plea for art and the art-museum, a clergyman replied, Yes, but *Holiness of Beauty* we cannot say. Indeed, will not the equation work both ways? Gross notion of Beauty in which it will not! Handsome to the eye of flesh, but beautiful no impure thing or person can be. David saw the omnipresence forcing him to feel, if there were any bed in hell he could lie down on without God for his fellow, his adoration and its object were gone; and Adam's fancy, that he could hide from the Lord among the trees of the garden, showed the short-coming of his apprehension, which made the Divinity but a larger man. The Infinite cannot suffer; and his necessary blessedness is proof that my sin, pain, compunction, is no solid, but surface, — a shadow not, as theologians so monstrously describe, to last forever, but pass away, having served the ends for which it was sent. We err, do wrong, answer for it, and are educated by it. Our iniquity becomes our grim minister, our folly a glorious benefactor. But we can do nothing against the will of God; for independent wills were breaks in Nature, with which the sublime totality we call Spirit were not. The doctrine of convertible species absolves itself of atheism, which lies rather in the opposite view of faults and blank intervals in the world. In the gaps no God could be; and if there be aught where he is not, he is not at all.

The next witness is Instinct, — a desire or direction animating Nature to suggest the same living unity at heart as in every point. This principle is identical, in however diverse creatures or things. The ant I saw dragging a grain of sand, as important to its hill as the Column Vendôme to Paris, and his brother pulling along over the gravel the carcass of a blue-winged moth; the bee in his hive or flower, or on a bee-line between; the toad or turtle basking in the sun on a rock; the bird and butterfly; the dog and deer; the fish and fox; man and woman, — all have this common quality we call Instinct. The little one that runs to me with a smile and kiss before it can speak, and the dumb beast that licks my hand or rubs its fur on my foot, are acting from the same impulse and doing the same thing. On one parallel child or animal pushes or runs. I cannot distinguish between the heifer's horns and the baby's doubled-up fists. Does this property stop with what we call sensitive existence? When we speak of somebody's monkey-tricks; when a man is called a snake in the grass or a bear, or one woman is called a lioness and another a cat, and we are told to beware of their teeth and claws, for they scratch and bite with words, — we feel a disgust at carrying humanity so low. But we must take it lower still.

Must I not feel that the plant, creeping toward the light, is a type of my groping my way faster, but with less certainty of direction, out of the same cellar? The roots spreading after water under ground, that have been known to pierce through the decaying wood of a conduit for a drink, imitate my seeking in a thirsty land for a finer river. Plants that shrink from touch are prefigurations of the nervous system, and mimic the maidens withdrawing their hands from a too bold or eager grasp. The fertilizing pollen shows vegetable sex. For the mutual attractions of human beings and chemical atoms we use the same word, *affinity*, — as in Goethe's wondrous story of "Elective Affinities," and Miss Shepherd's of "Counterparts," and a whole class of literature back to Plato's Ideas. The electric fluid loves iron so that it will run on a wire beneath the bottom of the deep: Jesus resembles to it the coming of the Son of Man; and some scientists suspect it to be the element of thought. No brain without phosphorus, says the physicist; and advises the student to a diet of fish for strength to swim and cleave the depths of *his* ethereal sea. No inertia that instinct does not bore or dive into, or come up through, to breathe. All the faculties of the mind — causality, comparison, memory, imagination, constructiveness, and music — act from instinct. It is the first form and matrix of divine inspiration. According as a man draws from books and systems, learning and recollection, instead of this living spring, he lacks or loses power, and drops from eloquence and pathos into oratory and recitative. What this quality is we cannot fathom or circumscribe. Microscopy and analysis detect it in the rhythm of the particles of a bar of steel and of a stone, as a universal nature, which is another name for God. It is one tune and many variations, like "Home, Sweet Home," through endless travesties of the pianist, — an unsearchable essence, an innumerable sum.

The third witness is Character, which, whoever possesses, knows he never created, but only, like the block under the etcher, yields himself obediently to receive. No virtuous man takes the credit of his own virtue. It is no manufacture of the mind, but a product and projection from behind the will, use whatever subordinate shaping we may to fit the case and circumstance: "And this not of yourselves; it is the grace of God." In proportion as my good behavior is my private intention, conscious of its charm or able to reckon its merit, it is at fault. It is beautiful, only as ascribed to the Sovereign Command. Jesus claimed no glory, for it cost him no struggle to cast off Satan. Think not to pay me for the service I render you! Your payment is an injustice and offence. Render a service to somebody else. Pass, as Franklin said, the favor on. I am a mere agent. I do the King's bidding, like one of the soldiers of that old centurion, who could figure Jesus only as captain of a troop before which diseases fled. Render your dues to the one Author, whom all channels of benefit and mercy represent. How ridiculous this complaint of people's ingratitude for your help and kindness! Are you the source of their advantage; or did you communicate it for recompense, as a hired servant that grumbles because he has to wait and dun for his wages? Are you owner of the house, carriage, or garden you invite them into? Your demand to be paid likens you to the Roman proconsul who embezzled the provincial fee on its way to the imperial treasury. Are you charitable? It is God's pity in you. From his winking at the times of "this ignorance" your lids learn to drop, while lynx-eyed pursuit of any sin is worse than the sin.

"Be to their faults a little blind."

There is an imperceptiveness finer than any sight. How men are hit with the pistol they wear and whip they flourish! Censure is the edge-tool which he that handles cuts himself with. Judgment and righteousness are a line and plummet nothing in the world can bear to meet. Governments are not carried on, taxes collected, houses and railways built, or any machine run with perfect rectitude. Demand ideal purity, and the wheels stop. The pump has to be fetched, says my friend, with dirty water; though it would seem as if New York had used too much! In business-dealings with my fellow-men I find a certain per cent of corruption. But I am too busy to stop. I cannot consume the day with question of every particular; it were an expense of nerves more precious than money. I am guilty if I let the community suffer so? But I suffer wrong rather than suffer myself. The Spirit bids me let off, and not sentence many a criminal.

How such compassion, returned for wrong, abounds among the purer sex! Therefore Goethe, their truest modern delineator, says: —

"The eternal womanly draweth us on."

In whatever calamity or folly, it is always some woman's hand outstretched to take us up. Lady is bread-giver. She that blamed us when we throve will feed and tend our hunger and disease. Every man has been a Mungo Park without travelling. This is the crown of the queen. No woman has reached supreme merit in song or story, policy or art. It was said of an able woman, if it had pleased the Lord to drop her spirit into the pantaloon she would have been a great general. But what match would Elizabeth of England or Joan of Arc have been for Cromwell or Napoleon? Yet, as organs of Divine forgiveness, we have a thousand women for one man. I do not wonder when the Catholics desire Heaven's mercy they call on the Virgin for her prayers.

All great character is the flow of Divine love and justice through the human soul. Looking at Niagara, an eminent statistician said, There is power to turn all the machinery in the world. But does not the gazer at that green tide feel the force of a mightier flood behind his smallest act of right? "My usual weight is a hundred and forty pounds," said the countryman; "but when I am mad it is a ton." There are no limits to the sacred rage for equity. Not by wealth or numbers, but its cause, Union beat Secession. "We have figured out this sum," said the slaveholder to Mr. Garrison, "and are sure to prevail." "It would seem so; only you have omitted one thing, that is God," was the reply. When the civil war broke out, and boys under age ran away to enlist and fling themselves in the Dragon's mouth, a joyful sacrifice for liberty and the land, was it their own will, or something that took it captive as a tool for its majestic design, and made a paradise for them of the field of death? A true spiritualism, not that which is but the sensuality of the spiritual world, nerved their arms. Their motive was not a thought of any shiny place they were going to, but conscious glory of the spot they were in. Virtue or duty is ever such heavenly joy; all notion of reward is foreign to it. Samuel J. May hardly expected his translation would make him happier. "I may," he said, "have clearer vision, but not more confiding faith." The saint only asks to be permitted to continue to feel and love as he does already. Dr. Tuckerman declared his idea of eternal bliss was fulfilled in his ministrations to the poor. When one dilated on Christ's anguish for man's deliverance, Charles G. Loring answered, it was his privilege to think Jesus the happiest man that ever lived. What a superstition that he was crushed by the penalty of sin of millions dead or unborn! Did that wine of the Passover, that water of the Samaritan well, or that corn rubbed in his disciples' hands, have no refreshment or flavor in his mouth? Was not the meat, they knew not of, a feast which no funeral of earthly life or comfort could offset? My neighbor's delight in feeding his own horses, the little girl's in tolling the fishes, the minister's who has bread of God's word to dispense, needs no supplement of supernatural touch. The disembodiment we call death cannot make it more celestial. God recompense it with palms and harps and crowns, gold pavements and streets of pearl? It reminds one of the Oriental prayer: "Have mercy, O Lord, on the bad; for Thou hast done every thing for the good in making them so!" My inclination to make a sacrifice of time, talent, pleasure, or life, is a gift from him too great for aught else as payment or equivalent to be possible. Let others spend their immortality surveying the precious stones of the New Jerusalem! We will sell every share in that city for new commissions in the war against woe and sin; and not covet, in comparison with the service we enlist for to the end, even the wine the Master told his followers he was to drink new with them in the Father's kingdom.

This disposition, not created by, but breathed into us, is witness of God. The carver at his table, though eating no morsel, has the best portion, as the most blessed and enviable person at the board is the host, who divides all his dainties among his guests. Here is a quality which no politic contrivance or utilitarian experience, no calculation of carnal solace to revenge temporary abstinence, and no generalization of remote selfish benefits of any sort, can account for. It is positive life of that Infinite One whose own joy is communication, and to imitate whom alone makes us communicants.

The great achiever is never wilful, but possessed. In wilfulness the will of God or man were lost. The great are conscious of destiny: what they mean is meant in them. Napoleon had a star; Jackson swore by the eternal splendor; Lincoln waited on Providence, and would not force events. Called coward by the impatient, killed for a tyrant because slavery owned in him its most dangerous foe, branded as a compromiser by reformers conscientious but unwise, — when he died, and the lots were cast for what he left, his coat also was found woven without seam; for no high phrase, extreme ground, radical or doctrinary extravagance, can compare with the character, which is God's fitting such a man to his purpose, — as he was so conspicuously to whose cradle the Magi were led at Bethlehem, and who will survive all his critics, new or old.

The fourth witness is Art, the expression of truth in the form of beauty, be it what it may we call beautiful, — picture, sculpture, music, or manners; for, take whatsoever shape, without inspiration it is not art. Poem or painting, wholly explainable into the maker's dexterity, is not art, but artifice. The part that could not be calculated or foreseen, in your grace or eloquence, which was the escape of God, where your pen like the Spiritualist's pencil was guided; the slip of your tongue; the point while you climbed you were raised into; that of which you knew not and the artist knew not, and no theory can clear up how it was done; which baffles as it delights, — is the interesting and immortal portion. In the composer's company you are lifted off your feet because he was. In Retzsch's engraving of a scene in Homer, the deceased hero is borne to glory by angels. So, when touched by any performance, we are exalted with singer or speaker, and tread on air. A bit of canvas, on which genius has put its mark, can no longer be measured by the foot-rule. A visitor of Rubens's Descent from the Cross, being told it was time to go, answered, "Wait till they get him down!" Who has not seen how leagues of land and water, hill and sea-beach, could be brought by faithful color within a narrow frame, and the universe of earth and sky opened to our glance by a few happy strokes of the brush? As Madame

Guyon was elevated by religious transport from the ground, as Mr. Hume in his trance ascends to the ceiling, so we go up, unaware that we rest below, see afloat by the magic of genius in an ether of joy. Raphael is said to be the only one who can make his angels look natural in mid-heaven, and absolve them of gravitation. Does he not make us, soul and body, just as light? The artist in his rapture heeds not laws of Nature in any mechanical sense, balks at no difficulties that make materialists halt, but revels in miracle. No impossible wonder of the story gives him pause. Paul Veronese makes the wine run red at Cana in his incomparable sketch; Raphael fetches down Moses and Elias to witness the Transfiguration; Schaeffer shows the hapless lovers in their penal whirl; and Allston displays Samuel rising to Saul at the Witch of Endor's incantation. What is the ecstasy which the cold canvas can impart after generations have gone, and the ideas are obsolete from which it took its cue? There must be in it a hint of truth which physicists do not suspect. All the spiritualism is a hound after reality more precious than protoplasm or animal derivation of men. Artists are not atheists, however artisans may be. They are possibly not church-members, sabbatarians, or liturgists; but they are believers and worshippers. A spirit passes before them, as before Job. There is a moment or place in their task where, in the Orthodox phrase, they know they are *assisted.* It is no flag fleshly appetite can plant on the celestial coast. It is what on their voyage a holy vision wins. This, with Jesus, was the transcendent bliss. Disparage not art: he was artist!

From no such official or wretch as the popular theology misfashions could have come the spoken music of those parables and sermons, conversations and prayers. Such sentences of solace and benediction were moulded by lips that had exquisite sense of the melody of words. Was there art in Plato's philosophy or Homer's lines? Put his periods beside any of theirs. The ring is as true, the tone as sweet, the rhythm as complete, while the matter is more momentous and sublime. Verse-wright or logician many a one, but no teacher without Divine breath.

Does it shock piety to couple art with the Saviour of the world? Who but the world's Maker is the supreme artist? His works are beautiful persons and immortal souls. Art is man's nature, and man's nature is the art of God. Manners are an art as much as tinted cloth or carved stone. The gracious element will flow into every various act and motion, as the same fountain has many jets. We hear of eminent creators grouty and inaccessible, like Turner; and of poets and philosophers being taken suddenly ill, and jumping into bed when callers were announced. But it was to avoid the intrusion of reporters and insolence of gossips. There is a rudeness gentlemen must use to the impertinent, a shell sensibility exudes, a *chevaux-de-frise* the tender heart sets up against unjust fault-finding or unwarranted approach. But without inward grace is no insurance of courtesy even in the feminine frame. Such arrant rebels were the women of the South, General Butler must print something about *she-adders* at his office-door; and in both the French Revolutions a special fury seized on women more than men. From the genuine artist, politeness, on whoever has capacity to receive it, will flow. William Blake, treating the companion of his walk with rare deference, had, with second-sight, still loftier salute for St. Paul passing them on the way. This magnificent style depends on no prim particulars of elaborate study. I can think of an artist, who may smoke, dance into all the positions of an acrobat, wear a cap in your presence, use expletives to pious folk profane, with such overrunning good-will in every look and gesture to his pupils and peers, — keeping no secrets of his skill, but telling every thing, as a scholar said he left his manuscripts open for all on his table; and giving to each comer alternately a piece of his mind and a piece of his heart, expending with reckless profusion his vitality in good advice; drawing smiles and tears alike with his pencil and his tongue, and setting everybody astir with his voice as with the drummer-boy from his brush, — that no one shall say where the authentic art begins or ends. That such a man, moved unwittingly by something greater than his exceeding wit, should deny God, were as if the finger denied the brain. *I have come to see your possessions*, was said to a land purchaser, who answered, I own none of these acres: I am a possession myself.

In all art we take example from God. "All the world 's a stage," writes Shakspeare. It is also a picture, which the Author leaves us to finish. It is a collection, the best in which we are puzzled to decide. From admiring the tawny lion we are diverted by the shining bug. Our eye is taken with the frowning cliff, but taken off by the billow dashing at its base; and again soon forgets the foamy rush, to be absorbed in the long stretch of noiseless flats clothed in green and yellow by the retiring tide. When paint is added to a boarded house, it is like covering a lank frame with generous flesh and blood. But God leaves the world no skeleton. How Nature hastens to heal every gash of coulter or carriage, or cannon-wheel! People take glasses to inspect the details of a landscape by Church, or battle-piece of Le Brun. How do they compare with the shadings on the back of a turtle, scales of a fish, neck of a dove, or wing of a fly? We say of a well-adorned creature, it is beautifully *marked*. The fierce leopard, prowling panther, stealthy cat, cumbrous cow, slow ox, are designed and drawn as if God could let nothing mean or savage drop from his hand without his signet, as a painter writes his initials on his least sketch.

"Did He who made the lamb make thee?"

writes Blake of the tiger. Yes, answers the soft decoration, supple motion, glittering eye. Divine intent in lavish charm is here, as in the meek ball of wool. How the spell for the population, of caravans and menageries, vindicates the wild beast we think fit only to exterminate! Are not the animals themselves artists, into whom a taste for beauty descends? Watts writes of the bee, —

"How skilfully she builds her cell!
How neat she spreads the wax!"

No, says the theologist; nothing but instinct. But wiser science discovers voluntary intelligence; and we find that birds alter and adapt their nests as men their dwellings to new situations. Are not the modulations of their songs, too, learned and enriched by degrees, — one note or trill, in successive ages of these winged citizens, joined to another? Surely the lark, thrush, linnet, and nightingale, are not deaf as a flute or hand-organ to their own melodies. They are no wood-work of dumb show to entertain us, but have something of the feeling of Braham or Malibran in their breasts, some organ of tune in their tiny brains, and appreciation of harmony. They must despise the senseless screams that pass in some of our parlors and churches for secular or sacred music. They sing and play more true than many choirs and organists. They are their own composers, and have no Mozart or Beethoven to give them the score. Is not their nerve and faculty the Lord's composition, part of the music of the spheres? The art that is God's exercise is his demonstration too. "He has made every thing beautiful in his time;" and, however our modern Orthodoxy may note exceptions, if there be a Hell, I doubt not that is handsome too.

The last witness is Experience. Everybody comes, like Falstaff, to need God, — One eternally alive to succor and befriend. I cannot quite credit the professions of entire content, with which, looking only to annihilation, some lay their offspring in the dust, and have their own coffins made. It is a cheerless belief, or disowning of faith, that no God makes his rendezvous in the human breast, or becomes conscious of himself in his children's mind. When we go down into depths beneath the sun and air, not to find him were madness and despair. He is there to bring us up, like divers with pearls in our hands. There are cases in which no man can redeem his brother. Mortal or angelic help will not avail. Something the soul must have for its reliance: one cannot lean on himself. Who does not feel the pathos of the situation when Rip Van Winkle says his dog is the only friend he has left! But there are extremities wherein no friend in sight will suffice. The Invisible Almighty we want. If some other, as Jesus, the Virgin Mother, or Guardian Angel, stand instead, it is but as his proxy to assure us of his pardon and support. Happy they who require no medium, attorney, or friend at court, being at home with the great Appointer and on good terms with the King; able to say, like one when admonished to make his peace with God, "I am friends with him, and we have never quarrelled."

We cannot rest in multitude, in the many. There is no single creature that is not many, of imperfect principles and inconsistent moods. "My husband," said a hopeless woman, "is hurt at what I did with the best purpose: I do not expect to please him in any thing." "I feel," said another, pointing as we sailed, "that I am that long, lonely island, looking over on other peoples' trees." But, in the sense of unity embracing the world, we are at peace. The doctrine of Spiritualism, held as of a swarm of spirits of all dispositions, without Infinite Spirit, can only discompose. Such a Spiritualist wrote me, "Truth cannot prevail without the abolition of the Christian's God." Spiritualist and Atheist! What a worse than Chinese puzzle this chaos and limbo of spirits, —

"Black, white, and gray,
With all their trumpery!"

The many only repeat the One, and are impossible without it. Take away the mathematician's unit, and all his mighty calculations sink. Take away the real Unit, and the universe is no more. It is easy to call names, to brand as atheist him that believes not in your God, who may be finite, fetish, devilish. But discard the vital Unity to adopt the elements and particles alone for your countless senseless fathers and mothers, and religion is the hypocrisy of an empty name. In the One only we repose, and meet any fate. A friend, dying of cancer in the throat, said: It is his will; and I have so suited my mind to it that, should anybody come in and say, *Alice, you are going to get well*, I know not how I could bear that!

We fondly trust each other, but no fellow-creature can bear our whole weight. We shrink from omnipotence, not knowing what it will do with us; but the Almighty is all-tender. Among men, it is not the strong that disturb us, but the weak. Strength of will and feeling raises and soothes. The feeble irritate and torment. The superficial chop-wave on the sea vexes and annoys and disquiets the sleeper as it dashes sharp and angry on the shore. But the ocean's groundswell lifts skiff or frigate gently, and how silently, as an infant rises and falls on the mother's heaving breast. The resonant surge along the tremendous rocks, as mellow as it is mighty, is delicious unsatiating music, never tires the musing mind, hushes the weary frame in the soft resistless swing which sun and moon stand ready to push to and fro, is a pleasant accompaniment of thought; and, with its rote in time, reminds of the roll of eternity. The image is with me still of one whose eye-lids drooped, as by some pre-established harmony, with the regular dip of my oars on the slopes of the sliding, watery heaps. So on this slippery surface of time we are borne by a Providence we cannot fathom or withstand. The Power that is measureless can afford to be kind.

> "Hark to the voice of the mighty sea,
> Whispering how meek and gentle he can be."

The shallow freshet, the brawling brook, cannot help being rough. O my brother or sister, precious are your regards; but if, in sore distress, it is the mildest treatment I need, if my heart is wounded within me perhaps by your ill-considered word, then with David I call for mercy on Him. His hand is as much easier as it is greater. Nature is that hand, into whose hollow creep alike the bleeding soul and the stricken deer. His breath is more healing than any human speech: solitude is that breath. Thousands charm and cheer me, but One sustains. Without Him we are confused, dissipated, and dissolved. In his Being we are and cannot cease to be.

But there are conditions of knowing God: first, intellectual. We call atheist the man who does not accept our definition. But we must see God, if at all, in his act. We cannot part him from what he does, or between Creator and creation stick a thought. Once he was supposed too pure to soil his hands with making the world; that he employed apprentices, or used for a proxy his Son; or, if he constructed it as a carpenter and owned it as proprietor, like an absentee landlord he left it to run itself in certain grooves of rule, while he took the air in some celestial Boulevarde, showing his hand occasionally to break his laws, playing a game of hide-and-go-seek with his creatures, and caught only in some marvel. The sacred hymnist prompted our thanks that we —

> "Are not left to Nature's light
> To know the Lord;"

as if an author could be published in aught but his works. God's revealing is in what theologians considered his veil. Spinoza was counted atheist because he could see nothing but God; as Novalis said, was drunk with him. Nature the wreck and ruin of a fall? No: his costume changed, summer or winter, every day. Peruse him in printed ink alone, when we turn the rock-pages of the globe, the album and picture-book for his children's amusement, containing not the seven wonders we read of in our primer, but showing all is such wonder-land where we live that nothing in particular as a miracle can be distinguished and defined! A good editor tells me my God is Brahma, because he is One I cannot get rid of or cut off from myself. But I have never been able to pronounce his name.

There is a moral condition of knowing him. A liar is atheist, conceiving only of some power he can circumvent. If you make partial, deceptive statements. I shall find out the missing links which Darwin hunts for in the earth's autobiography. How surely in every falsehood the Deity sees himself denied! The duplicity of the Pharisees was their own blind which they could not see him through; but his beauty shall break out all over you into eyes. The false reasons are not only insulting, but profane; and whoever gives no such is rare and divine. Every deceiver imitates the ostrich with its head in the sand and its body out. My friend in the cars did not know how clearly I saw her unwillingness anybody should take the empty seat by her side. The moon eclipses the sun, and is eclipsed by a sixpence close to the eye; and all double-dealing eclipses God. As criminals are described in advertisements, how we placard the uncandid on the inner walls! They, and no theoretical atheists are without God. We can readily think of people who keep on their premises a pot of varnish and plenty of veneer. From the shop of their mercenary mechanics comes nought but superficial mimicry of value, — the excellence skin deep, the meanness a foot thick. Be mahogany all the way through, if you would have your religion pass for more than pretence. "Oh, that I knew where to find him!" dost thou cry, O Job? Find yourself in his service, which is justice to his creatures, and you will not miss him. For the man who gave to the Missionary Society the money he owed for his wood-bill, saying he must pay God first, that Being must have been hard and far to reach. Weave your dogma out of prophets' tongues, you will not catch him: put your fence of form never so high, you cannot impound his Spirit. He will stay only in the truth of your own lips and purity of your eye. He laughs at your creed like the morning at the prism in which you would analyze and confine its beam. If he be not in your purpose, you can have him, like Greek or Jew, only round in spots. Your righteousness is the Real Presence. Theodore Parker over a sceptic's coffin said, "O Lord, though he doubted thy being, he lived thy law;" and all who had come to wonder what prayer could be uttered were convicted as less faithful than the man in his shroud.

There are doubtless professors of atheism, idolaters of science like Vogt, carrying contempt of religion so far as to class the apostles with apes. Self-esteem in their brain fills the whole space reverence should share. A French Communist general, being asked if he believed in God, answered, No; and he would not tolerate him if he did: it was one against many, a tyranny he would resist and erect the barricades in heaven, — feeling as Milton's Satan did about the God whom only "thunder had made greater." This was the insane anarchy washed out of the streets of Paris with the blood of sixty thousand men. The God that had been preached to them, of Calvinist and Jesuit, priest and cardinal and pope, undeserving his sceptre, was too like the earthly rulers whom liberty and brotherhood led them to withstand. "What, then," the French officer was asked, "do you believe in?" Elbow-deep in gore, "Universal Harmony," he replied, — with no Harmonist, only a tune as on a barrel-organ playing itself! No wonder a bar was set up for a trial, in which binocular, ambidexter, centipedal, believing Germany was appointed judge. Nevertheless, an obscure sense of right inspired that Commune, and every honest drop of blood shall have a resurrection.

All science of the understanding God escapes. No microscope or telescope will ever discover him. A devout scientist, apologizing for his brethren, said, "They are too much occupied and tired with their specialties of investigation to entertain the subject of Deity." But is it not their method which for any spiritual pursuit is at fault?

There is, to know God, a spiritual condition. Is faith his communication to us or our unfolding to him? He will impart himself in the ratio of our growth. Doctors tell invalids it will do them good to take deep inspirations of their own breath; and travellers say they get no just impression of Niagara or St. Peter's till, by often gazing, they grow up to what they contemplate.

So with our seeking our source. All things help us. I found a teacher in the little brown bird filling the sky with its song from a throat no bigger than a straw. As I wrote in the field a heifer came up to me. I offered her some clover. She shook her head, did not want that. I stroked her forehead. She jerked her horns again: it was no cosseting she was after. She stood and looked as I drove my pen, and was but immensely curious to know what I was about there on her domain. What was the green worm crawling towards me along the walk but some bit of an old sin trying in it to lift its head from the ground? Every dumb creature is one round in an angel-ladder we mount on to God and heaven. The beast has no dread because no idea of death. Our ability to face and anticipate destruction is proof we are not to be destroyed. Your joyless outlook at annihilation, like the Indian death-song, refutes your doctrine of doom. With one glance at the universe we feel some One is happy, with whom we shall have a good time. Some of us debated, if shut up to the alternative, which we should prefer, faith in God or in our own immortality. Let me go down, if only so he can remain eternal supply, to vanishing creatures, of dissolving views. But God were suicide if he killed himself in his children, murderer if he slew his children in himself, deceiver if he stirred expectations he must disappoint, robber if he waylaid us for any treasure of friendship, spurious benefactor if he snatched away what he had once bestowed.

> "Chip, chop, chain,
> Give a thing and take it back again!"

"Do you believe," one was asked, "in the devil?" "No: I believe in God." The man who doubts the reality of sin is held a pantheist. But he who regards sin as an essence is not a theist. Thought, which is imperative, and no respecter of persons, must charge him with being an atheist. Satan is agent and tool, not a chess-player saying *Check* to God. He is, and there is none else, — eternal equation of the universe. It is no subtraction, but seal of his infinity, that he can leave his own solitude and make persons in relation with himself, Person of whom they are part, able to love and pray. Were the Divinity a single consciousness devouring as quick as it produced, it would be a helpless and futile force. Its power to differentiate, hinted in the doctrine of the eternal generation of the Son, is its own authentication.

From the teachings of many churches and schools, we should suppose God's nature a collection of contradictory qualities, like those creatures which, though hostile, are caged together, to look askance and growl at each other; living only in a sort of truce or armed neutrality. So he has to keep the peace in this quarrelsome family of his own inclinations. He compromises between them, is the great Compromiser. God is good; but, we are told, forget not he is holy too, and that his holiness limits his grace. No! his holiness expresses his grace. He is equally benignant whether he comfort or strike, as light and lightning are but the same. A Methodist said to a Calvinist, "Your God is my Devil." But we all have really the same God. The overseer on the plantation was an obsequious person to the owner, cruel to the slave, — wreathing his face with smiles, with a whip under his cloak. God turns a shining look on high and low. He has not given you up! The writer in Genesis, and Paul in his Epistles, were mistaken and disrespectful in supposing he had failed with Adam and Eve. One described the virtue of a persevering ecclesiastical organizer as like the mill, once having grasped the log, not letting it go till it was turned to account of all its value. So God will never have done with us till we are converted to all we are good for. He will get the last drop of music out of us. Jesus was in error if he thought God had forsaken him. We remember the town-crier, who used to go round ringing his bell, and shouting, to inquire for some lost child, and set the whole population, on every wharf and by-lane, to hunting him up. I have known all the inhabitants in a village kept awake because some lad had not returned from the woods; and large parties organized for the search. The meanest and worst is as dear to God as the one we call his Only-begotten. Parents are supposed to have favorites; but the good father or fond mother will never tell the pet of the house, however by look, act, or manner the secret be betrayed. They are ashamed of their partiality. God has no partiality to be ashamed of. No sublime personage, king or genius, profound philosopher or special messenger, is an inch nearer to his good-will, a hair's-breadth deeper in his embrace, than the humblest breather.

God is the same in all ages and nations. We think he has some far-away Golden Age, like the commencement of the Christian era; and the Jews put it still further back with Father Abraham. They appropriated Jehovah, made a monopoly of the Lord, on that little strip of territory; letting the heathen — Hivites, Jebusites, and the rest — have some poor little wretched deities, Moloch and Remphan, of their own, but no share in Him who thundered from the mountain, and had led them to Sinai through the Red Sea; as the modern Chinese think all worship and civilization barbarous but their own. Almost all Christians fancy the Pagans under a curse, and not a few put the world's favored time eighteen centuries ago. To the question in the mental-photograph album, which is the last toy we play with, *In what period would you have rather lived?* they answer, *When Christ was born.* Those were the times of glory, when the star went before the wise men, and the annunciation came to Mary; the angels sang over the cradle, the Holy Ghost descended as a dove, and in tongues of flame, and there were healings and feasts and resurrections! Now the age of miracles is past. But is God less manifest now than then? Was there formerly more of him in the world? Has he lost ground? Absurd, impossible, impious to presume! What those wonders were we cannot exactly say, only that Jesus told his followers greater were to come; and just as great now as ever. Where would you rather have lived? in Bethlehem or Bethany or Jerusalem, rather than Boston? What illusion of false color through the kaleidoscope of history, the stained glass of imagination, we turn on the Distant and the Past! "Are you going to the Holy Land?" said one to my friend. "No," he answered: "why should I be flea-bitten at Nazareth?" As if the Holy Land were Palestine more than England or Massachusetts! The steps of Christ? They are no more on the slope of Olivet or along the shore of Galilee, road to Emmaus, or way to Capernaum, than in every place of need and path of progress, or enterprise of philanthropy. Asylums for the sick, and cargoes of flour for starving Frenchmen three thousand miles off, are as good and sacred as the upper chamber of the Passover or the Cross carried to Calvary. A mission to India or the Sandwich Islands, a commission sailing to San Domingo, or sitting, lords from England and peers in America, at Washington, to settle international disputes, — are as divine as conclaves of apostles dividing out their routes over land or sea to Corinth and Athens, and Thessalonica and Rome. The reports of committees, examining matters essential to the public weal, ought to be as religious in motive as any old Epistle to the Philippians or the Hebrews. Why should the living Present slink away so ashamed before the ghost of the Past? To-day is as good as ever dawned. Egotism —

abounding, all-devouring coveting of place and priority, loving to lead — alone hinders the Divinity, as Victor Hugo said Napoleon with his ambition annoyed God. We have no one king or queen, crowned like Victoria or William; so everybody wants to be empress or emperor. In what shining talents and splendid virtues this self-love is the only flaw, fatal to the rounded integrity! No egotist can be greatly loved. However modest, deferent, deprecatory you are, if a pushing forth-putting temper, a greed of precedence be the main-spring, people will know it; and the nearer you come and friendlier you would seem, the more they keenly feel, and make you feel, their distrust. Be not the fly in your own ointment. Lo! all the constellations of truth and beauty in God's heavens are waiting and wanting to come down to you, and you put yourself a mote in the object-glass of your own telescope, to shut out the spectacle and spoil the revelation! Leave your self-pronunciation at last behind. Simon Magus thought the Holy Ghost could be bought for money: will you sell it for admiration? It will not be the Holy Ghost, but some plausible falsehood — mock pearl, paste-diamond, pinchbeck metal — your vanity barters for its food to grow fat on. You are high and lofty, O my man of talent and fame! But any man, to move me, must not be so tall I cannot see *God* over him.

The lower creatures have the same God as we. They, like the poor negroes once, have been neglected in the pulpit and the religious books. Of that beautiful Mosaic Law, "Thou shalt not muzzle the ox that treadeth out the corn," Paul asks, "Doth God take care for oxen? Or saith he it altogether for our sakes?" With all due respect for the great apostle, I answer, Yes: God does care for oxen as well as for us. In this slighting comment on the poor patient drudges for man I have no share. Beast and bird how like us in nature as in structure! I saw some pigeons lighting on a narrow window-ledge. There not being quite room for all, it interested me to see how dainty and restless, with what clean and delicate step they moved, like men or women on a crowded bench. At last one or two got up as you do in a car, only on wings instead of legs, then flew off to a wider seat; where, the rest following, they formed in line again, and seemed to have an excellent social festive time together, as if they were giving a party or returning calls. I thought they behaved as sensibly as people do in a pew or at a picnic, and were as kind and polite as gentlemen and ladies. I saw a dog make signs with his right forepaw to his master across the street as if asking leave to come, and then spring over like lightning the moment he was allowed. Those our poor kinsfolk have a measure of inspiration. He whom we worship is God not only of the Jew or Gentile, but of the hunted deer and over-driven horse. "Not a sparrow falleth to the ground without your Father": is not that in all literature the tenderness most sublime?

> "Tiger, tiger, burning bright
> In the forests of the night,
> Did He who made the lamb make thee?"

Yes: the tiger has rights not to be tormented, which we are bound to respect.

Through all material changes God abides the same. The revelation of Him, before whose face the heaven and earth fled away, only anticipated science. Gross bulk, there is no more in the world: nothing is left but power. Matter is committing suicide in the materialist's hands. We stand face to face with the Infinite Force. We sometimes see in man or woman a Beauty that takes away our breath. It is a ray of the Divine Spiritualism to announce the retinue of spirits, without which the universe would seem a tomb; but all have one God.

Can we speak to him? Can we refrain, with this geyser in our heart bursting up to heaven? But he sees our situation. Beggary will not turn one hair white or black. "Which way do you call the wind?" an Irishman was asked. "I could not call it any way," he replied. How about the wind that bloweth where it listeth? Becalmed in Frenchman's Bay, our skipper whistled for the wind importunately and long, till it came in a gale from the hills. Who can read Cowper's

> "Celestial breeze, no longer stay,
> But fill my sails and speed my way,"

without a heart-echo? Earnest seeking is prayer. Charles Goodyear spent his substance, threw in his health, used up his family, and tired patrons and friends searching for a form of India-rubber to be of service in the arts; till, as Forceythe Willson said, "Nature, also worn out, told him, 'Take it, my child!'" When my search for a lost keepsake became agony, I found it in dust or desert or sea. God is constrained by prayer, and cannot choose but heed our request; for the genuine prayer in us is part of himself and no whim of ours, as we are part of him. It belongs to the constitution of things, and is one of the laws that cannot break. God, said one, could have made a finer fruit than the strawberry. No: in the French phrase, he does his whole possible. Can he help seeing us? Hearing us, no more! "Thou must hear me," Luther said. He bides tryst. You will not give your razor or the reins to a child. God will give us only good. When words fail us, the inward incense rises and rests ever in the soul, like smoke from the chimney, the cloud on Mont Blanc, or the powdery snow blown for ever round the head of the Ortler Spitze, the Alp-giant in the Tyrol. "I took him up into my room and prayed with him," said the minister, of the Liberal Tract distributer at the Tremont Temple; "but I have concluded not to be bothered with him any more." But prayer, that is perfunctory or used as magic, is jugglery and pretence. It must be patient and painstaking, like that in the Garden, to be heard.

We seek unity: but God is difference too. The Son is eternally generated, not as an individual, but an element in the entire substance and essence of things. Physical science as vainly as metaphysical strives to reduce this other yet not alien quality. The philosophic astronomer tells us of the fire-mist or nebula or world-stuff, of which the worlds were made. We might, so far as concerns solving the problem of creation, as well stop with the shining, rolling worlds themselves. Whence the vapor they are made of, is as hard to say as whence the masses and orbits complete. The point we make is a paradox, alters not our position, and brings us no nearer the Source. Can we get the universe out of a primordial germ? From some vesicle was the balloon of Nature inflated, and the whole bubble blown? By what breath without mouth or lungs! The bellows must be accounted for, and One they were handled by. A marvellous child thrust his pipe into that soap from which star and planet were thrown off! Such a view of the origin is a conception, but no thought. It is unthinkable. So is all derivation of Nature from design. We can speak of the design of an artist or artisan. There are models and patterns, after which weavers and carpenters arrange their thread and timber. But we cannot distinguish between the Originator and his work. Creator and creation who can separate with his eye or in his mind? I conceive of the fender, which I look at while I write, as constructed of iron, smelted from ore, blasted or quarried from the mine by a series of inventions. But whither did God go for his materials, and in what manner were they fetched? Did they lie at first within or outside the Being they were used by? For God there is no quarry to discover, and no date to lay his corner-stone. It is not supposable that he began at any point in time or space, or that there was any beginning, such as the Book of Genesis declares. *It commences now*, says the photographer to his sitter. But *He* never commenced. The universe was never less, nor will be greater, any more than himself. We may say, *fitness;* but any attempt to consider periods or compartments, as including all, is nonsense and folly. God has no era, and the epochs we name are for accommodation and convenience, not perfect science or history of his deeds. The Pyramids, Strasbourg, Vatican, had their architects. Ceiling of the Sistine Chapel was plaster once. But none has ever breathed to say where or how the Eternal Builder put his hand to the foundation of his palace; and Jesus is as ignorant of the day or hour as the babe in your crib. Mr. Huxley gives us a good phrase in the "Physical Basis of Life;" yet his protoplasm is itself no simple thing, but combination or composition of several elements, whose putting together is a mystery so beyond our search, that the adjective *proto*, or first, seems a sheer assumption and misnomer. The First hides under and behind every atom he employs. Besides, Mr. Stirling shows how proofless is the dogma that any one protoplasm serves for vegetable, animal, and man. Every species, through the whole range of organization, may have its own. Its *homogeneity* takes for granted the point to be demonstrated, and is recommended to the mind by the fascination and flattery there always is in any single explanation of all phenomena.

There is in matter no elucidation of the genesis of Nature. Spirit is the first term. Thought is the starting-place, not the result. Infinite Self, to which time or place is not, save as opportunity of motion and transition, is the centre, which is circumference too. All we know is a Becoming, which is in and from Being. Blessed that the secret is not found out by us; for then the object and continuance of life were gone. It was said of one, She ceases to care for a man as soon as she knows him. Be not regretful you have not ascertained the Divine method: no interest in existence for an intellectual creature would remain.

VI.

NATURALISM.

THEOLOGY has been a standing insult to Nature. But by what rights of primogeniture? It is no elder brother or better born. Nature is that word of God which *theology* means. The assault is suicide. It is a false contrast to oppose Nature to Revelation, every syllable of which comes through her mouth. Nature is not contrary to Spirit which it voices, nor to art which voices *it*, but only to artifice. The true distinction is that all religion which is not natural is artificial. Nature, or our knowledge of Nature, advances, while theology is stationary, — professes to have learned out. It sits by the roadside with improgressive complacency, as a lout reviles the sister that passes by. No wonder the theologian insists that Nature cannot tell us of God; for she never originated, and cannot indorse his schemes. Living close to Nature is good for health and worldly wisdom: why not for character and truth, and to import common sense into our creed? Here is Nature's revenge: that every system, so far as it leaves her, becomes artificial. Is this quality better in doctrine or ritual than in manners or speech? Much of the present belief and worship of the Church lacks genuineness. It has no charm for a sincere mind, or challenge for the attention of a strong one. Those who wait on the ministrations complain, as some have done at watering-places, that the table is poor, the food scant, and they have to carry their own provisions, though but a cracker, to partake of in secret. Said my friend, who was over-persuaded to go to a showy church, "I had to spend my time looking round at the building and the bonnets; for I took in the sermon with the millionth part of my mind." Many Churchmen and Church-women so belong to the great class of artificial people, it is not strange those who can abide nothing but reality choose to be unchurched, and that thoughtful persons fall away from ordinances and tests. Artificial folk we know too well in society to wish to meet them in the temple. Their love is painted fire; their protection, a Quaker gun; their loyalty is for the spoils of office; their philanthropy rises when the tide turns against slavery and oppression; and they will be for woman's rights when the majority of men are. We have all been cursed with artificial friends, following and smiling in our prosperity, as when you go forth on a bright day every lazy creature creeps out to bask in the sun. But the overcast sky of our fortunes shows their affections to be affectations. In our extremity they desert us. When we are sick and weak, and they have no hope we can do any more for them, they drop off. They will not need us, and think we shall not complain or call them to account when we are gone; for "dead men tell no tales." Their ties with us are for ornament alone, like those knots and bands, cunningly carved in architecture, giving but the appearance of strength, only weakening the pillars by every grain in their construction cut away. Nature, from the lips of piety a term of reproach, and mark of man's depravity and corruption of the world? We speak of the *Divine* nature. But when we change the adjective to *human*, it spoils the noun, and Milton's "human face divine" is a contradiction in terms! Not so. Nature is substance, and every thing substantial is good.

> "All are but parts of one stupendous whole,
> Whose body Nature is, and God the soul."

But do the scholars who think Nature herself fallen consider what blasphemy to His body is their diagnosis? Nature is the proceeding of spirit, language of revelation, material and finish of art; for, says Shakspeare, —

> "Nature is made better by no mean,
> But Nature makes that mean: so, o'er that art,
> Which, you say, adds to Nature, is an art
> That Nature makes."

There is no distinction of natural and revealed religion. Either is the other, if one or both be true. It matters not whether our knowledge be growth into God or his descent into us.

But for what ideas are we to Nature in debt? First, that of Infinity. Does it come from Scripture? But whence the Scripture? From creation the prophet's mind had it, ere it could flow from the prophet's pen. All ideas are within, phenomena are but the occasions. Imagination is the artist sitting in his secret studio to mould and tint the stuff of Nature's quarry. Without the starry vault, whence the notion of immensity? This sparkling hollow what shape shall match? Taking a hint from geometrical figures, my friend called it *diagrams of light*. It seems an endless beach for the eye to wander over. It is an hour-glass through which stars fall like sand. It is a celestial railway to whose last station we never get. "Milky Way" we call part of it; and the new-arrived German pointed and asked if it were Milk Street. It is headland after headland from which we leap into the bottomless deep. It is a transparent lake we sail over, a trembling line we hang on, our downward gaze returning the image of the upward. Nature pale before revelation? God lighted her great altar-candle as well as the lamp of reason, or taper in any prophet's bosom, and the too often dark lantern of the Church.

Is Eternity an abstract conception? The world is a notched stick, a register of vast lapses. Said the Greek, It never grows old. But, fresh as it contrives to look, it bears marks of incomputable age. It is a genealogy and record of time,—man's family-tree. Had it been fashioned to cover its tracks and efface its own history; if the earth obliterated all transactions on its surface or in its depths; if it came before us spick and span, with the furniture varnish upon it just from the shop, like something turned from a lathe, created new every moment as sentimental philosophers say,—what could it give us of that feeling of duration which is our stepping-stone into eternity? But as I walk along the shore and note the crumbling cliffs, the fragments fallen in countless heaps, the cobble-stones they have been worn into, the comminuted pebbles, and the fine brown or white sand into which the granite mountains have at last been ground by the waves; as I notice huge upland boulders delicately poised as if their melting vessels of ice had let them softly to the ground, and others with bits of stone underneath acting as chisels with which they have ploughed their way, showing in the smooth grooves the unmistakable direction of the geologic scratch; and as I observe how Nature, ready to heal her own wounds, has clothed with beautiful lichens, in colors faster than of any art, their enormous sides, — I ask how long it took to do all this; and, from the futility of attempting any chronology, take refuge in the everlasting. I looked at a cedar rooted on the edge of the precipice, — an old Atlantic sentinel, standing guard of vegetable life over against the barren waste before Columbus heaved in sight of the Western shore, — with the knotted stump of a more ancient tree enclosed. We do not remember, said my friend, when we did this: it has dropped out of our recollection. We have turned over some of the pages of this "infinite book of secrecy," and detect everywhere vestiges of former life. We dig up fossil remains of animal and plant. We find, in petrifactions, other cemeteries and mausoleums than man has reared. We discover in caves rude tools of primitive fashion. We explore in the rock, once mud, the prints of the feet of pre-Adamite birds. We calculate the periods requisite to build the coral reefs and lagoons of the Pacific Sea. Mr. Darwin, trying to explain the origin of all existence from primeval germs, has to confess missing links; and knows not how long they were in Nature's chain, or what gulfs they spanned in the bridge of the never-ending march. Of our idea of eternity Nature is the suggestion, if the Eternal One be the cause.

Has not the idea of Omnipotence like derivation, — the will, we are conscious of, confirmed in things? All this motion hints the self-moved, the Infinite Determination. How admirably dextrous he who keeps half a dozen balls in the air! But what the vigor and suppleness by which these larger countless ones are kept from falling or interfering? To the invisible wind, sweeping and striking, rousing the ocean to send far inland the sound of fury with which it founders ships at sea or dashes them ashore, making the midnight sky the alarm-bell struck by its hammer, — whence or whither in its flight we cannot tell, or how twisted into the tornado over the plains and among the gorges of the hills; simoom of the desert, hurricane round promontories and among the islands, or cyclone and typhoon of the Indian seas, — we owe the conception of strength. That we may not miss this realizing sense, the earthquake does not confine itself to the tropics, but travels north to shake every city and village by turns. Volcanoes open to show the pent-up vapor in this boiler of the planet is not exhausted; and make us shudder at the force, in rivets of iron and rock, beneath the mighty deck we tread. On every side are signs of unexpended power whose leash is in the Almighty hand. We ponder over the long dykes of trap-rock that lace the granite coast, and ask what heat and fierceness thrust them up from their fusion far below. In one spot on the American continent the terrible pot has overflowed and spread in a chaotic mass all about; and in some places the granite, through which the molten streams were forced, has itself melted again, and risen to break in two the trap by which itself was broken at first. As a ship signals to us her condition, so does this aerial vessel of the globe inform us of her story and state. Does she not hold out colors, the flag of power, to which the banners of nations are vanity? I know not what innate sense I may have had of a resistless will; only that the resounding breeze which woke me on my bed in the dark woke also my childish soul. Gentler tokens of equal energy more affect me now, in the tide coming and going every day. I sit and write on the sea's edge. As I look up, the waters have ebbed, the sea has lost its arm. In the empty bay the long sea-weed, that had stood upright with perpetual courtesy in the waves, lies prostrate for leagues, and paints with pale green the wide reaches that take their names from long since deceased tenants that saw the picture as I see it now. No loom ever wove carpet like the stripes and patches of brown, yellow, and black that variegate this marine verdure, through which the sluggish channel, shrunk to a thread, winds its way, turning the neighboring islet into mainland accessible to foot of man or beast. I bend to my task in that musing work, which makes hours pass as instants; then lift the eye, and lo! the inlet is full again, so that fleets of kingdoms might ride on it. Without raising its voice to the murmur of one louder ripple, the sea has rolled in. What mathematics shall reckon the liquid tons heaped against the hemisphere while I have not heard the ticking of the clock? It seems no unworthy task for the sun and moon to carry this water-pot of the planet on their shoulders, to fill the pail now for the East, now for the West; and of this refrigerator and salt sanitarium make the most for mankind.

But it takes not things of tremendous weight and size to stir this sense. A little bird, lighting on the tree-top and filling the whole air for miles with the song from its slender throat, while the sun climbs to the zenith, excites the feeling of ability and vitality which there is no way to estimate or play out, more than of the turning on their axes of planets and suns.

What did those who have pronounced upon Nature's defects know of her resources? They were like an infant-school pretending to all the knowledge possessed by their mistress. How invention has gone forward, and our conception of Nature with greater stride, wiping out inadequate notions on which the old creeds were based, since this conventional disparagement began, and compelling perpetual revision of theology; though Conservatism resists, like the mop of Sydney Smith's famous Dame against the tide!

But one want in Nature, it is said, we must confess: there is no sign of forgiveness or mercy. We depend on the miraculous communication for that. Can there, then, be aught in God not signified in his works? If Nature remits no penalty of broken law, is there proof that God does; or is any voiding or suspension of law an equal fiction, in the world or the soul? Goodness is manifest: the universe overflows with it. What at first we count hostile turns out to be friendly; and this love or goodness is the only attribute, including all we call tenderness or pity, such as seems to quiver on the lips of the Phidian Jove. The mercy is not in letting us off from the proper punishment in full measure for our fault, but in so constituting us, and ordaining the issues of our acts, that no sin can be fatal; a fatality of eternal woe for temporary transgression being the monstrous wrong and cruelty for so many ages palmed off on human superstition for the justice of God. Have children a right to parental sympathy? To Divine compassion we have the same claim. It is no gratuity he could fairly withhold, at his arbitrary choice. It is not his option, but necessity. It appears in all his providence as much as in any special grace. It is what physicians call Nature's healing power. The instinctive effort to expel any bane from the system in the shape of disease, — a cough, sweat, fever, eruption, which is the evil demon going out of doors; the marvellous recoveries from nervous functional organic prostration, Nature being, what man is erroneously called, the resurrection doctor; the formation of a new tooth, bone, nail, or claw, when the old has decayed or been torn away; the abundant juices that run in the same season to a second crop of grass, berries, blossoms, or fruit; the throes of remorse to drive out iniquity before the setting in of mortification or dry rot, — all show salvation in the make of things as much as in any supernatural display.

Character must absorb and be nature before it is worth. *Good-natured* is our term to describe perfect temper. Dr. Spurzheim's observation forced him to say he preferred a wife good by nature to one good by grace. Benevolence, to be relied on, must go deeper than will, into instinct and blood. Then there is no need of what revivalists call change of heart. I have heard Orthodox people depreciate the amiable qualities I regretted they did not possess. Change your heart, O friend? So much the worse for me were it changed! "Keep that position," says the artist to his sitter. Keep that disposition, I am moved to say to some I love: it could not be any better. "She has not experienced a change," mournfully one said of a dying negro woman who was a Liberal Christian. "We hope not: none was required or would be a benefit," was the reply. I have seen in a young child, just cutting her teeth, an expression of patience, which was the identical trait we read of in the Book of Martyrs, with beauty not surpassed by Daniel in the lions' den, the three in Nebuchadnezzar's furnace, Paul in the stocks, Peter in the dungeon, or Jesus on the cross. I should not have admired John Brown on his gallows any more.

But did not the Christian dispensation bring in merit of a quite new style? It were sad had virtue denied itself, or ever been born. "Cradle of Liberty," said Kossuth,—"I do not like the phrase: it has a savor of mortality." The heraldry of holiness is too old to trace: it has not altered its coat-of-arms. Have we nobler than Plutarch's heroes? Were our soldiers at Bull's Run better than those at Thermopylæ? What modern captain braver than Cocles kept the bridge? Where a case of more unselfish sacrifice than Curtius leaping into the gulf? Is maid or matron now more jealous than Lucretia of honorable fame? Purity, loyalty, patriotism, and generosity are everlasting excellencies, the monopoly of no religion or age. The oak did not become emblem of courage battling with harder storms than the north-east can unloose, nor the sweet-brier with its roses and thorns a symbol of intangible chastity, in our era. There were brave men before Agamemnon, and virgins before the mother of Christ. To what time or denomination does a good man belong? He is Quaker of the inner light, and Catholic in the outer worship; he sees Unity of person branching wider than any Trinity; he is at home with Methodist fervor and Episcopal decorum; he likes Congregational freedom and Presbyterian order; he believes in Orthodox discipline and Universal redemption; he agrees with the Spiritualist's presence of unseen friend, and in a rising from the grave of body and dust into a glorified form. All parties covet him because he adheres to none, and is above any, having the freedom of the city of God. No society or ceremonial suffices to hold or bind moral integrity. No meeting-house is big enough for the soul. No more empty the pretence of the babe's nurse to appropriate the grown man, Washington or Lincoln, than that of the Church to keep her charge in leading-strings, when it has outgrown the nursery-room of ecclesiastic rule. I remember, when a boy, how I envied the horses outside the sanctuary on Sunday. Though they, too, were tied, it was with a longer tether; and my pasture was dry compared to their green round of grass.

He makes better men than churchmen, was the complaint against a popular preacher: was it not panegyric? Said a Radical to a young girl in a Catholic school, "You cannot be religious too soon: you need defence from whatever quarter against earthly vanities and lures. I beg you, be no sectarian: I do not want you for a proselyte; I would rather a thousand times you should be defended than agree with me in opinion." All who are religious are at one, and need only the atonement they have received. By a humanity deeper than strife, Rebel and Federal soldiers exchanged comforts, in the intervals of an engagement, across the fortification lines; so we stretch hands over rival frowning battlements, and recognize each other by a surer than Masonic touch. The wisdom of Natural Religion is justified of her children. Wordsworth doubtless was a good member of the English Church, but spoke from his heart when he wrote,—

> "And I could wish my days to be
> Bound each to each by natural piety."

When Safford was astonishing a circle by his swift computations, and one asked by what training he solved the fearful sums, "By nature," answered the chief of American mathematicians standing by. We notice this divine property of reverence even in the beasts who look up to man as their deity. Well, if the bowed head or lifted kerchief, or hat held before the face in great cathedrals, express always a deference as sincere. Even the worm trying to raise its horned proboscis makes some figure of aspiration. The alarm with which our cruelty has managed to inspire almost all the lower creatures is inverted veneration. The highest reach of spiritual culture is nature; for it is absurd to call natural that savage state from which man is moved naturally and irresistibly to depart.

The consistent theologians took bravely the consequence of their accusation of our nature, that outward Nature is evil too. We ridicule the mystic fancy that man is responsible for the obliquity of the ecliptic and might say, *I snow and rain;* but it is matched in the older doctrine that the world was ruined in his fall; that the pits and brambles, barren swamps, hot deserts, and icy poles and ragged cliffs, came of his sin. Milton sings of the tears Nature wept over the eating of the forbidden fruit; and we have all seen and felt on our cheeks, as if on hers, those plashing drops, blotches of wet falling wide and slow, from which he doubtless took his line, though probably nothing dreadful and deplorable had occurred. It is our mood that Nature is cipher of. "The heavens mourn," said a Democrat, on a rainy day, "over the disastrous vote." "These are tears of laughter," a Whig replied. The rifts in the globe are too grand and beautiful, too redundant in health and fertility, to have a curse for their cause. Who would have the world round as a bullet, smooth as a ball of yarn, bright as a bead in the sun? These drifts of sleet and mist shall be not puddles of mud only, but sweet springs and lilies and strawberries by and by.

> "The dews shall weep thy fall to-night,"

says Herbert to the Day: but how many morning-glories from such dews arise? Byron's like figure of Ardennes

> "Grieving, if aught inanimate e'er grieves,
> Over the unreturning brave,"

might be of gladness just as well. The gorges are better than a polished surface; the billows, than an unruffled sea; thorns and thistles, than the spontaneous production, in which man himself would vegetate and rot, and his soul never rouse from sleep. The flower we could snatch with hasty impunity were not so lovely as that whose virgin sweetness we win from its sharp defence with a bleeding hand. Only from "the nettle, danger," can safety be plucked.

Abolish the so-called evil, and you abolish the good. How many virtues — of patience, forgiveness, commiseration, magnanimity — are conditioned on human defects! God understands himself and his children in them also. Beware how you make Nature evil. Driven out with the theological fork, she returns and prevails. Truth to my nature, good or bad, is my only task. Is it a wasp's duty to bring honey? Is the copperhead or hooded snake accountable for its venom or fangs? If the Scribes and Pharisees were the devil's children, their only obligation was to make good his designs.

But do we not see native depravity in the child, — irritable, wilful, wanting what it cannot have? What achievements are wrapped up in that will, affections in that sensibility, arts and sciences, endless inventions and improvements, in those wants which grasp at every shining object, and are discontented that the moon will not come down! You are angry with your child because it will not be polite as you dictate. But the fault is yours, not its. Will you beat it with brute strength? Would you mould it in your fingers as wax or dough? Do you not own that new individuality Divine Personality shapes because it needs another instrument, and desires no repetition of you, whom one said, It is enough to have once? God will lay you down, and have done with you, if you push and encroach. Force not the little master or mistress to come and kiss the gentleman, as if the salute or caress, when not voluntary, had value for your courtesy as merchandise in trade. Let the gentleman take that castle himself, if he can, in fair truck and barter. If I cannot win your babe to my arms, I will respect its freedom, as I would the affections of your grown-up daughter or son.

The doctrine of Natural Religion is not unchristian. Jesus was the pre-eminent specimen. From the unfolding of his own soul came all his wondrous works and words. Had he been anywhere to see God out of his bosom? When he said, *Before Abraham was, I am*, he meant no pre-existence you do not share, only you are not inwardly developed to perceive it so clear. All persons are convertible into equivalent glory, if not into whatever he was. When Lucy Stone, in the riot, told her friends to look out for themselves, and was asked, "Who will protect you?" — "This gentleman," she answered, turning to the leader of the mob, who instantly proved as good as her word. It is the touch of sunshine that makes the roughest bud open. Paul was hid in Saul all the time. Fickle Peter was not misnamed a rock: the superficial wave has but to retire to disclose the granite ledge; and under unstable feeling lies unshakable resolve. To the nature within nature we appeal. In a graceful dancer I admired the flying feet that struck so surely every note of the tune which flew from pipe and viol through the air, with pre-established harmony in nature between the melodious chords and those of the human frame. Like answer in our spiritual constitution just education will find to every law of purity and line of truth; and we shall know that each genuine sentiment and resentment of the mind has its part in the music, and is a string in that harp, made of living fibre, which the angels play.

Nature, to our meditation, supplies the moral that goes with the fact. With this power we must be on good terms. Nature pardons no mistakes. She will not give me an inch of rope or hair-breadth of billow to save me from drowning or oversetting in my boat. But on her fidelity we can depend. Point for point, to the end of the line, it will answer to ours. Her penalty is the other side of her reward. The mechanic puts his board to the circular saw. If he puts his arm, it will cut that just as well. If his hand is caught in the wheel, it will be carried round as swiftly as the strap. The car will crush my toe on the rail with the same coolness and iron equanimity as it does the boy's copper cent. The Almighty's buckler is for his children's defence; but they must not rush on its thick bosses themselves. Had there never been a line of Holy Writ, Nature would have hinted obedience of her laws, with every child's finger that went into the flame, or moth that hovered about a lamp, or flood that came and wind that blew and beat upon the house; with every spring freshet or lava-stream that tore up the fields and burnt or bore the villages off, a teacher of Theology.

VII.

MATERIALISM.

WHAT is the starting-point? "In the beginning God created the heavens and the earth." But the materialist says, In the beginning the heavens and the earth created God, or the idea of God in the human mind; having first created the mind capable of that idea, fancy, or fact. But derivation from dust is a theory that disposes of no metaphysical difficulty. In an ever-changing universe, something must self-exist. Is or has matter any *self?* In the play of Ruy Blas, the hero bursts, in a closing scene, into the warning cry, "I am here!" Out of no act of this mighty play of the world can the *I* be kept. To no after-piece can it be postponed: it is an impossible feat for any Roman Lucretius or French Encyclopædist. An Infinite Self, root of every other, appears with the first motion of curiosity, runs like the ghost under the platform, reappears at every point, — a giant that carries us all the time, a spy we never escape, a sapper and miner of whatever godless hypothesis we build. Does the traveller go on foot, this has outstripped him by rail; does he run post-haste, this, like the telegraph after the thief, has sped with the lightning; does he drive his stakes in the wilderness, he wakes up mortified with this pioneer ahead. The Romans were right to make Terminus itself a god, and our poet is right with his "god of bounds." It is a contradiction to talk of any bound of God.

In this almanac of Nature, what is the date? We cannot, without a sense of absurdity, date mind from matter. An inmost sentiment, deeper than sense, stronger than logic, wider than what we observe, and higher than all we understand, forces us to date matter from mind. The masters of wisdom, Plato and Aristotle and Spinoza, join in this verdict with the chiefs of inspiration, Moses and Job, Jesus and Paul. Your primordial atom assumes order and an Ordainer; your protoplasm implies a Protoplast and plastic art, an Architect of the many-chambered house, a First including the many, and a Self-motion without which is no motion; your substance, One that stands under and holds up; your conscience, a Detective pursuing us from the trees of the garden through every web of sophistry or thicket of shame.

Matter is multitude, which it is preposterous to put for the original term and make the parent of unity, instead of the result. What is the depositor but the soul, from which all this fund or bank of particles proceeds, and by which it is held, something it dropped by the way and shall resume at will, like cast-off clothes or an old manuscript, to go through the mill again? Matter is the mind's decayed self, buried for a while, and awaiting a resurrection. All this scene of visible glory is but a receiving-tomb. Lower life is the sepulchre of worn-out higher, with angels at the door to blow the wakening trump, at which the rock itself shall rise to consciousness, the clod clap on wings, and lost spirits learn hell is but a way back to heaven.

You are sure of matter? But who are you, and what is it to be sure; or what is matter sure of? The physicist despises superstition and idolatry, but talks of our origin in the *elements*. What idolatry so deep, superstition so stubborn, polytheism so manifold, or pantheon so wide! Deification of the elements as factors of whatever is called God or man? Give us back Jove and Juno, Mars and Minerva, Vulcan and Venus, for better deities. Let us study religion with Homer for our text-book, as nearer the truth than the senseless atoms. If the elements are more than instruments, let the carpenter be made by his tools, the painter by his paint, the chemist by the gases he combines in his retorts. If we shrink, with the old sufferer, from saying to corruption, "Thou art my father," and to the worm, "Thou art my mother and my sister," it is a noble hesitance. We subordinate our Author to ashes in subordinating ourselves. To make the first term countless is like making the variations precede the tune, and the accompaniment prior to the player. A lifeless womb of life is unthinkable. The gem is not made by the rock that imbeds it, nor the flower by the soil it grows in; and the phrase *spontaneous generation* is a figure drawn from *choice*. There was a mother of the matrix we were shaped in, and hewer of the rock from which we were hewn. The wonderful Person contains road and sky, is at the goal and the outset, stands for the post and slips in behind the limit, and constrains us to conclude as we commence. Matter may be our nursery; but who is our nurse? Matter is but the door of invisible force, lying always in fineness, not in gross bulk. Are the subtilties made of the masses which they toss? Are light, heat, electricity, magnetism, product of some creative crucible? The composition is the clod. A French chemist reduces all not to atoms, but to atomicities, or active powers, — shall we say, to One Atomicity, whose name we dare not speak? The materialist starts from the particles, and gets into the presence-chamber of the King. Encourage him on his way. Give materialism rope enough, perfect liberty, and it will hang itself. It thinks to commit murder, and commits suicide.

Yet physical philosophy is not without benefit. It has made the wordy Sahara of metaphysics green and fruitful. Into the void of abstractions it puts form and color, a language clear and picturesque. Let us give thanks for its portfolio of sketches of the actual world. This earth is so fair, I reserve my opinion if heaven be better. I take not the preacher's assertion. Let me pause before this picture. Hurry me not with premature descriptions of the next. There are moments of visible revelation, when life is unmixed blessing, the cup is full, time disappears in eternity, there is no such thing as calamity, the soul is content and asks no more of God. A gleam of glory from the unveiled constitution of things sets the gate of paradise at our steps. We see death as the last scud of vapor that flits away. God makes his garment of matter so fine we little children can only clutch and gaze.

Materialism humbles, too, our pretensions of a separate nature. A Hebrew scorn of animals, founded on a notion of their inferior origin, and existence for man's use, infected the Christian teachers, though not Jesus himself. To the naturalist, more than to the theologian, we owe the growing interest in their welfare. It is the crown of civilization to apply the word *humanity* to a kindly treatment of every lower tribe. What but the science we condemn has taught us that this is no figure of speech or act of grace, but simple justice to creatures of the same dust as ourselves? Zeal to gather specimens may sometimes be cruel, and the eager pathologist pursue sharply the homologies of structure and function. But a new sentiment is making the knife relent: the pinning and vivisection once so remorseless now submit to the law of economy of pain. In regard to human beings too, materialism proclaims equality. It is no autocrat or aristocrat, but democrat. It shows one womb and cradle for all men. A narrow spiritualism, regarding the soul as not a flower or outgrowth, but æolian attachment of the body, allowed cruel diversities among men. The Church suffers from its fancy of gifts in one, impossible to another, carried in the case of Jesus to the extent of miraculous generation and introduction to the world. But for him God would not love or save the rest of the house. The other members of the family have sinned past cure. The case is gone by default: the sword is unsheathed, and the throne burns with devouring wrath. But if this dear Son will bow to the stroke, and sprinkle his blood in the flame of that almighty forge, restoration to favor may be had! Such gratuity at another's instance and intercession, I decline. If God will not love me for my own sake, I will not be loved. If he hates my nature, let him hate. If, says Mr. Mill, I must go to hell on any ground that goodness in God or man is not the same, to hell I will go! Would you have your father or mother embrace you for your brother's or sister's sake? Could you accept the affection tendered you on account of an older child or first-born? This primogeniture is no better in one place than another. An iniquity on earth, it is no magnanimity in heaven. We want a generous Father, or let us have none. Christ died for me? I would die for him. He were worth dying for. If he died for us, it was because God saw that we were not worthless, but worthy. We want no sacrifice but of our own kind. If it was not my blood that flowed on the cross, it has no virtue for my sin. It was a drop of the circulation of the race, and therein its power to redeem.

With the eternal All-mover, atom or immensity is the same. He is weigher and gauger of his own substance and dimensions. The number of his meters is the note of his infinity. The hand raised in prayer or stretched for help is more continent of him than the heavens. Omnipresence which the materialist admits is only mechanical extent. But piety makes the lowly heart larger than the sky. "God is everywhere," said the Sunday-school teacher. "Is he in this room?" asked the little boy. "Yes." — "In my desk?" — "Certainly." — "In my hat?" — "No doubt." — "In my pocket?" — "Of course." — "No, he isn't: I haven't got any!" God's presence is co-equal with the sense of it. The materialist's experiment of the endless subdivision of matter — observes our metaphysician, Mr. Harris — resembles travelling in a circle with the hope of some time coming to an end. Is not material multiplication, to reach the immeasurable, nonsense as sheer? Materialism is a counterfeit depth, and atones for being shallow only by being obscure. Its professors complain of metaphysical abstractions. They substitute physical ones. The definitions of Spencer are more prolix and less satisfying than the categories of Kant. Nothing but confusion can come from making things procreators of thought. Without parentage and rule of mental conception, they are starving orphans, masterless steeds. In materialism is no rest, but endless chase, that brings no game to cover. It is the wild huntsman blowing a ghostly horn in a barren pursuit. But spirituality is peace. It finds the weight and specific gravity more truly than did the old philosopher in his bath.

It makes a difference to have the centre of gravity fall within or without. They who seek external foothold for the soul remind us of the toy whose perpetual attempt to recover its erectness is the amusement of the child. "Discontent is immortality." But it is not a famishing discontent. "Prone to action and to rest," says Pascal, "through action we seek rest." Blessed constitution, without which the apple would not have been eaten, or the fenced garden forsaken for the world, made so wide, as Goethe says, on purpose for our wandering! Man would have been satisfied to vegetate and rot where he was born. The poise of the other hemisphere was wanted by the Genoese sailor as well as by the globe. By every discoverer, North or South, the same momentum has been felt. Finding the fate of Sir John Franklin, the explorer traverses himself. Captain Hall, in *The Polaris*, searches for the counterpart of a map on some inward membrane. The student of geography or of the animated kingdoms lays out the metes and bounds of his own nature. Self-knowledge is the aim of his knowledge of animals and plants. The physicist goes round about the problem which the metaphysician directly grasps. Naturalist and supernaturalist would tell the bounds of God's acre with diverse method, each with his own rod and chain. The only question is if there be any Owner of the field, or the world is a wild lot with no claim. Marvellous canvas which no pencil ever touched, and a stranger set of cartoons than in any Vatican, with new sketches in numberless slides! Whoever finds the problem easier so may be congratulated, as a child put off with empty promise. In Scott's novel, the lad begged the lady to give him silver, the only money he was acquainted with, and declined her gold.

A thoughtless observation stops with the exterior. No personality is no origin and no destiny. Who is there to be immortal? Whom go to? Why so foolish to try to put our foot beyond the border, break the hedge, or hang over the precipice where is no support but empty space, or climb above the top of our tree of life, unless there be indeed a path the vulture's eye hath not seen? On this point Idealism and Materialism once shook hands. It was a singular meeting of extremes, stranger than when Herod and Pilate became friends. But the permanent position of the material school was with Idealism a temporary phase. To reduce all to unsympathetic power, tossing out this ephemeron of man, to keep up an hour like the stray butterfly that wearily drops drowning in the tide, is mean and disrespectful. It makes the universe look poor, a conundrum not deserving a guess; a nest of boxes, with much pains opened, to disclose nothing in the last. Contempt of the Creator and of his creation comes from self-contempt. The miracle of his glory is to beget children, as Saturn adorns himself with his rings.

Materialism is an apology for ignorance. It has but one maxim, that everybody is devoured by the Sphinx. It is celebration of surface and despair of knowledge. It scoffs at the deepest sentiments of humanity, by dropping God and Heaven as fancies or whims. But he who specifies what we can have no notion of has some notion of it himself. Every negative is a positive. God is unknowable, you say. Is God to you but a word? What business, then, have you to say about him so much? It is saying a great deal, to affirm he has no inventory or manifest, and is inferior to any householder or master of a ship. You have no right nor title to *say* you know nothing of what you know nothing. The subject to you does not exist. The materialist has no account to offer of Nature or man: only that the particles in one arrangement present beauty in form and color, without life; in another, unconscious organs; in a third, creatures deceived with an imagination that they are not machines. What is the imagination, that inner eye? From him no reply; but that the atoms in one collocation digest, in a second secrete, in a third assimilate, in a fourth feel, or reason, or love, or illusively appear to will.

Materialism climbs over the sides of the pyramid, or sits akimbo on its top, but explores not the interior, and denies it has any door. It is a spy reporting the nakedness of a land flowing with milk and honey. On the materialist's chart, the whole spiritual region, like one point of the globe, is put down as "No man's land."

What of any interest or importance in human life can he explain? A certain multiple of those elements, his only counters, composes a round stolid mass, wheeling eternally dumb through the sky. A few of them, otherwise disposed, form a human figure that sees and speaks, sparkles with genius or glows with desire, and sends shocks of affection through another with which it has a deeper than chemical affinity; or thrills us with combinations of argument and imagery, never heard of on the planet before and making all things new. One of these shapes, with its few score pounds avoirdupois of flesh and blood, we call Moses; another, Cæsar, Isaiah, Shakspeare, Christ. But law-giver, commander, poet, prophet, redeemer, or saint, comes out of the retort according as the atoms are mixed, and the blind fingers sift! Such a theory is too great a demand on the faith which materialists despise. My credulity is great; but, like a millionnaire in the city angry with the assessors, it refuses to pay so enormous a tax. How cheaply the unspiritual theory appraises those quick faculties of my friend, the nimble-tongued woman, that never fail in any jet of talk to deliver to my prosing dulness something fresh! Can the quality of that young maiden, who just left my board, be analyzed? Can that purity, untouched and intangible by aught evil, be convicted as an outcome of the soil?

From these novel speculations, we learn that conscience is no voice of God or communion with rectitude, but calculation. Utility transformed makes that angel of light; and self-interest is the wonder-worker that turns out self-sacrifice from its lathe, projects every passage of devotion, and casts every scene of heroism in the whole history and long tragedy of mankind. The iron selfishness, which some alchemy contrives to convert into the gold of disinterested deeds, is itself transmuted clay. I can read Hebrew from right to left, but not spell creation with this alphabet. I cannot get one from many, but the many from the one. Where is that One? as Philip asked Jesus: point him out! He is the artist that does not thrust himself into his work. I went into a studio and admired the sketches, in charcoal and water-colors, that lined the walls. But where was the friend that drew these *fac-similes* so lively of the house and headland, the boat and the bay? No sign of palette or easel, painter or brush, anywhere to be seen! The design so exquisite, the skill so perfect, the tints so true, and every shape solid in this re-creation of Nature; but the hand withdrawn? Room for all to appear to advantage but the one that did it all. For her no nook nor corner where I could conceive she was bestowed! Shall we doubt the First Artist *is*, because he nowhere draws himself?

We cannot separate motion from will, mobilization of an army from the general, or of the funds from a financier. The wires of the electric cable are not wrapped closer than this faith. An English authority affirms it as an indisputable axiom of science that life comes only from life, never from death. But life is indistinguishable from movement; and who has reached the limits where life and death part? Death is still and cold; and how stark and stiff we have thought large part of the creation! Sepulchres are hewn in the rock, whose helpless mass seems fit enclosure of the corse that shall leap or walk no more. But motion is no absentee from the stone. "The dance of death" continues in what we consider dead, and disproves death with rhythm the unarmed eye cannot see, and a music of spheres, infinitely smaller than the orbs Shakspeare celebrated, which our ears cannot hear. A finer procession begins where the funeral ends, and elemental melodies laugh at the melancholy dirge. Tyndall's thesis, that heat is a mode of motion, resolves the universe. The figures in this cotillon are appointed by an intelligence identical with command. There is a swarm not only in the beehive or the city street. Every wooden block is occupied and spinning under the feet that seek it for a support. The sea stretches off glassy and treacherous, as a place for unwary mariners to drown and die in. But the existence that sports in its huge bosom roughens the surface with schools of fish that make mimic waves on its swell, and spring out for a moment, with the universal disposition to break bounds into the air. From the bald eagle that sailed by me this morning, to the fly I discern only by his pincers on the back of my hand, is no interval nor cessation of activity. There is no passive voice in the world. Patience is a nobler motion than any deed. We never have so much will as when we say, *Not mine.* There is no stay. We must up and on: the bed or chair is intolerable unrest. In the arena is ease:

the rising sea drives me from the seat where I am writing my theme, and a heaving ocean of desire lifts me to enterprise and accomplishment ever fresh. My boat is tossed and tosses me; and in my heart is a pulsation chiming with my oar, a jet from the infinite pulse. The beat in my wrist refers me to that in my breast. To what does that refer but a will co-extensive with wisdom and equivalent to love?

I sit in a skiff on the last ebb of the tide: the minnow swims through the transparency below, and the fly floats through that above; an infant-crab creeps, and a minute flounder, simulating the sand, ploughs on the bottom, while a horse-shoe steers along with his rudder of horny tail; bits of eel-grass glide with their shadows; the long sea-weed waves on the surface in the wind, its glittering tips casting down prismatic tints, spots of rainbow that move over the bottom of the sea, which is pierced with little holes through which the clams suck, and breathe back with bubbles that ever rise and break without noise; the drift of clouds overhead is reflected in the mirror under foot; a slight ripple glances the last subdivision of the ocean-swell that lifts my little vessel softlier than a babe on the mother's breast; the surf a mile away tumbles on the rocks, beyond my island break-water, with a force no frigate could resist. And all this on a morning as gentle as ever shone. No will nor meaning, says the materialist, in the whole! Then how prolific is ignorance, and what a busybody death!

How much motion is represented, beside what is seen! The wave rises and washes some invisible particles from the cliff. But what imponderable tons in unreckonable ages have been washed from every promontory and ragged seam! The rude sculptor of the sea, shouldering to his work, chips finer than any chisel an atom at a time, smoothing into what beauty, carving with what grandeur, the mighty block! The green tongue of land that divides the quiet bay from the stormy deep has been moulded into curves passing any mathematics to compute. Yet all the tendency to this exquisite result is without intent! We are not able or allowed to spell a syllable in the volume that has no preface or finis. We are looking over an album in which no photographer had a hand. We are walking through a crystal palace whose pillars were set with no plumb-line; and it required no eye in the making of what we behold! But will is power knowing what it is about, whoever may please to esteem himself accident or resultant of a blind force, that cannot, like the Cyclops, even feel round. Through countless variety all the cogs are carried with one wheel. The strength that raises a child's finger rolls the billow and the orb; and the hydrostatic paradox is wherever Infinity is balanced by a drop.

Spirit cannot be parted from matter. We worship God as Spirit; but we cannot conceive him out of Nature. No more can we so conceive the human soul unclothed, but, as Paul said, clothed upon. Hence the difficulty always felt of imagining immortality without the body. So for their dead kings the Egyptians built, in the Pyramids, houses more splendid than any palace, and embalmed the flesh. Was theirs a superstition of which we are rid? There is, in Greenwood Cemetery, a mausoleum of such cost that the fortune intended for the occupant is inherited by her dust; and a Greek temple in Mount Auburn casts into the shade with its beauty many a country church. Our horror of the resurrectionist arises from our superstition of a resurrection. The good Boston doctor, who bequeathed his body to the dissector's knife, doubtless had been annoyed by it. When the Indians were removed, their being driven from the graves of their fathers was the peculiar aggravation of cruelty on which Congressional orators dwelt with a pathos it was poetical to think the roving tribes were conscious of themselves. Yet furniture for future use, weapon or ornament, was put into the warrior's tomb; while the Chinaman, after his California toils are over, can fancy no rest for his remains but on the side of the globe where he was born. The resurrection of the body — a spurious phrase, substituted for the New-Testament resurrection of the dead — is printed in all liturgies, and the mortal relics committed to the ground "in hope of a general resurrection at the last day." Is it possible friends suppose these dissolving frames will sprout from the soil or be mechanically restored? This gross belief is, however, not without ground. It is founded on an idea as true as it is necessary, — that without form or matter spirit is lost; the mistake being that this identical matter, our familiar garment, will recover from the trance of death. So we cannot quite give it up. In my neighborhood, a little boy, attempting to bathe in a race-way of the ebbing tide, was swept away and drowned, — Nature herself undertaking to be both minister and service, shroud and procession, prayer and dirge, sexton and grave, with her salt caves and sounding tides. But from such disposition of the dear body the town was in revolt. Crowds hung along the beach, peered into the channel beneath the draw, and put forth in boats to hunt it up out of its wide wandering sepulchre. Field-pieces were brought and discharged from the deck of a vessel sailing to and fro in the harbor, hoping by the concussion to start the morsel of humanity from its lurking-place in the briny ooze, so wholesome and sweet. Before the time the apostle names, the Sea was called to give up her dead. Was it all sympathy with the afflicted, otherwise in many ways expressed? Was it a feeling that the soul could not survive the loss of its perishing robe? Did it hint the lingering strength of the notion that associates it so indissolubly with its habitual form, and imply a rational view that its projection without form is impossible to conceive? The physicist laughs at the Romish or Episcopal official's notion of perpetuated flesh; yet the physicist admits no individual immortality without a reassembling of the particles we are each one composed of now, thus meeting the ecclesiastic in the same philosophy. If both could learn a human person's independence of any given set of particles, neither need scorn the other; and the discovery how delicately the threads are woven in Nature's loom, how her strongest is her finest stuff, and how she hides her everlasting principles, the thunders of her power, in imperceptible atoms, and not in bulk, suggests continuance in safe investment.

The whole is inseparable from the one. Materialism is disintegration. The infinite divisibility of matter is an axiom in mechanics: is its infinite multiplication an account of the universe? An Anti-Darwinian said it is not from one, but an ocean of germs. But, to get the one out of many, thought labors in vain. What is the whole which the materialist posits as greater than any Personality, or God? It is the general impression of the world. But this is no whole. It is infinitesimal part. To talk so of the whole is absurd. We say we see the earth, ocean, or sky, with but a trifling arc or section of either in our view. When a traveller came in sight of Sebago Pond, wide stretching and ruffled by the wind, she asked if it were not the Atlantic. We say Columbus discovered the Western hemisphere in an outlying island. That referred to the continent; the continent, to the globe; the globe, to the constellations, swimming in immensity like mites in the waste or motes in the air. The integrity of Nature cannot be reached by our observation or generalizing. No induction of particulars or deduction of logic is its measure. It is Thing of pure Thought. Like integrity of character, it is no construction of distinct portions, or polyp-growth resolvable into endless individuals; but implies simplicity of absolute centre, from which all the virtues radiate, and of which every word of wisdom or deed of goodness is a beam. The man worthy of his name is never in pieces; is not many-sided, but circular, meeting you with one line of beauty at every point. God is the sphere in which innumerable circles, great or small, are contained. In every earthly inch and throughout celestial leagues is one uncontainable Container, reducing countless objects, circumstances, persons, and events to the Being from which they proceed. For Being is no multiple, but always and for ever One.

But, the materialist will ask, does the Spiritualist attain to unity? Is he not vagrant, in variety beyond all compass, entangled in the meshes of the net whose drag we cannot escape more than fish can the seine in the stream? Here is the reply: We cannot comprehend or imagine the Person or Unity which is God, but we can think it. Eternity, Infinity, is our Thought, though like the peace that passeth understanding, or the heaven eye hath not seen, nor ear heard, nor the heart of man conceived. My identity with it I feel, but cannot describe. Of the enthusiast who declared "I am God," it was said, he is right, though the words were false the moment they left his mouth. Our doctrine admits no proof, all proof being less certain than itself. It is open to criticism and scorn, spite of which it will not cease to be affirmed and to affirm itself.

We cannot explain the lowest forms of life by importation of properties from the air and the soil. My friend picks up in the pasture a red berry which has a pleasant taste, but whether it be poison she cannot tell. Who can elucidate the difference which determines the flavor of an apple or peach; or of meats, which some have not a palate keen enough to distinguish with the eyes shut; or of wines, for which a certain judge had a tongue so nice as to detect a savor of iron from a key having been dropped into the cask? The wisdom, from whose herbarium all the grasses came, like varieties of architecture and stuffs of the loom from the master's designs, ordained the many-colored orb of human genius to outreach all the patterns of palaces and colors of woven silk and wool.

The derivation of spirit from matter implies a time when spirit was not. Some lonely little vesicle wandered in the void womb of a universe! When I can put myself into my own crucible, rake myself out of the ashes of my own furnace, cut myself into pieces, and from Medea's kettle recover my youth, take my perceptions back into their materials, and be revivified from elemental dust, I may expound the process of creation of which my intuitions and imaginations are the end. But our cradle is farther off than our tomb. It were easier to find where Moses was buried, though no man knoweth his sepulchre to this day, than where he was born, if by birth we mean that by which Moses was made to be himself, and not Aaron or Pharaoh. Our knowledge finds everywhere a wall, if our wonder do not turn it into a way to Infinity. I sit in a vein of trap-rock, through which the granite has been eaten out by what the Greek poet called the foaming tusks of the sea. Midway in the horizontal shaft the once overhanging cliff has fallen to fill a section of it up. The stone has disintegrated into soil, and in the soil vigorous oaks have sprung to overtop the level whence came the support of their own roots. The total is beauty, which no camel's hair pencil with all the pigments could improve. Give me the methods, material equivalents, and exact time required for the picture so as to leave adoration out, and I will set you then the harder problem how beauty has come into a thought, a character, a gesture, a gait full of grace, or the human face divine, with no intent to lift our eyes above the earthly floor. Is matter such an accomplished posture-master it can take all the attitudes of perfection and faultless propriety of motion unawares? Delsarte would generate eloquence, like electricity from cushion and cylinder, by a study of the language of facial and bodily expression, to every syllable of which only passion and inspiration first gave vent. This theory puts artifice for art, cuts the train of oratory and action from the locomotive of feeling, would conjure things signified out of their signs, subordinate the everlasting to the mechanical, and dispense pulpit and rostrum from the need of any inward affection. But no such juggle can create truth. We cannot extract mind from earth, as by successive processes in a refinery the black juice of the cane becomes white as wheaten flour. Reason is absolute. It accepts not its costume of matter for its creator, any more than would the French monarch the state robes which Thackeray in his pen-sketch sets up for his royal self. The marble mountains of Carrara move not out of the sceptic's way for any dispute or ignorance of their origin; and the moral sense is so positive that from all speculation Kant retreated on it for fundamental trust, like Wellington on the Torres Vedras from the open field. How selfish utility mounted into spiritual tenderness and strength would puzzle Minerva to tell. "I cannot allow myself," said a man, "to eat a pear by myself: I have to carry it home." Who told Theodore Parker not to kill the little spotted turtle basking by the brook? Ezra S. Gannett would not let me have my newspaper back till he had folded it precisely as he took it from my hand! I sit among the rocks before the spectacle of the sea that rolls and breaks in thunder at my feet. In no other way is sublimity brought so near. But why am I uneasy and discontent? Why not abide and enjoy the marvellous scene, letting the day pass, and Time shake his hour-glass as he will, while such luxury of the imagination, beyond all feasting, is mine? Because I am alone, and my companion is needful to perfect my delight. You say it is an elixir of utilities; it is the compound interest of selfishness; it is a dividend on the policy of mankind: but that the main chance were susceptible of such gradation, and brute appetite could graduate humanity like a lily from the mud, we should all have been a pack of gluttons and thieves! I decline this origin of glory. I will find in no such dross the making of my heavenly crown.

In all nobility is an unborrowed charm. A child of five summers takes my case in hand for counsel from her curly head, and warns me not to stand on the platform or jump from the moving cars. What concern has the little maiden in my hoary head and nearly spent life? Has she calculated the account of profit and loss in my departure or longer stay? Is not the gentle disapproval of my rashness part of a generous instinct which comes out to touch me more in the sober smile than in the monitory word? I should as easily suspect a miserly computation in the motherly hen's scratching for her brood close by. The abysses of the sea are beneath those white caps blown up by the south wind; and from more fathomless deeps of the human bosom rises every spell of honor and truth.

I am positive, says some reporter, in whom we may mistrust some mixture of will with knowledge. But the *will* which positivism, materialism, phrenology, and the metaphysics of Jonathan Edwards, not knowing what to do with and unable to explain it, unanimously deny, declines to leave the lexicon or the world. We make a convert of the man; but the will is not convertible into any particular motive. If it would only confess itself to be a sequence, a link in the chain, no cause, but one of an endless row of effects, how well we should comprehend it; and in our philosophical cabinet lay it as a labelled specimen on the shelf! But it declares itself to be more than intelligence. It testifies not that it has, but *is* motive. In a saint, like Jesus, it declares itself part of the will of God, as it must be in every man, who is his child, in every filial act; for this unscientific, wilful veto on the will cannot stop with human nature, but must defy the Divinity. If the universe have a throne, and be not an automaton, freedom is the birthright of man.

But how get from our idea of God to the fact? We deny the chasm! As there is no void in Nature, but the opposite banks that frown at each other are united by space and air and magnetic circuits as closely as by timber and steel at the St. Lawrence River or the Menai Straits, so subject and object cannot be severed. Some identity makes them one. "Know thyself" is a profound proverb, because self-knowledge is the knowledge of God. The prodigal came to his father when he came to himself. No absence of God where is a man, or of man where is a God! The same immense, positive, universal Root abolishes all but surface difference, and allows no negative. Life is the fact; and death, the shadow it appears to cast, is part of itself, the ghost of life, as all apparitions are shades.

There is a doom on every scheme of pure criticism. Not by counter-criticism, but want of vitality, will it fall, as trees said to be winter-killed perish of the summer-drought that has drained their sap. As in morals, so in the intellect, the worst fault is fault-finding. A strong organism insures longevity. I saw a prostrate trunk, half-rooted in the ledge and soil, each branch of which on the upper side had made a soil of the parent-bole, and shot up into a perfect tree with boughs and sprays of its own. Any thing is possible to bountiful being, to amplitude of soul. But the poor and juiceless denier, subsisting by attack, like the mosquito on the blood of its victims, leads a precarious life, and will soon be blown away by the wind in some little heap of his fellows as useless as himself.

But must we not define, stake out our roads and bounds of our dwellings, and have gates not only to open, but shut? "We cannot live," cries the conservative, "out of doors." We may well consider if we do not live too much *in* doors for our virtue and our health! Has the close air of churches any better quality than that of other houses or shops? To what, asked my friend, do you owe your recovery? To perpetual open air, I replied. Air, light, water, earth, the four elements with their ever-flowing magnetism, the only medicine-chest from which I have got any good. All close communion is unwholesome. Camp of Indian, haunt of Bohemian, wandering of gypsy, are more salubrious. I grudge every hour frost and storm drive me in from the roof where —

"Tenderly the haughty Day
Fills his blue urn with fire;"

or "fretted with other golden fires" at night. "I call this going in, not out," said Edward Everett when he walked abroad. We need ecclesiastical ventilation. When the lamps burned low in the North-End meeting, and the oil was complained of, the merchant told the worshippers to find the difficulty in their deoxygenizing breath. Was the atmosphere any better for the mind? But the old confinement has given way to a gracious allowance, in some quarters, that we can worship in the woods. Thank God for this big playground for his children's recess! Not a few roods of land in Boston or Hartford, but the earth is our common, which no Internationals can cut into strips as numerous as the population. Beyond private rights of legal possession it is an undivided patrimony. One, asked if he were owner of a line of coast, replied, How absurd to presume to own shore or sea! My idol, like that of ancient idolaters, is made of stone. But it was fashioned by no tool in human hands. The elements of wind and wave were its sculptors; the promontories measure its stretch; and through unmeasured leagues of its proportions it is vocal with the praise I lay, a sacrifice, on its shrine.

Every thing is affirmative. Denial is but the hem of definition. *Nay* is the condition of *Yea*, which is unconditional. Every creature adds: the coral insect, his reefy sepulchre; the worm that eats the mulberry, his silken tomb; the spider, his web, that pays in beauty before the broom sweeps it away. The bee is a sugar-refiner of Nature's most concentrated sweet, like human creators of good finding in his hive his grave. The objector, the contrary person, has no business.

Your amount of righteous will is your warrant. The pious man says, "I have no will." He should say, No *wish*. It was not his will, but his wish, Jesus resigned. Self-renunciation is not surrender of will. The will is never so strong as in giving up, for principle and the common weal, self-interest or sensual delight.

Every thing is excellent in the ratio of its positive force. Free Love and Free Religion are the phrases of the day. But freedom is of no worth save to express truth, and conform to the divine order. Love and Religion are not choices, but inspirations and necessities, the laws as well as liberties of our being. They are stones in gear to grind our daily bread, but falling they grind to powder whoever would shift them to the service of his passing whim. Personality is the secret and circle of the world. We doubt immortality because we count personality the accident, not the essence of our nature. But it is the composer as well as the tune. By statutes, that cannot be repealed because never passed, every genuine concord comes: in a symphony of Beethoven, in a harmonious affection, in a word fitly spoken on the smooth wheels of opportunity, or a pure and happy deed. To sacrifice yourself is impossible. God cannot sacrifice you! Only some unworthy propensity — obstinacy, vanity, pride — can be sacrificed, as much below yourself as the ram Abraham caught in the thicket was below Isaac his son. Never was man less a victim, and more a victor, than Jesus on the cross.

The opinions of most people are accidental. The minister or professor does not succeed, and imputes his failure to the system or sect he trains under, or to partners who will not see his merit, — unlike the brave clergyman, who said he stuck to Orthodoxy because he was Orthodox: "the company was not much!" If the person is greater than his creed, he carries it. If he is less, and wins no promotion, he bolts. If the platform is old and rotten, it trembles under the tread of every strong man. But the soul is one with its faith.

VIII.

SPIRITUALISM.

THIS seems a misnomer. It means the materialism of spirits, so much of heaven as can be manifest to mortal senses. But pure spirituality is impossible, in God or angel or man.

"For soul is form, and doth the body make,"

writes the poet. Seneca says it is a mistake to think the surface is the inferior part of a man. Goethe declares: "O Philistine! there is no inside." Beauty and wit and love come out. All the explorations of science are on planes of inconceivable thinness. As the soul opens, it knows it is not in the body which it uses and contains; but is as much more than that as the atmosphere than the earth, or ether than the stars. The Turkish cadi asked Layard, "Wilt thou see heaven with thine eyes?" Death will not benefit us if it blinds.

But Spiritualism does not abide fair experiment, like electric, chemical, or planetary laws. It cannot endure sceptics, in whose presence all other operations of the world go on without superfluous modesty. It has not been made to bear on any practical welfare of man, — to rescue those exposed to wreck or famine; to comfort any in sorrow, save its own devotees; to detect the sealed number of a bank-bill, though great reward was offered; to add a mite to the store of knowledge; or to charm intellect or fancy with any rare rhetoric of words. Whether Jackson or Morton discovered anæsthesia, a disembodied spirit did not. It was not beforehand with Leverrier to announce the new planet, or with Daguerre in the photography it applies to cherubic portraits. The great souls it re-presents to us have so retrograded as to make the anticipation of our own immortality an alarm. Franklin, in its introduction of him, is inferior to Poor Richard and his old newspaper, and makes no show so grand as with his knuckle drawing the spark from his paper kite. Swedenborg does not see, nor Washington behave, nor Webster speak so well as in the flesh. Milton's poetry and Parker's pith are gone. The revelations make backsliders of all men.

Is it that the struggles of the departed for self-publication fail on account of imperfect mediums? It was said of an artist, All his pictures are full of the east wind. Over all *their* communications runs a blur. Spiritualism seeks the shade, twilight, drawn shutters, and a closed-up box for its performances, as it did midnight in church-yards. Its children are not of the day. I have heard of painters who would put their drawing of a flower where only a single ray would fall on it for the best effect. But the cardinal blossom I picked required no such bolstering of gloom. The more it was brought into the light, so that the sun shone in and round and through its leaves, which no palette can match, the handsomer it became. For people or pictures one law: how do they bear being exposed? Michel Angelo told the anxious sculptor to set his statue in the public square.

Yet Spiritualism is a genuine attempt to handle that problem of existence which puzzles the young child whom we see putting on its considering-cap to know why it is here, and who is responsible for its appearance. Somebody it is evidently determined to call to account. The riddle it begins to guess at we have not finished, and Gabriel or Uriel will never solve.

But are the facts of Spiritualism fairly dealt with? "They are not in Nature," says an eminent naturalist. That is, he has not found them. Does he assume to know all that is in Nature, and exhaust in his classes and categories her sum? The gods laugh at him, as he does at any preceding tribe of naturalists asserting for their survey eminent domain. Said my classmate, to the senior Professor Ware, of the *a priori* proof, "This is unintelligible." "Would you not better say," answered the venerable head that swung its pendulum so justly between opposing views, "that you do not understand it?" No superstition of the Church is so gross as that of the scientist that he has mastered the creation in his formulas, and can rule out phenomena not encountered in his field, on the ground that they are not among the contents of the creation. Is he as chosen clerk to take an inventory of her effects? The theories that have been already surrounded and overthrown show how scientific and ecclesiastic dogmatists are blood relations falling out, as vice fights with itself in another person. He is fool, as theologian or physician, who fancies no circle yet to be drawn will circumvent him. Give us your criterion of incredibleness.

But there is a second objection to Spiritualism on the score of religion, urged by Christians who hold the supernatural view, and are disgusted with the spurious miracles and pretended apparitions of the new faith. This is a family quarrel about a supposed will of God, under which one party claims all his curiosities, and a monopoly of prodigy, with which it is sacrilege to interfere. We forget the absurdity of isolated portents. Whatever has happened may occur again, and must accord with law. Half a dozen ghosts in Palestine, to please a few spectators on the Hebrew stage, and none beside in all history throughout the sphere, were as tough as yesterday's most astounding tale. Christianity and Spiritualism, as popularly professed, rest on the same marvellous prop. Both maintain human survival with external proof. As the eye sees that the duck or hawk which rises from the water is the same that dived; as Sam Patch came up from Niagara as he went down, — so the ghost is seen to be the man we knew. But immortality is no matter of chronology. Bare continuance what noble spirit would accept? So the Florida cedar, that took root before the land was discovered, were better than a man. To be immortal is not to be the same, but another higher self every day; so that by none, without a discerning love, we could be recognized. Goethe said Schiller had taken such strides as to astonish him. Milton's seeing his "late espoused saint" in a dream is grander than any of the gross apparitions. Let us behold our dear ones in pure vision "still far high advanced," rather than coming back in their earthly features and old clothes. These bodily resumptions or perpetuations of familiar forms are but one step above the Morgue. The resurrection is no act of fleshly preservation, nor heaven a huge pyramid of Egyptian embalming. The soul will not stop with being translated: it must be transformed. The guise the departed return in hints a reduced condition, as if their absence had been one long *diminuendo;* and in going to the *other* world the exchange had not been in their favor. But God has only one world; and, in that, no conflict of laws, but progress through whatever dark or devious passage. Jesus is descried by his followers exalted in a glorified form. If my vanished friends be not more wise and worthy, but only sentimental talkers with but a fragment of their former character and remnant of their wit, show them not at all. Piety were charity, to walk backward with a mantle for the shame of celestial simpletons and dotards, the sunken wreck of once fair women and brave men. Better go *under* than go down. A sailor, hearing ungenerous terms of salvation announced, took his hat, and said, "I make over my chances to the rest of the company;" and, sooner than be the sort of angel some depict or disclose, let us ground arms in the battle of life, surrender our being, and face annihilation with a smile.

It is a rational faith that the planets are inhabited and our vanished kin all around us. But are they eaves-droppers or tale-bearers? Will they give us ineffectual stammerings about their lot and our prospect, and lament their inability to tell us clearer or more? When they speak, the message will be unambiguous as the last trumpet or the first song! The soul stoops not to extraneous support. It does not endure being shored up. Out of the immortal nature immortality has no proof. Another's rising is no evidence of mine. Shall I cling to the skirts of Jesus, if God sees nothing worth saving in myself? I do not wish to live if I am not part of himself, or can fall out of his careless hands. Righteousness, strength, or sense I have none. All is his. The moment I claim it, it is gone. The saint owns not his sanctity. Christ resents being called good: the beauty is lost that has seen itself in the glass. But if I incur God's displeasure, I wish no one's rescue but his own! I have value in his eyes, am part of his investment; and the miracle is his projection of a creature individually distinguished from himself, when there is no personal distinction but for thanks, worship, and love. There is no demonstration, then, of prolonged existence by sensible signs. But through aspiration the soul has for outfit a life-preserver in its own conscious tie with its Author. The lines it walks on are shot from the heavenly shore. No argument can be so strong as this interior sense. Though the graveyards should heave, and tombstones lean and fall, to let up the swarming myriads of the buried in all time, it were no assurance of my destiny comparable to my thought of God as my relation.

But, amid the dissolution of old beliefs, Spiritualism has rescued millions from the sceptical gulf into which, as by a reaction-wheel from irrational systems, they were plunged. Better make our "prophet a mahogany plank," than conclude there is no prophecy. Ridicule of Spiritualism, as a hysteric laugh over the charnel-house, is a poor substitute for the wildest dreams and most baseless visions. The gloom of chambers abutting on the grave, which to some is all that learning and culture and study of Nature supply, leaves scant superiority of reason or advantage for scorn of those who expect to appear in their familiar habit. The ascension-robes were prettier to look at than the pall and shroud. I was called many years ago to say the last words over the corse of a dear sister, whose kith and kin thought all that was left of her rested on the bier. They requested the service should be as simple, the words as few, the implication or committal of belief as little as it could be made by reducing, with selections and omissions, the Liturgy to its lowest terms. But why any ceremony at all? Wherefore not, without priestly pretence or hypocritical form, shovel the ashes into the hole? What lingering relic of superstition, not quite as dead as the senseless frame, detained the dust, needing no more speech than any other clod? We are so made that into the hardest unbelief Hamlet's query of futurity will intrude. The human breast is a camera-obscura, from which every ray of celestial light cannot be shut out; and Spiritualism has great odds in its favor against the Calvinism which put all the generations of men, with the exception of some Enoch, Elijah, or Jesus, under ground, to await a final summons. "You will find your mother," it said to the orphan, "when the affairs of the planet after myriads of ages are wound up."

To this "hope deferred, making the heart sick," came the whisper, "Your mother wants to speak to you: she is present in the circle here." By no strategy were the lines of an army turned into such rout as was suffered by the believing host intrenched along the lines of apocalyptic pictures and apostolic tropes. The Spiritualist's view was a stereograph; the Calvinist's, thin as the earliest sun-sketch. This scarce less than eternal sleep; this motion indefinitely to postpone our lessons and lay our love on the table; this dubious getting up out of decayed members and a conflagrated world; this reassembling from the débris of Nature of countless particles wandering and lost, — presented an unwelcome spectacle to the musing mind. As well lie where we were, or let our atoms thrive in other growth, as be disturbed so! Rip Van Winkle's shorter slumber, to wake and find all so changed as to make his arousal a doubtful boon, seems a satire on so awkward and unconsoling a faith.

If the Spiritualists be asked for proofs of their creed, they point to facts still taking place, as wondrous as any Jewish tales; and Science shuts its eyes to phenomena it can neither explain nor resolve. Convicting thaumaturgists of some tricks does not bring all that is strange and incomprehensible under the ban. Nothing is more common in all history than the mixture of imposture with truth. Spiritualism must have the examination it asks. It cannot be dismissed with a jeer. Belief in the persistency of persons it has kept up. There was creeping over us a cold and cheerless monotheism, not only in the sense that there is but one God, but that a numerically one God is all there is to lift the earth and fill the sky. Spiritualism peoples space with his escort and family. No longer so ghastly are the moon and stars. Nature is a swarm of creatures in glory, seen or with vanishing wings, as in pictures of the old masters; so that the danger now is the Deity by its own offspring will be eclipsed. But the old swamp of a universe is redeemed. What were unfathomed ocean caves, and flowers wasting sweetness on the desert air, to the wilderness of an uninhabited world! Somebody had been before my friend, and was perhaps with him, to see the meek "Rhodora" he thought so lovely, when he came. The charge of irrationality on supposing occupants everywhere about us, though unrevealed, let us fling back on the contrary notion of inoccupancy. If it be powder in my ears, O infidel! it shall be nitro-glycerine in yours.

But do they actually, or can the departed lawfully, step over the dead line? Were not two modes of being confounded, if so mixed? The answer is in no theory, but must be in the facts; and if contempt of Spiritualism is a cover for scepticism of the soul's futurity, we must inquire what our basis is. If God could make me out of a shell, he can make an angel out of me. If my body be a resurrection from the grave of a trilobite, something finer than enters its own tomb may come out. If clay has mounted into my soul, how high shall my soul mount? What is the last graduation of the scale, on which nebulæ rise into stars, and this well-clad planet is the phœnix of its own cinder-heap; and Newton gets out of the balance he was so light in as a babe, to weigh the constellations in his hand? Let the objector consider whether two kinds of facts are not classified together. The miracle of an uncommon is not of course an illegitimate event. An apparition is not usual. But would it violate any known law? The lame, blind, deaf and dumb, are cured by long treatment sometimes. Would sudden healing break the world's order? Blasting a fig-tree, or multiplying thousand-fold loaves never baked and fishes that never swam, were an affront to reason, a floating of things from their foundations, a lie of Nature, so that we could not depend on her word. When the discovery of fossil remains and shells of extinct fishes was alleged to prove the planet more than six thousand years old, a clergyman asked why God could not have made the fossil bones and shells just as they were in their beds, having never served any living creatures for homes? It was asked, in reply, why God could not have created Herculaneum and Pompeii under ground, never having been cities on the surface or the habitations of men! If any Being could do this, his doing it would be a lie, after which we could put in him no confidence, tell us to trust him however prophets might. He had appointed us to meet him in a particular place, and not kept his tryst. We should not know what other promise he might break. God is faithful, and does not go back on us or on himself. He goes forward, and leads us to higher revelation without end. But seraphs coming as ghosts on earth, or mortals going as ghosts to heaven, are no burglars. Earth and heaven are but mansions of one house. It is God's extension to us his debtors.

But the spectral demonstration there are those who neither relish nor need. They are above the middle air, in which these heavy-winged cherubim fly, that are like herons among birds, soon weary of soaring and ever ready with their long legs to light on the flats. Doubtless these frequenters from above of our lower atmosphere will turn out to be amphibious creatures, not permanently content with either element; mediators on the fence betwixt the spheres, or a sort of insurance company for such as doubt the superior life. Spiritualism is spirituality run into the ground. Yet some must have celestial things made plain, as figures are chalked large for the dull-eyed or near-sighted. All Divine revelation is condescension to those who cannot gaze undazzled on the sun. Who are the philosophers to disdain its lowest degrees? The sage rebuked the savage for fondling his Deity, and addressing to it endearing words. But God rebuked the sage for repelling his child, really drawing nigh to him at the only point his ignorance could reach, as little ones walk to their parents with weak and wavering steps. What are all our approaches to the Infinite but as of babes that step and stumble, and venture on? The boy or girl you see on a door-step, trying and straining to get hold of the handle of a bell, is an image of our best prayers. O metaphysician! are the Spiritualists coarse and you refined, or are they substantial and you vague in your speculations on the transcendent theme? The Future will decide the relative value of the stuff from their looms and the webs from your brains.

Meantime let those who care less for the outward

facts and more for the inward thoughts be thankful for the subject, which no meditation or disclosure exhausts. I too much enjoy my reflections to wish the matter cleared up. "Grandmother, what is *glory?*" cried the lad learning the Lord's Prayer. I do not quite want to know. Let the New Jerusalem not be measured for me! I desire not to be informed how many sorts or regiments of angels there are. Let something even of the certainty of bliss be reserved, and of the eternal blazon withheld; nor the story be told till it become trite. The gladness of the supernal visitants to see us, and be able to manifest themselves, gets a little tiresome. We hope there is some secret they have not let out. We should be disappointed with Paradise, if what they say of it were all. Shall we complain that the Divinity is veiled, or in eclipse; and the road of our destiny runs and turns out of sight? Let us rather rejoice in the hidings of his power, in promise of fountains we can never drain; and that the path is no turnpike stretching monotonous over the blazing hills, but winding and tempting through lonely hollows and thickets of mystery! The descent of the valley of the shadow of death, so cool and private, is good for us, as well as ascending among the seats of the elders. With what rest and refreshment, on mossy beds and along noiseless streams, may it not prepare for new action and advance! I bless my Maker for my joy to *think*, exceeding all pleasure of other appetite or possession, festal scene, beauty of prospect, or travel by land or sea. "I want more light," said my friend. But I am sure enough, because sure as He wills. I read in the religious sheet a lamentation over one, standing outside the accepted Christian faith, as therefore less convinced of happy survival of the dissolving flesh. O critic! is the vista clear and the journey mapped out for you? Are there no queries to be put, surprises to encounter, or discoveries to make? Yours then were the lot to be deplored!

Shall it be said there is something ungrateful in this craving for circumstantial knowledge beyond our present lot? One world to be in is enough at a time. Let us not grasp after the preternatural, which will be natural in due season; nor seek unto strangers after news of our ascended friends; nor covet a support for ourselves in the dark valley beyond the rod and staff leaned on by our race; nor wish to degrade for our convenience or curiosity those promoted from the earth. A man once fell from an immense raft of logs on the Penobscot, and disappeared in the foaming stream. A few days after, his employer, seeing what seemed his ghost advancing toward him, with the well-worn implement for arranging the logs in hand, cried out with horror, "Do not come back: you are welcome to the fork!" Is there not something in the coarse and comic expression that goes seriously to the heart? What is the design of our friends' going, but that they may reach a higher state, and we get along without them, in outward presence and person, as well as we may? Shall God repent of and foil his own purpose, by ordering at once their sensible return? It were to belittle the majesty of bereavement, and discrown death of its glory, for a consolation so fleshly and weak. Parting is a lesson: shall the book it is written in be snatched away before it is learned? The grave means something;

and, though it never held a soul, were too empty of significance, if the tenant walks out the day after his burial to mock us with his mortal shape. Let us not grasp at the treasure God hides, but be patient till he give it to us again as to the rest of mankind in his own way. To cleanse, not continue our fondness, he takes away our idols, and denies the familiar embrace. Our beloved leave our senses to lodge in our souls; and the holy imagination, that works in their living substance to shape them more finely than before, were baffled by gross presentment of their wonted form.

That our virtue may be pure and sublime, God withholds the "eternal blazon" we seek. The saints of former ages trod their way unhelped by marvellous shows. They knew no distinction of nature and the supernatural. *Nature*, in human knowledge of a lawful creation, is a modern entity; and from the *subject* they mused on so intensely till the fire burned came the *object* that could be seen and felt in the air. It was their faith, not the fact, that was extraordinary, amounting to a second-sight. If angels went and ministered unto Jesus, in visible form, as of flesh and blood, he had the advantage of a succor forbid to us, and detracting from the truth and honor of his example. Who was there to lift him from his agony in the Garden; or help him, but Simon the Cyrenian, to bear his cross? When he was mocked with the purple, and pierced with the thorns, and drank the gall, there was none to stand by him but God. Invisible sympathy sufficed. The same is too wholesome, and needful for our goodness from Him, that we should wish it neutralized or lowered in quality by carnal aid of apparitions to touch us with warm hands. The struggle with pain and temptation is hard; but let me have no superiority in it to my kind. "I am a stranger and pilgrim on the earth, as all my Fathers were." If I can share their fate, I am content with their lot. They ventured forth on unforeseen perils of an untried existence; and I will follow in the same straits, hoping through fog and icy currents and driving storms to reach their warm Polar Sea. How corrupting is this mistaken vanity of being carried in some spiritual elevator above foregoing generations! The improved arts and increased comforts dispense not with our working out our own salvation by effort and patience equal to theirs. What we call the progress of society may hinder as much as it furthers the soul. Want of that vivid feeling of Deity which solved the world in wonder, and stamped any former time as the age of miracle, is proof of a decline in one direction, to match whatever general advance.

Spirit is its own proof, which no rarefaction of matter can reach. What signifies a street-full of ghosts if they teach me naught? The lively Frenchwoman said they were but mortals who, though dead, had never been able to go. Spiritualism has offset the scepticism of the market, but not disentangled the soul from sense. Its spirits are bodies; and boundless liberty between the sexes is the doctrine of one of its seers. Life is the test of honor or shame to our faith.

IX.

FAITH.

THERE is a feeling which it needs no science but close observation to know is shared by lower creatures; by the cat rubbing round your leg, and the dog you may call Fido to signify his loyalty; by the horse that owns your stroking of his neck, and the cow that takes your hand into her mouth, as well as by the babe sinking unalarmed to sleep on its mother's breast. It is dependence, a consciousness of succor and support. We call it religion, no definition of which suffices that makes it an act of the intellect or confines it altogether to man. It is the owning of superior power and goodness; a sense of God in the soul: not the motion we make, but he makes in us, finding himself in our heart. It is a narrow measure that would put this Divine seizure into our understanding, and a false date that would derive it from our will. No picture in Nature more touches a child than a fountain bubbling noiseless from the ground, carrying up a perpetual pillar of whirling sand, as firm in the water as that which moves in the caravan's sight, or once led Israel through the desert. It is an image of the well springing up unto everlasting life.

But this Faith is thought by many to be in suspense or passing away. Physical philosophy has drilled and blasted the old rock men rested and built on as eternal; and people run every way from more expected explosions. Rome was not more moved by those terrible Gauls than is the Church by these uncomplimentary barbarians — geology, astronomy, and ethnology — making havoc of her traditions and savage work with her sacred books. Study stops no more for priestly remonstrance than the train for a boy's pin on the rail. The last rag of belief seems about to be torn from us by ruthless hands. Not only Mormonism and serpent-worship are descended upon for gross offences, but a right to arrest Christianity is asserted by the new police.

But the primitive granite cannot be blown up. Because it has been found out that the world was not made in six days, but was a job too long to be done by any demiurgus; that mankind cannot be derived from one pair; that no single flood ever drowned all Nature; that history is not fall, but an ever-ascending order; and that the Bible has flaws for Colenso to point out in the Old Testament, and Strauss and Baur in the New, — is Faith destroyed? No more than a building by an architect's removal of a rotten underpinning to plant his structure on the ledge. No record is exempt from critical tests, and the command of thought to move on. Jupiter and Venus, Mars and Mercury, and Saturn himself, are driven into lifeless names and sparkling points in the sky; tormenting witch and enchanting fairy are gone, and not a few of our cherished forms and notions must follow. But

Faith survives out of dissolving superstitions, as the trees out of last year's decaying leaves.

Nor does Faith, like a feudal prisoner, live at the mercy of science, but is sovereign. Where were knowledge without motive of curiosity and confidence in something to be known? Lessing liked truth or certainty less than the pursuit of it. Why care for it but from prior persuasion of a correspondence in the world with ourselves; that things and thoughts are made fast with the same glue; that creation is no confidence-game to cheat us with marked cards or loaded dice of laws broken in anybody's favor; but, without one juggle, will justify to the end the inquiry it prompts. If Intellect be father this Faith is mother of sciences and arts. The scholar is led by some surmise, like the lamp in the miner's or hunter's cap casting its light on the dark. This column of fire and cloud in the mind gave Columbus his second-sight. The laws of matter come as ideas, those ghosts of the mind, before they are verified in facts. Newton's unity, or God's in him, revealed Nature's to him; and no falling apple was more than a signal-ball. "Whither now?" asks the child of the angel, in Greenough's statue. Hope is the mind's angel-guide. Darwin admits the missing links, but clings to the organic unity. His faith cheers and halloos the hound of his understanding. Huxley cannot meet objections to his protoplasm; but thinks the builder's brick, for this palace or mosaic, though too small to handle, will yet appear. He will furnish cement or mortar from his own mind. Because Goethe is no dualist, but a believer in the One, he finds in the sheep's skull a transformed vertebra; in the fruit the leaf, and in all the colors of the rainbow varying mixtures of light and shade. Do we call the child *cunning*, for the interrogation-point in its face? How it coasts along and circumnavigates its own little globe of flesh, finds its continent an island, becomes an individual, parts from God and begins to be afraid, and loses for a time its innocent wonder! Age is not in years, but self-sufficiency. Our octogenarians are lads in what is called the dark age, and misses in their teens. But the man reflecting becomes the child again. The moon-faced marvelling of the babe is shallow to that surprise of the unfolded mind which no deep-sea line of metaphysics can sound. The man believes so much, he is called infidel; and atheist, for being intoxicated with God. The sanctuary cannot hold him, as the queen's court could not Talbot's troops. The *fire* is quenched by the sun of miracle. Cork up some supernatural drop to which all Nature beside is but "leather and prunella"? What is liquefaction of the blood of St. Januarius to the circulation of the blood; or the turning of water into wine at Cana to that on the Danube and Rhine; or the money in the fish's mouth to the Australian mines; or the blasting of the fig-tree to its growth; or Joshua's brake on the sun to the rolling of its car; or the spectre to the moon's light; or a revolting resurrection of the body to the immortal life of the soul? I believe in Christ's healing, because all goodness heals. Said Edward Everett to an overweening solicitor, "You make me sick." True men and women are all physicians to make us well. Faith in God's works let us have. Any supposed counter-works or anti-works imply duplicity in his constitution. Like the love Shakspeare boasts, this world was builded far from "accident." The paper account of it may be but *crédit mobile.* But the Bible is not fountain nor river, but reservoir; and, though it become a ruin, the spring is deeper than that lake Nyanza Baker found at the head of the Nile. The stream flows like the Euxine to the sea: it is a Danube to force its way through mountains of prejudice; a St. Lawrence brawling over rocks of controversy; a Niagara dropping to a different plane and deeper tide over the pitch of some tremendous reform, like Luther's; a cataract ready for a new leap in that German mind, scorned as unpractical, but showing its double genius to speculate and act.

We must not confound with the substance the accidents of faith. A scholar suggested to a churchman the unimportance of some rite. "Nothing is unimportant that we stand on," was the reply. But why stand on trifles, any pulling of which from under our feet may trip us up? Forms and formulas are burrows of insincerity. "What is the difference in your farmer since his conversion?"—"This,—that when he used, in cutting trees on Sunday morning, to carry his axe on his shoulder, now he carries it under his cloak." Chunder Sen arraigns English hypocrisy, sending the brandy-bottle with the Bible to India.

Doubtless, faith must be nourished by scriptures and institutions. But it is congested when they become ends instead of means. Mr. Brindley had not much sense of beauty when he said the use of rivers was to feed canals; and the beauty of virtue is gone when the canal of the Church is made the reason and end of those affections which are the currents of the soul; and God himself is considered part of the Establishment. Faith is the motion of love. Visiting a nephew of General Hardee, the writer on Tactics, I heard from the wife a complaint of the Northern soldiers who had trampled her orange-grove and spoiled the crop. I took some large oranges from my pocket and gave to her children, saying, "Here are some that have come back." — "I am beginning to have faith in these *Yankees*," she cried. A small kindness may be mother of a child of goodness that grows to be larger than herself. But whoever had a human friend he was not obliged to turn from to God? Said a nervous woman, "I have sometimes to tell my husband to go away." But so we never tell Him.

But has Faith any hold on the future? Let science answer. When Copernicus was told, according to his theory the planet Venus should have phases as well as the moon, he said, "Wait till you have a telescope of sufficient power." Those phases were among the first things the improved telescope reached. From a resinous property he detected in the refraction of the diamond, Newton predicted the discovery that it is carbon. When the new planet appears, Leverrier, like Wordsworth's saint, but "sees what he foresaw." Morton risks murder for the blessing of ether to mankind. Our punctual crossing the Atlantic by steam, and traversing its monstrous bottom with the electric cable, was once a prophecy. Quite alien from such cases is the prevision of that immortal sea we shall navigate when this poor flesh is a condemned vessel? Is Nature a subject for foresight, and human nature not? The anticipation of gold pavements, and houris, and luxurious boards, is the coarse working of the instinct. We must not expect to take our old coats and shoes with us. "How much did he leave?" "He left it all: he did not take a cent!" But in spiritual immortality is nothing base. It is the unselfing of the soul. Our hope of it is our honor of God. He does not play with us to give us a good time at any theatre of Vanity Fair, nor let us lick the hand just raised to shed our blood, but will justify our aspiration in a fact as sublime. "Whom God deceives is well-deceived," say you, O Goethe? Deceit of the inmost in us were self-deception in him. Forms will pass. When the sacrament of the Lord's Supper was called in question, a pious woman said, "If they take away the bread and wine, what shall we have left?" But the light will remain, fall the shadows how they will. Sunday may lose its emphasis. Men may get along without ministers. "Your kingdom," said Charles Sprague to a clergyman, "is passing away." The triumph of the Church, as of its Head, will be in going from us. But the kingdom of God will not pass; and that kingdom shall be a home.

Faith is unity, the real atonement. Faith is one, in distinction from particular objects, be it fixed on God or Christ, Saint or Virgin, angel or mortal. The motto for a seal, *I die where I am attached*, is graven on a vine twining round a pillar. But the fidelity is in the vine itself, whether climbing on a trellis or a tree; and my trust in my partner's loyalty is as noble as in my Redeemer's sacrifice, or my Maker's faithfulness. The same principle clambers to heaven or clings to earth. It may make an idol of a stone or fetish of a man, but parts not quite with its own nobleness. Holding to a bit of carved wood, painted image, woven flag, or printed creed, it implies invisible excellence or sufficient help, some reliance on the constitution and Constituter of the world. In the yacht-squadron my friend's fancy saw a troop of hooded shapes gliding ghostly over the deep. I saw clouds of canvas bellying from the well-moulded hulls, guided by mortal hands of eager captains, who believed in the laws of wood and iron, water and air, and the triumph of the best model and sail and skill. In the sloop and schooner, that tried conclusions, leaving the rest in a helpless heap behind, was a figure of minds far ahead of their generation, of that proud majority which is but a confused multitude and lagging crowd. All faith is in law and lawgiver. Subscription to miracle, though exacted and crowned in the Christian Church, is unbelief. My friend exposes glass on his roof, and in due time the sun gives it a beautiful rose-color. If the sun do it this year, and refuse next, we could put no confidence in the sun, nor know but it would rise in a new quarter, or its furnace-register give out. Who could lean on a Being that played fast and loose? How foolishly we talk of his making laws! His laws were never made. They have not their birth in time, but are necessary in him, are himself, and cannot change more than he, — not card-castles he like a child is amused with building and throwing down. Not lack but fulness of faith rejects tales of unnatural transformation of water into wine, and green leaves into withered, or any substance unknown into silver coin. These are juggles, to which Perfect Wisdom cannot stoop. It is time miracle, as a test, were withdrawn. Those who cannot abide it the Church cannot afford to lose. Doubtless there are interpretations, like Dr. Bushnell's, by which the supernatural turns out to be the natural, and the portents are made as orderly as the procession. But will you lay persons, who can neither take them raw, nor cook nor construe them so, under ecclesiastic ban?

Faith is distinguishable, next, from its statements. What men contend about is not the substance, but the form: the five points, thirty-nine articles, the scores of sacred books so uneasy ever since they were bound into one, the *discrepancies* in doctrines, narratives, or genealogies, and uncounted clauses and texts. My friend told me he thought "God must be sorry now he had a Bible, finding men quarrel about it so." Expressions, unsatisfactory to those they are invented by, generate strife. Every church in Christendom is convulsed over the undermined language of its collect or creed, and all who stand on it are in fear of being blown up. Written dogmas, not shifting to correspond with the march of knowledge, are flanked. They cease to be sentiments, and become tenets grasped and held by the will. Some persons escape from the untenable forts of theology; and some try yet to man the hopeless guns. The war becomes a *mêlée;* and no man knows his opponent. The excommunicator finds himself at heart excommunicated, with but some tatter of a phrase which for a weapon he has clutched. By the bishops that judge Colenso is he not secretly indorsed? Priests, like politicians, illustrate Talleyrand's saying that the use of language is to conceal thought; and the art of *putting* things confounds candor with trick. Part of the clergy in every establishment outgrow and chafe under the old cut of the uniform which from policy they still wear. Others, like mourners going from black to slate color, attempt to vary their costume by degrees, to take time by the forelock, and meet the coming wave. My brother would fain be free. On judiciously selected points he is outspoken, and wins credit of courage and being independent. But his boldness is not boldness. He is not loyal to his last and innermost belief. He thinks the time has not come, or the people are unprepared. He will work at the soil successive seasons before casting in the seed. But, had prophets waited till everybody was ready, would any reform have occurred? It is a battle of sentences, theologians now fight, more than of thoughts. All are on the defence. They are mouth-pieces of ancient divinity, holding proof-texts as shields over their heads. You are brave only in spots, O Orthodox or Episcopal friend! Now and then, here or there, you deal a lusty blow at prejudice. But you have no mettle of principle, always, everywhere, and all over. Dare to say as you think, — that there is no warrant but expediency for governing the Church; no system of divinity in your symbolical books; no authority for faith in the Bible or any printed word; no evidence of immortality but in the immortal soul; no God apart from Nature and man; that every spirit can say with Jesus, "I and my Father are one;" that the Divine unity consists eternally in its offspring, is in its activity, and in loss of its relations were itself deceased, — and your congregation might be as thin as ours!

Though we seem earth-wide and heaven-wide apart, faith is one motion in our minds. The collision is between the trains of word and theory. Some fresh conviction struggles for life out of worn-out schemes, as, from the gravel, which a past vegetation crumbled into, I admire to see the sweet rose and soft mullein spring. Happy is he by whose imagination, in some new proverb, it is voiced. Lonely as the seer that sat astonied, or as John the Baptist in the wilderness, he will be for a time. But soon he will appear a forerunner one party would expel and another win. "Go out," says the pope to Döllinger, yet begs conference with the man more formidable than a rival pope; "as if," wittily answers the great heresiarch, "the Father cared to have my body with him when he has excommunicated my soul." "Come," cry the Rationalists to the robust Romanist, "to swell our revenue!" The Papal fear and Radical hope prove a common ground beneath personal pretensions and a belligerent vocabulary.

For, thirdly, Faith, distinguishable from all particulars of object or statement, is indistinguishable in itself. Other properties may be christened by its name. Pride and passion, sensuous music, gay architecture, Sunday clothes, keeping one day holy, seeking God in a single place; making the curtains of a temple, the gems of a Shekinah, or the rafters of a meeting-house holier than all space; removing the temple not made with hands to some heavenly distance, instead of trembling with joy in it all around and every day; thinking the Divinity can undergo shrinkage from the universe to a conventicle, — all this may be considered faith. But by the narrow mode its quality is not touched. In every age and nation which we call heathen, — through Buddhist and Brahmin, Mahometan and Chinaman, Indian of the Eastern or Western clime, sun or serpent worshipper, — a like feeling runs from one Source, with whatever stain in the stream.

Faith is repose in the perfection of the world. Job, cursing the day of his birth, and wishing to cover it with night and be his own pall-bearer, was an infidel. Schopenhauer, flinging stones at the creation, as a worsted work that just rubs and goes, is prince of denying spirits. My friend, rejecting Christianity, is not a sceptic; for he worships Truth, and never flinched in his persuasion, like Wordsworth's, that every thing is "full of blessings." He has less doubt in him than that infallible Pius IX., unable to foresee his own dethronement, vainly beseeching a conference with the recusant German scholar on points in dispute, and trembling before rebels he would cut off but that they are protected by the foremost nation in the world. This friend fights a duel with history, assails the logic of events, considers mankind mistaken in what it remembers or forgets, holds his own recollection of more worth than the oblivion of ages, and Cato-like tells the gods they have prospered the wrong cause, which is an accident that does not occur; but, by his temper of devotion and trust in the Most High, he is saved from all just accusation of unbelief. When shall we learn that one thing is sacred, — our thought? We assassinate our own liberty when we condemn our neighbor's. Liberal Christianity hates its offspring, like a parent scolding an inherited propensity in his child. But beware your prescription of terms! Has the man no faith who sacrifices life to duty, thinking all is over, and expecting nothing beyond, — facing annihilation, and not asking to continue? Demand articles of faith? My love has none; nor, when perfect, has my health. If I descend to particulars, and talk of my head, stomach, or heart, disease has begun. Soundness is the light and happy bearing of the whole frame, and faith of the undivided mind. Curiosity about our beginning, or dogmatism about our end, is defection from Faith, which contemplates only existence; and, no more heeding death than butterfly or bird, sees only a path of morning-glory without end. Faith goes on, not needing to take an observation. It is no resignation of office or winding-up of affairs, but proceeding to do business, and not take off our clothes till we go to bed. It is like the Western pioneer, or traveller that halts for but an hour. The Yankee in Italy glanced at the Apollo Belvedere, and told his attendant to check it in the list of curious objects, as he must pass on! His business was more important than the statue. The wanderer along the rock-girdled beach never finds just the place to pause, while Beauty coyly glides before to toll his feet. The man of science cannot rest, though he find out the chemistry of the sun. The earth's poor clerkship or unreadable record keeps Darwin on the stretch. The intellect would circle the old with ever new generalization. Artist or inventor has visions that shed scorn on his performance; and no character, even of Christ, without room for improvement. Faith means this conscious room. The infidel is he that asserts finality anywhere, makes a term of any achievement or conception, sees or puts a block in the eternal road. To affirm any stop or period is unbelief. How many the unbelievers in full communion on the church-books! Some astronomers say the earth will drop into the sun by and by, and be burnt up. Is he a believer who asserts a destruction of the world, ultimate loss of millions of souls, the running out of human nature, and ending of the race of virtue at the tomb, like an Olympic game at the goal, with the partial saving and crowning of a few victors elect? Choice, confidential friend or private secretary of the Lord as he may deem himself, he does not properly believe at all. Faith is not such a murderer of hope. To vilify our kind, or despise ourself, is not belief. David, crying out he was conceived in sin and shapen in iniquity, was a blasphemer. He was a matricide, shouldering on the woman that bore him his own guilty lust: and they renounce God, with him, who quote his language to the point of a general fall and woe.

Calvinism is a system of disbelief. To say God was disappointed in his works, repented of man's creation, got off the track with his engine, and botched his business so as to have to do it over again, is worse than atheism,—if Bacon be right, that, rather than have us think ill of him, God would not have us think of him at all. Faith is the feeling that creation is no bad job, bubble that has burst, or mine that will blow up,—but a master-piece, with no flaw. "The experiment has not succeeded," the Harvard professor used to say to his class, when acid and alkali failed of the intended combinations in his retorts. Has the great Experimenter nothing else to say? To declare that tragedy, not triumph, was the end of Jesus; that such a Son went under, with the heavens deaf and dumb to his prayer; that the ruling Power said to him, Dust to dust is the doom, and your talk of ascension is a foolish whim, — so that, as in Richter's dreadful dream, now there is no Christ, — Orthodoxy would hold to be dire unbelief. What is it, then, to reckon the entire humanity cast away, with the exception of a favored minority snatched like brands from the burning, — God hard of hearing to myriads of souls in immemorial æons? A father's harsh chastening of his child brings universal blame; and lately, in the West, certain citizens hung to a tree, not waiting for the law, an abuser of his boy. Yet we are all bound for prison, in the sentence of the schools, — except the redeemed, who seem like courtiers obsequious to a tyrant because personally safe. But to crook the knee to such a despot for his power were the meanest slavery on earth. Faith is, that there is no such fatality; but as the sea in God's chariot of cloud is a cleanser of the air for man's breath, while making every wave a span of beauty to bridge all lands, so an ocean of purity is sufficient antidote to all sin. Faith says that no hurt goes to the centre, no stain is too deep to take out, no wound which Divine surgery or cautery cannot tent. The soul cannot mortify. The stuff we are made of is so stout the texture never rots. I heard a reformer say, There is essential evil, heart malady incurable, an everlasting scar, a consequence of folly we can never get over, but must be left hopelessly behind, like one that gives out on the march, or a vessel that lags in the race. Melancholy want of faith! Total depravity or everlasting penalty? Why argue against it, when, if it be, there is no God, there being nothing total but him! Even sin has a ministry, and is one of God's sharpest tools. The vilest criminals on the scaffold without hypocrisy commend to him their souls. "The mystery of iniquity" teaches some clear lessons. If our preaching lose edge in making light of it, the edge is turned in declaring so universal an experience of no use. Men sometimes do wrong or doubtful things from an impulse, for which they cannot account, but from which they learn wisdom. The faults of Paul and Augustine made the mould in which their excellence was run; and "Uriel," in the poem, well doubts if the old deities know not, though they tell it never to the younger, that naught is ill.

Faith says that destiny is not doom. The jail, to which the convict goes, is no object of his faith. He bows to the verdict, feels the sheriff's hand on his collar, surveys the machinery of the law in jury and judge, hopes for no reprieve; yet his faith stops in no visible circumstance, but foreruns beyond calamity to rescue at last. It is no demonstration nor conclusion in the head, as when the degrees are measured in a triangle or contents of a geometrical figure; but it is the rejecting of all dimensions in our lot. The sailor's endless rope, the mechanic's revolving wheel or universal joint, the spiral stair lifting at every turn, is its type. It is the Tower of Babel that does reach heaven.

It is the horoscope of paradise; and, as the astronomer's glass can compass no bound of sparkling constellations and conjunctions, so it overleaps every wall of time or space.

It is not in propositions, but persons, — powers alive, whose relations are truth, designs goodness, and enterprises joy, — to lay some ocean-cable, to reach a North Pole, or knock at the gates of shining mansions. People talk of faith in the Bible. It is impossible. You may blindly believe all its books an inspired summary; but no scripture can be the object, nor more than the excitant of faith, as the quick-silvered cushion or revolving cylinder is of electricity. In a loose use of the word, I may have faith in material substances or in ideas and laws; but strictly only in persons, in being and life. There may be acceptance of, but no faith in miracle, — only in an Ordainer whose mode is order; a self-consistent One, who turns not to contradict himself, and cannot be outgeneralled by an alien force. Faith is faithfulness, or living by an inward law. David calls God's word a light to his feet. But no parchment or paper ever held that word which comes in visions, goes running swift to the ends of the world, and is published only in deeds. The Greeks had hill-top signals of flame, and the old racers handed the torch to each other. But there is a candle God must light in the soul. He goes round his own city, and has the only key to the hall. None else can apply the match and kindle the jet. Opposite rules may be gathered from between the sacred lids; formulas are swallowed, and nice customs courtesy to great kings. Louis Napoleon bent, and dodged the shot. But there is a Marksman no respecter of persons, and careless if monarch or peasant come in his range. There is a bridge whoever passes pays toll, a tax impartially levied, a custom-house remitting the duty for no bribe, a road with no free passes, and a concert where no dead-head hears the song. The mercy is not that the law swerves, but that it does not slay. The storm rises in the teeth of the wind, with thunders to wreck the world. How the wheels rattle, and the steaming vapor rolls round the sparkling heat! But the crash goes by. Up the valley for miles the sun turns the rain to silver drops. Rainbow on rainbow hangs double assurance on the flying cloud. The green gloom hurries seaward, and white sails scud home faster for the gale. In an hour all is clear and sweet in the sanctified sky. Is it law, or is it grace?

All the faiths have one root, like all the mountains, shooting from one bulb. *God judge betwixt me and thee* ends dispute. Inquisition or victim appeals to the same court. Father Taylor, seeing a half-dozen white martin-boxes of churches in a country town, said, "You have war here!" But, like hunters or explorers scattering their forces to find the same game or gold, every sect adores one Spirit, whether by Quaker dumbness, Methodist shouting, or Romish cross. One painter uses high colors for his landscape, and another low. Is the first Episcopal, and the second Rational? Both are true. My neighbor's Orthodoxy is a piquant relish in his society. Dr. Bushnell can swallow creeds as Mirabeau did formulas, seeing the centre of the target they all hit. Elihu Burritt or Mary Lowell Putnam can translate languages at once into each other. No word suffices for the thought; so we use many, as a surveyor his triangular series for a measure. When *love* repeated and overworked sounds sentimental, we say *truth;* and *Allah* is refreshing when *God* has become trite.

Our faith is better than we. We pretend surprise at the gyrations and self-inflictions of fakir and dervish, and barbarities of bull-fights, still the sport of Spain. But we murder Indians, and drink blood, like the base woman in Scripture wiping her lips and saying, "What have I done?" No speech of Owyhee or Japan is more brutal than the last report of slaughter from the commander of our troops, whose abolition of humanity no savage ever matched. But American religion takes it as bread and wine from the communion-board. The air is full of spirits, buzzing like so many bees in our bonnet; but none help us to be merciful or just. The Church says to the world, Stand apart, *I am holier than thou*, yet brings forth no better fruit. "*That is a Magdalen*," said a visitor, pointing to a picture on the wall. "No: a St. Cecilia," was the host's reply. "Well," rejoined the guest, "at this distance, my eyes are so poor I can scarce tell sinner from saint." We ask dreadful questions. Are communicants nobler than those who partake not of the elements? Are members of good society more generous than Bohemians? Are preachers less jealous than artists or actors? I suspect a reputation for sanctity, under which men do unsaintly things. What is uncleanness but conscious cleanness, or a *sense of dirt* that cannot bear a mote, and insanely spends life in removing every speck? But innocent childhood plays in the mud. Only the invalid is annoyed by foul weather. Hazlitt says the Italian lazzaroni let the fleas, that craze nice ladies, creep unmolested over their naked limbs. Unworthy men most warmly resent offences, swear at whoever imitates their mistakes, and confronts them with a copy of their own sins. "To the pure all things are pure;" but nothing to such as have "their own mind and conscience defiled." Am I elect, my seat secured at the table or among the dignitaries on the platform? In that persuasion I am lost. Do we lift our eyes to God? He is as low under our feet as high above our head. After mounting over the Swiss passes, Splügen, Stelvio, and Great St. Bernard, I came to the Finstermünz, a tremendous gulf grander than the lofty pitch. The divine glory is in his condescension. His humility is sublimer than his exaltation above the clouds. Our conceptions affect our conduct. Some creeds demoralize. But the idolater goes into the kingdom before the money-maker; and his wit was not far, who, being shown two portraits of thievish stock-operators, wondered that of Jesus was not hung between! Consistency would require too many crucifixions. We are hurt by our conceit of progress; and suck a subtle poison from our songs of deliverance,

> "Which kings and prophets waited for,
> And sought, but never found."

Are we so well, and were our predecessors so badly off? So the Orthodox chants, and the Liberal follows suit. But there was light and color in the world before we were born. Mists rose to be clothed in beauty.

Gently fell the twilight and dew. There was joy in life and hope in death, or content to cease and give place. In the Christian era came Hamlet's question, "To be, or not to be." I have heard Christian men and women say they have no complaint of annihilation, if that be for the universe best; as the Indian folded his arms, sang his death-song, and went over Niagara in his canoe.

Be it what it may, that is not sad which we can sing about. Something delicious is there in a funeral hymn or dirge, with trumpet and muffled drum, of the dead march over the soldier's grave. A friend told me of the sweetness of the dying chime of bells, in a foreign town, as a figure of his fading life. Does not this feeling mix in the cadence of every bell that tolls? The child said it tired her to think of living for ever. The Oriental Nirwana is understood in the Occident. But being equal to cessation is the strongest proof of continuance. The creature has title to live, that can surrender its life. Can a fly do it? Said a hearer of my sermon: "men are not worth saving." But the doctrine of depravity is proof of nobility. Who found it out? No goat or wolf, serpent or tiger, is ashamed of itself, or ever saw the plague of its own heart. The man that first discovered his sin went further than Columbus. Nothing but virtue could ever become aware of vice. Does not good taste detect discord in music, deformity in a posture, or disproportion in a building? How else is ugliness discerned in the character? Chief of sinners are you? To decide that, you must be expert professor of morals. That forth-putting woman does not move us like the gentle-voiced one by her side, unanxious to lead. Set up your ideal standard, see yourself overhung as with the constellation Libra by the higher law, hold yourself amenable to a perfect tribunal, and worthy of hell-fire; and then declare yourself worthless and corrupt utterly? This self-depreciation is native grandeur, the foil of goodness and bond of honor. Self-condemnation is God's absolution; and pleading guilty, acquittal at his bar.

Presumption of our own righteousness is a pest. Who has not seen in the house some king or queen who can do no wrong, and will take no counsel; is omniscient to decide every point, with brazen impudence bluffs off objection, lies every day with pretence of information, and ends in that chronic wilfulness, or insanity of the will, for which no asylum is provided, yet mortal cannot endure, and gets rid of by a divorce or putting the globe between? This head-strong self-confident temper check on its first appearance in your child. Tell me not, O fond parent, you would not break its will! In wilfulness the will is not preserved, but destroyed.

Faith is a moral quality, whose antithesis is disloyalty. Hypocrisy is the shell after the kernel is eaten out. Something more than intellect must keep the faith. Unfaithfulness is worse than death, and opens a deeper sepulchre than can be dug in the ground. The deceitful companion is farther off than any stranger. As a man leaves a temple, you feel the traitor going out of the inner sanctuary. Though all seem fair on the surface between you, and you laugh and play with him still, he cannot without repentance return. All religious faith has the same spiritual property to resolve bulk of theology and body of divinity into simple persuasion that our Author will be true. Amid the glory of Nature, no sentence, of others or my own, will express my conviction. Before the stress of my trial no rampart of sect will stand. My metaphysics dissolve like fog burnt off by the sun. My citadel goes as a Minot's Ledge light-house under the storm. But I see the arm of God by day, and I feel it in the gloom.

We make out a case for Christianity by calling Nature unmerciful. But what, if not pity, mean these warnings, — before earthquakes, eruptions, or billows hastening to cut off the beach, and mutterings of the tempest prior to the bolt? "Breakers ahead" is the cry of alarm. But how curiously the peril is announced to the eye by the whitening wave, and in the night to the ear by the peculiar sound, — the rattle of the *sea*-serpent answering to that of the land! Mercy is no after-thought of a Being who has to make up his mind, but the constitution of matter and human nature. A man carries a few wild roses to a sick woman's room. Long years after, sick in his turn, he finds the flowers out of their ashes blooming in her memory, as she returns his service a hundred-fold. Nothing so natural as the supernatural help that makes all duty or calamity light. Is your task or lesson, act or speech, easy? Watch the kind of ease! There is the facility of garrulity, and that of the Holy Ghost. Faith sees blessing prevail over bane, man's wrath a note of praise, evil a servant of good, and the assassin's dagger in God's hand, to save a nation when a martyr is made of its Chief. His providence no belief can sum. I take an inventory of my religious effects. They are not a cent on a dollar of my debt. I cannot pay, and must break. What an assumption, that you can put the account on a page of rhetoric, in a syllogism of your logic, and balance the books with God!

Faith is not a constant quantity, but an unvarying quality. There are no gulfs between men. As the slate and granite and trap-rocks all come to the surface, so the antiquary can forego his search, find all opinions present, and have a section of the world in every age. Comparative Theology has not exhausted its illustrations. The Chinaman's sending his body across the Pacific for burial repeats Egyptian embalmment and the superstition of all nations about the grave. Brigham Young, as naturalist and householder, is our King Solomon; the medium, a relation of the witch of Endor. The tripod becomes an extension-table, with raps instead of voices; the sibyl's cave, a wainscot at twilight. Mr. Home can show us in himself the bodily ascension of Jesus and Elijah. John was mistaken for the Messiah whose shoe-latchet he was not worthy to unloose, and Christ for Elias or some old prophet come again. The grandfather reappears in that blue-eyed babe of two black-eyed parents. In short human nature is one, despite all variations. He is a Hottentot, we say of some stupid groveller; he is a Turk, of some cruel husband. The Esquimaux, drinking train-oil, feeds no more grossly than the man in broadcloth. Seeing his brother's unhappy self-exhibition, a great man said, "There is something in him like me." "His blood is like ours!" cried a French peasant at the execution of Louis XVI. "Yes," said Fox the English preacher; "and therefore it should not have been shed." Goethe declared there was no sin he could not have committed, and John Wesley saw himself in the thief. *I am a man, and nothing human from me alien*, brought down the house, on the Roman stage. There is a parallelism in the proverbs of all nations. We have a hook for every eye of old speculation, and can button our creed with one fifty centuries ago.

Action or opinion has its ancient counterpart. Sheridan has the dash of Hannibal, Grant the prudence of Scipio, and Sherman does in Georgia what Xenophon did in Persia. Stone tools and weapons from antique caverns show the same art with our shops, railways, and mills. The exigencies of California mining have reinvented ancient tools. Our iniquities are as inveterate as our merits. We marvel at the Jew's contempt for the Gentile who was wiser, the Greek who was more polished, and the Samaritan who was more gracious than himself. But our Chinese prejudice is thicker than the famous wall. Are not *heathen* and *pagan* terms we apply to better men than ourselves? When the Presbyterian priest would force his way into Calhoun's dying-chamber, "Fool!" cried the statesman, "to think he can teach me things I have considered all my life!" We fancy the problems are solved. But every question is open. We float with our Fathers on the same sea of wonder, and sail out of and into the same horizon of shade. We cry for the same solace, —

"And with no language but a cry."

What a benighted man, to talk of pre-existence, do *they* hold Plato, who have learned the precise fact of man's creation from the dust! But Orthodoxy in our day repeats the doctrine. Dr. Beecher thinks it were mean for God to create us with a blot, like the blood-stain no water can wash from the floor, or a piece of damaged goods. So we must have sinned in a prior state; and our punishment is in the depravity with which we were born. Jesus pre-existed, we say. Why not everybody, if *he* was a man? He abolished death. But God chooses no favorites. We die like those before us. There is no unmixed truth in sacred history, nor unmixed error in profane. On a column, in a carriage, cupola, or balloon, I am upheld by the same earth; and in all my metaphysics or common sense I have one Uplifter. Isaac Watts sings of the "basis" that belong as much to Paine or Voltaire. Men try to be sharp and get the best bargain. But I stand in awe before the justice none can escape. You can take no advantage of God. You will have no joy beyond your measure; and I have not suffered too much. His car rolls on a law harder than steel, resisting every hammer or file. To the mind's eye matter disappears. Order and motion alone remain for his vehicle and will.

Sects are as ships, whose common is the ocean, but each with its own mooring in port. The thinker sails where he will. The Free-Thinker encounters the Creed-Bound on the high seas of literature, politics, art, and general conversation: only they run in when clouds rise, to cast anchor in dogma; and he, like a Red Rover, holds on his course. But both are one in

Faith, which starts with Spirit. Unbelief dates from the dust, and has only that mechanical notion of Infinity which it shares with the brute, who also sometimes seems in the creation to feel overpowered. But it is only a Finite extended. Nothing is infinite but the soul. Space is but one of the fields it works in. Our intellect is classified by what it begins with. "Hath the rain a father, and who hath begotten the drops of dew?" asks Job. It makes a difference if I consider that the rain is my father and the dew my mother, — that my generation is in the particles, not in my being thought of before I came, and coming because of me there could be a thought. There is but one question; and the battle is drawn. All who hold the elements for their origin are on one side, and those who derive from the Elemental Power on the other. Even the animals, in their worship of man, have an obscure feeling of a source above the clay. "Be patient," I said to the dog who offered me his fore foot to shake: "your paw shall become a hand by and by." We speak of the body we are members of. A man's culture is measured by the largeness of the community he consciously belongs to. Friends and relations, our social class, the municipality, the commonwealth, the country, the Pilgrim stock, the Anglo-Saxon, the human race, and all intelligence from the seraph to the beast, are so many ascending marks on the scale of dignity. Never was a nobler name than "Commune" but for want of the *commune vinculum*. If justice be the bond, the cause is international. If division of property, irrespective of industry, worth, and ability, be the aim, it means universal robbery and poverty. It is arithmetical or geometrical progression of all the pirates that ever beset the land or roamed the sea.

Faith is not a conclusion, but a quest. It is confidence in a right we can reach, which grows more fine and tempts us on for ever. Mr. Martineau's title, "Endeavors after a Christian Life," was ridiculed as implying what he had not attained. But who has attained? Attainment were a block in the path, a blind alley, the great stone rolled against the door of the sepulchre. If Jesus be not more and better than he was on earth, then he is dead, and never rose. I never meet a man but to inquire my way. I am thankful not only for the Inner Light, but for the road which generations have made and trod. We complain of every stone and turn in the winding and uneven way over which we walk or drive. But do we think how much digging and blasting it cost? Only to its termination in any forerunner's steps let us object. Even the great Example is not the finality, possibility, and flying horizon of the human mind. For creatures who are in a new coil of the chain of habit every year, what a dignity death adds to life, as a winding-up of involved accounts, and setting us up in this business of character again! The Church is but provisional, and must not complain of those who find no communion in the cold passing round of the loaf and cup, but are driven to the oracle within. "Is it wicked," said one, "to play croquet on Sunday, and not go to church?" "Yes," was the answer, "if it be a wicked thought." But pious scandal of your neighbors is worse.

Depravity may be unconscious; but sin is the sense of sin, and faith is the feeling of spirit. Great is our debt to the explorations of matter that distinguish the age. But the results only point to a higher method we must reach. The microscope throws the glory of the telescope into the shade, by its revelations of that vital structure which concerns us more than all the splendor of the sky. "This star with a tail spinneth round that other: let it spin," we say with the Turkish cadi. But if the secrets of health and disease can be disclosed by the physiologist, he more than Herschel or Leverrier shall have our thanks. Yet mind and conscience elude the keenest lens. God or man will never be seen through a glass, even darkly. The protoplasm, which Mr. Huxley describes as the physical basis of life, is composed of several principles, behind which the mystery of being is intrenched; and when you shall have got the tiles of all fashions used in this castle of creation, the Power that lays them in order is still to seek, whom no magnifier will ever detect among the atoms or the orbs. But what we cannot grub up out of the dirt, or overtake on the comet's trail, our nature shares. God, says the physicist, is unknown and unknowable. But to the spirit nothing is known so well, in that self-knowledge of God and man, knowing each himself in the other, which is the foundation of all knowledge. What is knowledge? An impression on the senses, picture in the eye, or sound in the ear? I know the ship when I have numbered its sails, and shrouds, and masts. I can call it sloop or schooner, frigate or brig. I know the bird or fish or plant, when I have analyzed its organism, and assigned its class. But I do not know the Deity, at whose least whisper of duty in my breast I am eager to work, ready to suffer and die! The youth and beauty of our Israel, that fell in high places or low ones of battle, *knew* not why! I deny the materialist's definition. As to your "knowledge," said the cadi to Layard, "I defile it." Limiting the term to an understanding of external objects put in rows deserves the contempt of all to whom the unseen is real, and ideas are entities which cast as shadows the sun and moon. Nature is no dualism. Yet the words *spirit* and *matter* must be used. The only question is, Who heeds the laws of language best? Science, the foe of Superstition and destroyer of groundless beliefs, is friend of Faith, and relays its foundation beneath frost or flood. It is teaching that force is not quantity, that there is no such thing as size, but every thing according to our optical apparatus — giant or dwarf — and the resistless energies too subtile for sight or touch. All is the same Proteus in manifold modes. Every entry that is opened, shaft sunk, tunnel bored, organic or inorganic latch lifted, leads to one point, which is centre and circumference alike, — a Unity we have as yet no better name for than God, but whose suggestion is not from time or nature, but the soul. O student of these fair appearances, observer of this ghost of God we call the world! before you close the catalogue, account for yourself. Will you tell us why *you* are here? Who woke your curiosity, and started you on your track? Was there no Instigator of your researches, or Source of your delight? What is the name of That which persuades you not chaos, but cosmos, is all?

In Paul's trinity of graces, love is greatest. But the love that fondles is not so good as the faith which forgives and expects, and abolishes antipathy. The feeling to a fellow-creature which makes him dear, though he will not further or vote for you, nor come to hear you lecture or preach, is worth more than all the superficial amiableness ever poured out. This confidence is the essence, the great wheel on which all lesser ones turn, the kingdom to which all else is added, the condition on which our actions will take care of themselves. "What are you doing?" it was said to a noble young person. "As usual, nothing," she replied. But it was enough such sweetness of spirit, purity of look, and beauty of manners should exist. There would be no wrong or waste activity, and no pride of accomplishment, as in the busybody that meddles with other people's matters, and clothes himself in his own righteousness. Who needs your haste and sweat, and superserviceable interference?

The creed touches the character. In the rebellion against Rome of Protestantism, in the recoil from Orthodoxy of Liberality, and the large field we have won of unfettered judgment, our dogmatism has begot indifferentism. We say, No matter what a man thinks, if he lives right. Liberty has become, instead of a means, the end. One being asked which he preferred, faith in God or freedom, answered, My freedom. But when free love, free trade, free rum, and free religion are the mottoes, we ask what curb will keep this wild horse of freedom from running away with us. You look to your harness when you are going to take a ride. Keep a tight rein on this span of free-inquiry and free-will, to hold them to the King's highway. Without conviction, liberty, like a ship carrying too much sail, ploughs under. What is the use of your independence? What is the freedom of the seas for? To sail about aimless and shoot into every inlet for sport; or like that *Alabama*, burnt and branded for ever into English history, to make free with other folk? Freedom is a bastard unless its parent be Truth. No matter what our opinions are! Is it any matter what a man eats, but not what he puts into the stomach of his mind, a French novel or a psalm? Many ways to heaven? Some to hell! Stop, as did the young man in the low theatre when he read in capitals over the door, *To the Pit!* Are you going to the rehearsal? There is a rehearsal for every thought, ere the act, be it music of charity, or murder in the Bussey Woods, or on the Brookline road. What but sabbatarian superstition stretches into intolerance the tether of the law, to shut up a public library from those who have no church? What but bigotry made one ask, "Shall we have only Unitarians and infidels on the platform to celebrate Italian emancipation?" Yet a certain minister proclaims his adherence to the same old articles held forth a hundred years ago, saying he would nail them on his church-door for a sign. So indeed it were well to do! The farmer nails mischievous birds and beasts of prey, hawk and fox, on his barn-door. The trader nails base coin to the counter. I saw counterfeit money hung up, a long row of bills, in a city warehouse. Luther nailed his propositions, a placard against the papal bulls, on the German cathedrals. Such doctrines as *total depravity* and *particular election* abolish the Declaration of Independence, and deserve any exposure of shame. Were the Five Points in New York named with any reference to the Five Points of Calvin? They lead to the same despair! We were shocked by Taney's opinion that the negroes in this country have no rights white men are bound to respect. But the abolitionists might have spared him the length of their lash. This belief was founded not only on his construction of the Constitution, but his notion of slavery as a heaven-ordained institution based on plenary inspiration of the text. Why should not *we* curse Canaan if God did? What was the judicial decision but part of the theological one, that mankind have no rights He is bound to respect? Was the Divine proceeding in dooming men for moral inability the pattern for us to match, like reverent copyists in galleries of the works of the great masters, or tapestry-sewers in the French shops? This the lost image we were made in to stencil in our demeanor and stitch into our heart? Has the child in the cradle no claims on you? More indefeasible ones have we all on God. I ask him to justify my existence; nor will he that resented not Job's expostulation condemn my demand, but satisfy me my creation was wisdom, and his bestowment of life a boon. Though my fate, like an engulfing billow racing after the vessel, were hard at my heels, one thing is needful: his conduct must be such as while I live I can imitate without harm. Is he unforgiving, remitting only with blood? I shall be the same. Did he punish Jesus in our stead? Let us hunt up scapegoats, and in every court let the guilty go! For our salvation must Christ's body and blood be partaken in the elements, though the taste of wine wake in the once delivered drinker the wolf of appetite? Is the Pope infallible? Then a kingdom must lie in chains, at least till the world learn to laugh at a pontiff no more able than the astrologer in the story to predict his own fate, and his authority be blown to pieces by a new-born nation's breath.

From men's persuasion comes their course. Whence cruelty to animals, but from an opinion derived from the Hebrew books, and customs too, that we are their absolute lords? Trace a human quality in beasts, make them our relations, and our new estimate will stand them in better stead than a thousand Bergh-societies. Truth is moral. "Is aught wrong in the temper of my articles?" asked a bold editor, knowing, with Goethe, that the spirit we act in is the highest matter. "No," was the answer: "your sharpness is not for yourself, but your cause." All the weapons of God's armory we are to wield against false prophets. Wrath and ridicule do not belong to selfish men to use, but to enthusiasts for the truth. Let them buckle on the steel against His adversaries, and draw the sword, and poise the lance of holy indignation and scorn. Would you bless your fellow, do not so much give him creature-comforts, but enlarge his view. Any belief, like that in immortality, is sound that promotes the common weal. God made us not for handiwork alone, but to behold his beauty.

If perfect love casteth out fear, perfect faith casteth out sorrow. Do we weep when mature fruit is gathered? Does the husbandman mourn over his sheaves? What means your stubborn grief but that there is no garner for the soul? Is it not only the shock of corn, fully ripe in its season, that is gathered, but the flowers and the buds? Yet we pluck them from the garden and the field; and the human blossoms, like those that had unfolded in a coffin on its way, fulfil their promise out of our sight.

X.

LAW.

USE different words as we may for diverse aspects of the creation or moods of mind, there is no distinction between law and person, or law and love. By law we mean the Divine method or habit, not an alien power to constrain. If our growing knowledge convince us that there is no departure from the line, we do not believe that line is arbitrary, or was ever laid down by One who would fain leave it if he could; but is itself expression of his own essence. Truth, beauty, goodness, — these three in the language of the schools are one and consubstantial.

We are placed in the world amid forces we cannot measure, of Nature without and our own nature within; liable to be run away with by the elements and our own passions. The reins, which are knowledge and will, are put in our hands; yet we shall be unseated and ridden over unless we take heed: and the danger is twofold, — from other driving as our own. As an old author says, we are like ships in a storm, in danger from the waves and each other. There is a superstition that it promotes health to sleep with the head to the north, to correspond to the axis of the globe. To ride backward or look from a piazza on the sea makes some persons sick. Farmer or sailor knows he can make the elements friends or foes, — difference of pilot being the only reason one vessel comes to port and another founders in the same gale. "Man will be happy," said Spurzheim, "when he confines himself to understand and find ways to execute his Creator's laws." We are at school to them from our infancy. They are the only university. The child finds that his throat is the wrong place to put down the gravel he plays in, that the fire or candle does not agree with his fingers, that edge-tools will cut hands taking them by the blade, and that he sits down very suddenly on the floor unless circumspect with the muscles upon which his leg-practice begins. Nature and our nature are like two mutually adjusted clocks or harps.

This sense is in the proverbs and cries of all nations. "Be careful!" says our companion when we step over the threshold, or on the stairs, or lift the baby, or open the knife, or reach for the razor, or cut with the scissors, or fasten the rope, or loose the main-sheet, or belay. "Look out!" cries the Yankee coachman; "*Prenez-garde!*" the French omnibus-driver; "Fire, fire!" the rock-blaster. The steam-whistle screams far off to clear the track; the red or white flag of the signal-man warns horse and man at the crossing; the watchman springs his rattle at mid-night-disturbance; the bell is rung by hand or by lightning in cities, in a conflagration. In Teneriffe I heard the Spanish sentinel cry every hour in the night, "All is serene!" as if the citizens must be wakened every little while to be assured they might sleep soundly. "Get out of the way!" we shout to our dearest friends. The chariot of law will bear us if we sit in it; its wheels worse than any Juggernaut will grind us if we be in the opposition to *His* Majesty's government. It is not the train that I see arrive or start, but His statute of which that is the apparition. A hundred locomotives go through the tunnel every day; but with every gesture and breath His decrees pass. Do you think retribution is postponed till the world is burnt up, and the trumpet sounds and the general judgment dawns, and all nations assemble at a final bar; and, if these things do not take place, you will escape, run toll, and go scot free? Your punishment is at once. An impure or intemperate man wrestles with a law, and is surer to be thrown than if he assailed the engine. The people say ironically to a man who has blundered against a wall or run his craft on a ledge, "Did you hurt that rock any?" More than by any disobedience you can the Divine command! The prudent profligate, who thinks not to injure his body, and is said only to corrupt innocence in the partner of his guilt, is dying out in the centre, like the rotten cocoa-nut, whose husk only hides its ill odor. The preachers say, "Break not the heavenly laws!" But a law was never broken. The law breaks us, if we try which of the two is best. We fight a duel with God. Jacob wrestles with the Most High, and finds his own thigh out of joint. You think you are *sharp* when by some ingenious trick you make what you call a good bargain. You are stupid not to know it is bad. "I calculate to do about right," we say. That *about* is often a large circumference, a good way off from the centre. It is no honor to hit the target on the rim. "Memorialize congress," it was said to a smuggler complaining of the confiscation of his bark: "they will do you justice." "Ah," he replied, "that is what I am afraid of!" Whether congress will do justice, its treatment of French and other claims makes us doubt. But there is a Legislator who will. No fraud or robbery, violated purity of a woman or stained honor of a man, outrage that makes us ask if any God live and reign, but he will atone to every victim and make the unholy victor quake.

We speak of those who are *responsible*, being in power. In some power the weakest of us are. We call it the will of God when our disrespect of his order turns its blessing to a curse, as the Turkish captain condones the mismanagement that casts away his ship, with pious ascription to fate. "Just my luck!" you say. No, your fault! "His providence!" No, your *im*providence! Piety to accept the miseries which impiety inflicts? Not so, if impiety consists not alone in profane swearing, but in disregard of conditions the Being you worship ordained. It is time to cease from our false baptism of the calamities, we draw on our own heads, as his appointments, and the unchristian christening of our mistakes as his inscrutable wisdom; as if he struck us when we wounded ourselves, or slew us when we committed suicide; as if the typhoid fever, as his angel, came out of the well that communicates with the receipt of ordure. If death be his messenger, we often despatch it. If he make out its warrant, he leaves it, as Horace Mann said, to every one of us to insert the date. It is no absolute will.

You determine it for yourself, and by your conduct for your husband, wife, child, or parent, — lengthening out their days with gracious manners, or with insult stabbing the heart to bleed life prematurely away, and bringing down gray hairs with sorrow to the grave. Father it upon God, will you?

I accuse not Deity of these horrors and ghastly facts in human life. Human carelessness is the misdoer and homicide. It kills a thousand to one beyond every assassin and highwayman, robber on the land or pirate on the sea. In neglect of sanitary rules at the table and in the relation of the sexes, in private unsanctity of the young, in unfit or defective exercise of body and mind, in all its undermining or overloading, its detraction from human vitality outrivals the waste of war, all whose flaming standards measure out for mankind the fields of conflict, but not the wider reaches of their fault. Who shall weigh the woes inuring, like wrecks and heaps of sea-weed cast upon the shore, from inconsideration of the Truth?

When a powder-mill explodes, or a ferry-boat blows up, or a locomotive dragging one train crashes through another, it is published as an "awful *accident*." No accident, but human *heedlessness;* not deliberate murder, but thoughtless manslaughter. The mixing of broken wood and iron, and splintered glass and suffocating steam, amid gasping men and women, is as regularly according to law as the rising of the sun, or ebb and flow of the sea. Only it was attempting to proceed against law, instead of with it. The law goes on more terrible than an army with banners, and the fragments are left bleeding and burning behind.

There are no accidents. Disorder is but the result of our blind neglect of *Order*. Our defeat is in order then. The carpenters on the staging, who had not nailed the support, fell to the ground by the gravitation that steadies your seat. The equilibrium is disturbed? Not God's or Nature's, when we miss our footing, and are overset. "I did not know," you say. Of all parties the Know-nothings was the worst.

But is there no mercy? Never, in the sense of releasing from this hug of Omnipotence withstood. Suppose the unwilful authors of the so indulgently denominated mishap could have been let off from the legitimate issue of their unlawful course, the attractions of matter cancelled, the hot vapor held back, and the coals of fire forbidden to kindle: we should not know what to depend upon. God and Nature would be playing fast and loose with us. All our calculations would be disturbed. We should be put completely out of our reckoning, and not be under tuition, but at a juggler's show. Education were impossible. When shall we learn that justice is not one thing, and pity another; but Mercy and Truth meet together, Righteousness and Peace kiss each other, and the Divine compassion no exceptional attitude, but the undeviating step?

We complain that the innocent suffer from the errors of the guilty. But we see not the Hand holding the balance of redress, death being the pivot, and one scale hanging with even weight on the immortal side, however tremulous the beam. Who shall say that to the blameless departed compensation is not made? There is no murmur in their song. They have no account of vengeance to make up. Earthly law may exact recompense; but no standing grudge beyond! We tread on graves. Our road is ashes. The rolling stock, the running gear, glides swiftly over the spot of disaster which has left no trace. The travellers, who knew not it was a way-station for heaven where they stopped, on a higher plane proceed.

There was one for whom it was not unmeet, like Elijah, to go in the chariot of fire. In the spiritual fabric he spent his last thread. He was like one turning the wheel when the wool gives out on the spindle. The fibre of his frame worn out, it was meet he should be dismissed from the field for refreshment, and that music of welcome for those who have well done. One virtue, of patience, that went against the fire of his nature, and high pressure of his speed, is for him struck from the list. The hireling longs for the shadows that point to the great emancipation of the freedman's dawn, where the Lord will deal gently with him who has dealt severely with himself. For Ezra Stiles Gannett let there be on the dry page of discussion trace of a loving tear.

But the whole sweep is beyond us. We can reckon the orbit of the most erratic body in the sky; but Providence mocks our mathematics. Yet science is doing the work of religion in reducing phenomena under the range of law; and no libel is so gross as to charge it with serving the cause of atheism, or unbelief, in disclosing the invariably regular march of all appearances and events. Is the living God to be proved only in arbitrary ordination and wilful favor to individuals or nations? Must he be a Parent who has pets, a partial Schoolmaster whose generosity to one pupil is injustice to another, a King who smiles on his courtiers, and for critics of his authority has only frowns? Shall some exceptional act, some whimsical decree, some miracle of love to a chosen man, in worse violation of order than any physical prodigy, demonstrate his presence? Thanks to investigators who say, No!

Still less is the cause of Faith served by ascribing any occurrence to a malignant power. Yet a new phrase, in startling capitals, has lately saluted our eyes on placards, and from the orator's speech, and in public prints, — *Fire-Fiend*, — a natural expression to personify as a demon the element of awful and sudden mischief, but involving a hurtful mistake. Fire-minister or fire-angel is the true religious word. The acceptance, with which the other name has been reiterated shows how prevalent still the false feeling which invented it, — that God the Good has a rival power of evil in the world, with agents of destruction in its employ. But two forces are not; only one in Nature, making servants of all substance. Nothing in the universe so potent as fire. It has lately in a day laid in ashes a city which some thought the most beautiful in the States; and, not content, swept villages in Michigan and Wisconsin away with its burning broom, as it turned to ashes in an hour the cars on that fatal Eastern train, and poured out from the broken pipes the suffocating steam; consumed to the water's edge the gay yacht on Long Island Sound; and lurks everywhere, ready to spring forth quicker than a panther or assassin for deadly mischief, unless sharper than any creature in ambush it is watched; indifferent whether it destroy treasure or life. When the dog-star rages, men fall like flies under the sun-stroke. Is it not diabolical? No: it is divine. Without it there were nothing human, no life extant of any sort. Unseen Spirit we believe Author of all. But physical philosophy has shown the sun, the great body of light and heat for our system, to be the source of all vegetable and animal life, the Almighty's instrument in creation; and the sun shines because it burns. Sixty or seventy tons of red-hot coal a day supplied the motive-power of the steamer that brought me across the sea. What amount of fuel is thrown into that furnace a hundred millions of miles away, to draw the planetary load! There is no bounty of the harvest, and no beauty of the blossoms, no benefit of changing seasons, no clothing for our body, no daily bread, comfort, necessity, or luxury, but his chariot brings it. From his genial rays the growth of wood to build house and ship or kindle on our hearth; or out of forests to lay away the mines of concentrated combustible to warm us in winter, and turn ten million wheels and spindles in our factories the year round. It is all fire, angel and minister of God, cashier of the bank that never fails. In the cordial pressure of your hand, beating of your heart, blush on your cheek, sparkle of your eye, animation of your look and gesture, is some portion of its beams. I do not wonder at the Oriental adoration of fire, the Persian worship of the sun; and I admire the keen retort of the Eastern sage to the Englishman who rebuked his idolatry: "You, too, might worship the sun if in your foggy climate you ever saw him." Could any idol be allowed, it would be no block, picture, or graven image, but his blazing orb. Jets of flame, blue and crimson, which no science can comprehend nor logic expound, lead our thoughts into unfathomable mystery. Cold is death: the marvel of life arises with warmth.

If fire be the strongest of the elements in its excess or misplacement to harm, it has no peculiar commission to injure nor monopoly to destroy. The water that buoys will drown. The air, soft as a zephyr, can rise in tempest of ruin. The earth, our floor, may cave in to bury us alive, or slide from the mountain and carry off dwelling and inmate. Every thing will bless or ban us, as we put ourselves in fit or cross relations. On its right hand, it welcomes; on the left, it sends us accursed away. It may be benediction or scourge, cornucopia or vial of wrath. According to our behavior, it frowns or smiles, furthers or blasts, gives us a reception or sets up a bar of judgment.

We owe a tender pity to the sufferings of our fellow-creatures. Never was a tenderer call for sympathy than comes from the city, beside the sepulchre of its matchless prosperity so speedily dug. Yet what was the conflagration but a dreadful calling to account of the hasty ambition for wealth and success that put such walls of pine and masses of shingle, and thin veneers of brick and stone, the best of which were only nominally fire-proof, and wide sections where if one building went a hundred must follow, at the mercy of a kerosene lamp kicked by a cow? — as in Portland a fire-cracker was the equally insignificant occasion of doom. If we charge a ledge or load a cannon, and lay a train of powder, or attach a fuse, and then apply a spark, we know what to expect. We should understand with equal certainty what will come in such ill-constructed and unguarded quarters of many of our towns, when some flung-away match, or midnight reader's candle at the bed-curtain, or careless ash-heap, or smoker's pipe (getting every year to be a more general and unbearable nuisance), or burning gun-wad, times the flame, it starts in a corner, with draught and wind to give it instant velocity and terrible voracity in its course. Chicago endures the penalty. But she is not alone, if even especially guilty. She is conscript for our battle with the avenger, choosing that point of attack and warning us with what other onslaught the war may go on. She is scapegoat of our sin, bearing it into the wilderness of her desolation, if we repent. She is one summoned for correction as an example. Avoid her funeral-pyre by seeing to the security of your own edifices and streets.

Fire a fiend? What bore the tidings of calamity and the cry for help but that same fire in the shape of lightning over the wires, more rapid in its office than devouring flame? What sent back instantaneous promise of aid and certificate of value but the same stream, the essence of the element that had made the havoc? Fire is the most alarming of cries. It is a good servant, but a bad master. But let us not forget it is in its nature beneficent alone. A great cause of death, M. Coquerel tells us, in the siege of Paris was the cold, want of fuel in exceptionally severe weather; and the lives of children were saved by a few sticks to make a fire to prepare and keep warm their food. If the vengeance of violated law comes through fire, careering on the wirlwind's breath, beating down arch and column and marble front, and escaping all control, we must not call malign the executor of justice and instructor to obedience.

Men shrink from this idea of wide-spread woe as punishment. They prefer to call it a disaster, visitation of Providence. It is a *sentence*, as much as when a man is sent to the gallows or jail. God's officers are in waiting, his detective's touch on our shoulder. It is easy, you say, to be wise after the event. Well, next time let us be wise before the event! In the enormous size our cities grow to, in the superficial quality of our carpentry and masonry, in the too late arrival of our engines at the spot, we may be less safe than in the times when we had but a bell with no electric arm to ring it, every man's buckets hung in his garret, and all good citizens rushed from their rooms to put out the first gleam of danger or restrict it to a narrow space. Wisdom after the event! Have we yet to learn that petroleum oil will explode with a scintillation, that a huge flame will leap across a scant passage, and when it gets roaring headway will smite the stoutest bulwarks like a surging sea to bear down all before it?

But in the anguish is saving grace. It reveals the interconnection and solidarity of mankind. Quarrel as they will, and vile specimens of human nature — roughs, thieves, murderers for booty, plunderers of the poor, selfish refusers of assistance save at exorbitant prices — as any seething of the social elements throws like scum to the top, these fellow-creatures do not desert each other in time of need. Humanity is not extinguished but excited by misfortune, though we share the shock. As the great Lisbon earthquake sent a ripple over the ocean to American shores, London and Liverpool capital feels the blow of falling Chicago. But London and Liverpool are not withheld from charity by their loss. Everywhere none more ready to give than those who have suffered, to those who have suffered more. It is a noble temper in this mortal clay, a shining refutation of the dogma that the soul is totally depraved. It is God himself, who is love, moving in his children's hearts. It is an Internationality, or super-nationality, all whose members rejoice or mourn together.

It is curious to see how widely through the country and the world, from a single town, run manifold branches of this great system in modern business of insurance against fire. But the failure of insurance companies under the strain, and the disclosure of the fact that particular corporations will agree to cover thirty times their own capital or assets, may suggest a query how far we are covered, and whether commissioners, like some boiler-inspectors, are not too easy in their search.

Fire, then, is Heaven's servant, and no fiend. The old Theology must answer in part for its being so misunderstood. The ungovernable fury of fire fairly unloosed; its hideous waste of wide regions, leaving groves and fields and habitations blackened heaps; its terrific overflow from volcanic peaks into streams of lava, to scorch and whelm in ruin vineyard and abode; its dismal smotherings of man and beast; the ground trembling and rumbling with its pent-up force, impatient to escape from the centre it constitutes of the globe, with famous judgments, as on Sodom and Gomorrah, — have doubtless furnished to writers of Scripture the hint of the popular hell. It was an apprehension from Nature, not inspiration of the Holy Ghost. How much more grand and true David's conception of it, as a minister bearing the Lord's gifts and corrections alike in its hand!

Fire a devil or factor of Beelzebub? What is this warming of the heart, all over the land and the world, but an inward fire lighted from the supersolar spark, and having in it a million-fold the heat even of those fierce, unquenchable tongues that sucked up the verdure round the Lakes, licked into dust the metropolis of Illinois, and feasted on the blood of thousands of lives, to mark this hemisphere of the West with one of the chief astounding afflictions in the annals of mankind? Fire in the wrong place — on the floor, and not on the hearth; in a powder-magazine, and not a factory-chimney; in a defective flue instead of a poor man's hovel — is no comfort. The inward fire — in our hate, not our kindness; in envy, not generosity; in lust, not love — is no minister of grace. Yet even it has caught, to burn out the often foul chimney of a human breast, which will draw better when it is clean. The remorse we deprecate we could not spare. Fan the flame of a fine compunction. Let the fire, that has levelled a city to the soil out of which with such indomitable industry it was raised, be met with the brighter glow of charity. As in the prairie on whose edges she sat, their crown and lustre for a thousand miles, fire is fought with fire, so against the outward element let us set the interior flame of good-will. Because love was not burnt, Chicago shall be rebuilt. Charity shall be the master-mechanic. Courage shall be restored in her citizens by the world's generosity. She shall rise from prostration, with the help of a hundred cities, more fair and strong than before; and, with her hands stretched to the lakes and the sea, feed us again with meat and bread, if we feed her sore want and hunger now.

If there is a law of Nature, there is a law of love in human nature and the Divine. When we talk of natural law, let us not forget that which is not less natural because it is spiritual. The overflow of sympathy in the shape of bounty surprises giver and receiver. Yet it is no accident nor choice, but a necessity firmer than the ravage of flame or axis of the globe. What merit in that succor which is the constitution of the human heart? If we speak of the whole humanity, and not, like Paul, of a sin-distracted soul, the law of the members is the law of the mind. The flame that made a cinder of the great city, and used forests for its kindlings, was but the lamp that law is read by. If without such light the inward engraving might get effaced or obscured, the conflagration is a blessing. If the fire were sent not only to consume town and village, treasure and life, but to burn deeper this lesson, its art is glorious beyond all other encaustic pictures.

The Divine law is remedy, not fatal disease. The Samaritan that will not leave the robbed and wounded traveller to perish is not a man sitting on his beast and riding between Jerusalem and Jericho, but mankind as a comforter for every afflicted man. We heal our own flesh when we pour balm into anybody's wounds. The apostle's figure is true: Christian goodness is kindness to one's self; and the Western paper's sentence was scarce a conceit or hyperbole, — that even Chicago is essential to the world.

Our help to the needy is a meter of civilization and religion. It gauges our discovery of the Personality in which we all meet together. No individuality but must pass and melt in the consciousness of an equal destiny and source. But this is no mechanism. The ocean will not flow where is no inlet; and there are souls closed up against this benevolent tide. They are shut out just as much from their own joy. Virgil's line, —

> "Happy if they but knew their own welfare,"

illustrates the deeper self-ignorance of those who cannot learn pity when in such blazing letters. But they are becoming the exceptions. How fellow-feeling increases and benefactors multiply! All the prophecies that illuminate the Bible grow pale before the fact of the millennial day. It is easy for a hard heart to dispense alms to a wretched object. But to lavish supplies to beneficiaries hid by the breadth of the earth is a revelation of the sons of God. After the death of Thomas Starr King, a man in California, leaning on his tool, and with tears running down his cheeks, cried out, "How I loved that man!" "You knew him, I suppose?" said the traveller to whom he spoke. "No, I did not." "You have heard him speak, then?" was the rejoinder. "No: I never saw him," said the rude miner again. When affection like that shall spread as a common sentiment, the misers will be in the minority, the kinship from one touch of nature will be owned; perhaps the Divine need will cease of startling us by flagrant cases to commiserate, and society be born again.

XI.

ORIGIN.

ALL thinkers consent that the Bible book of Genesis gives but a fable of the creation, or the conception of some poetic mind, not any miraculous knowledge which the Creator bestowed. That the light and the heavenly bodies and every living order arose from some distinct, instantaneous fiat, science cannot admit; nor that there was ever such a *nothing* as the catechism supposes out of which the universe came. We can as easily conceive that God was born as that the world began. It was not made in time, but by the Eternal Builder, in whose productive essence it is everlasting as himself; nor can we insert any notion of age or chronology between his being and his work, however we may trace connection in its parts, or the progress of a single planet like the earth. Physical philosophy, in attempting to show a commencement, commits the same error with literal faith; and is guilty of a blunder all its own, in deriving every thing from matter instead of spirit, as is so grandly asserted in the Scripture text. Reason allows not dust as the basis, but the deposit of mind. Only a thoughtless observation could bring forth the fancy, that figures in so many a verse, of "primeval chaos and night." There was no darkness before the dawn. Light and cosmos alone were primeval,—begotten of God. If the earth was ever without form and void, other spheres without number were shining and singing in the firmament. Never a wreck that was not the refuse of former beauty, never a clod but from the decay of somewhat awaiting a resurrection; and all that we call dead is cast-off clothing, mending for some new garment. It is the dropping of decay, which fresh vitality shall resume. Matter, which is multitude, follows Spirit, which is One. Our students overlook on Jacob's ladder the descending angels, prior in office to those that ascend. Creation is the condescension of the Most High to become the Most Low: not dust rising into Deity, but Deity stooping to dust. We can get the finite out of the Infinite; but the process cannot be reversed. The manifold is the One, but without the One were no number.

The fruit on the tree of life is from ideal planting. We are told that from material investigations has grown all benefit. But by some metaphysician, visionary or spiritual observer, every seed has been sown. Only to the kingdom of God have all the other good things been added. A pure perception, of which nothing visible was cause or more than occasion, in the mind of the physical explorer,—Newton, Kepler, Oken, Goethe,—led to every discovery from which inestimable utilities proceed. Abstract thinkers, as Kant and Plato, stop not in their service of intelligence till they lift the whole platform of action and plane of life. Matter is the false date that spoils our almanac. It makes every item of calculation deceptive. From the cradle of Eternal Being all variety springs.

The fault of the last theory is in trying to evolve the entire man from what is below himself. His animal organism may be so unfolded. But he is spirit too. Something is let down as well as lifted up into him. Will our friend, who is following back the race into some primitive germ, please to account for his own presence and curiosity, — for his wish and power to classify? Whence his hunger after something more than those creature-comforts for multiplying which the Baconian method is praised? I want an explanation not only of the object which is his subject, but of the student himself and of the study; and I find it only in some absolute Truth.

On purely physical premises God himself is no Original, but only a conclusion. But out of the finite, which is all the understanding and senses can compass, only the finite comes. No heaping of finites can get nearer the Infinite than does a drop. Some logicians throw contempt on the pretence of a finite creature like man to any idea of infinity. But what if it should turn out that he is infinite himself? In the Semitic, Hebraic, and Mahometan, as well as the too often pseudo-Christian thought, God and man are separate terms, so that the latter can reach the former only by some bridge. But the *cause*-way is the common nature of both. The mediator between God and man must be divine, and man must be divine for mediation to be possible. The phrase *immutable*, addressed so continually to Deity by our clerical sires in their prayers, seemed external, and implied this separate Being we are in relation with. But the Japhetic mind abolished this gulf, filled up the empty space, turned the interval into smooth continent, and saw the Unity which God and man together are. In the Greek gospel ascribed to John, Jesus says, "I and my Father are one;" and in that last wonderful prayer for oneness in which all should meet, he means nothing personal to himself as an individual, but has a vision of the measureless life. Strange that the Gospel whose authenticity is questioned should proclaim the spiritual verity which the Synoptics miss, though they do not contradict, and perhaps in the divine Fatherhood imply. Which narrative is the truest representation of the historic Saviour it is left to scholarship still to decide. But an insignificant minority of the Church has yet risen to the sublimer view. Even the Father is so outside as to be but a fetish unseen. The soul has idols as well as the sense. When I spoke of the Deity as changing to us with our own growth, some of my hearers were shocked, and one quoted against me the text, "without variableness or shadow of turning." But I replied that nothing which turns or casts a shadow is without God, or not part of him as much as the sun; that he is not only the fixture, but the flow; and that the same sacred book declares that he repented of having made man.

But does not Divinity descend into and communicate with the brute too? There are animals that mock man in their habits; warm themselves at the fire, build lodgings among the trees, and fling broken branches at their pursuers. The ants emulate us in their wars. But none of them put telescopes to their eyes, hold pens in their hands, raise temples, found governments, save in the rudest fashion among the bees, beavers, and crows; pass laws, have art to discover truth or put eloquence on their tongues, or imitate with any of their horny armory the cannon-wheel that ploughs the earth for the seed of freedom and right. But they all partake this universal motion and will, which, no less than thought, expresses Deity. The head of the Phidian Jove speaks not only of reflection, but power and pity, to indicate the artist's and the Greek idea. Personality, self-consciousness, action as well as vision, is the lesson written in the world; and some rudiments or relics of all our attainments may be detected in these inferiors, the poor relations we do not own, but may have yet to admit to a share in our proud generalities for mankind of free and equal birth-rights. Burns's adoption of the mouse for his fellow-creature hints in it some drop of the blood of which God is sacredly said to have made all nations. The St. Bernard dog, that saved the life of a wounded soldier by hugging him to his breast when every comrade had left, was entitled to rank among nurses. The Newfoundland one, that slept on his master's bed, but would not enter the chamber after the master's death, yet oftenest of any member of his family went to lie on the grave, might be classed among mourners. The one that gave me a daily greeting at the corner of my street, as cordial as any neighbor's, I certainly counted among my friends.

But in my recognition of these as members of the family reduced in their fortunes, who may have seen better days, let me not forget I have rich relations and a nobler kith and kin. Humboldt says, "I am an insect clinging to the surface of the earth." Did he think how nearly he adopted the theologic classification, —

"What worthless worms are we"?

I walk with the man of science up the rounds of organization from the dust. But let him not ask me to stop with the human form. I can show, of angels, no plates such as travellers fetch from their observations, or geologists give of fossil remains. But does nothing exist which cannot be so represented? The trilobite may be ancestor of my body, but not father of my soul. That the scale of being ends in man is impossible to think. It has no end nor beginning. It is that sort in mechanics called an *endless* chain. It is not a circle, but a spiral. Go down, microscope in hand, to the seed-vessel, to the animal cell, to the root in the ground, or dot or double-dot in the egg; to the sponge on the rock or increment of the crystal; to the chemical atom; to the infantile miniature of the plant betwixt the lobes of its little germ; to the undulations of a ray of light, or the splendid blossoms among the softest tiny feathers of the bed of moss; to the generation of colors by the crossing of flowers, or the hues in the marvellous sea-weeds that match the rose and pink, — are you nearer the bottom than when you set out? Can you tell if the bubbles you come to are the primal forms, or by whom they were blown?

Go up to this globe of reason in the human head, and thence to this well of love in the human heart, are you nearer to the top; or do you sit down weary as a child on the monumental stairs? We build cemeteries. Is there in God's works any graveyard that we can set apart and consecrate to stay for a burial-ground, save as a spot of perpetual resurrection? Transformation of species does not gainsay immortality; for this is possible only by the convertibility and conversion of man into angel through some selection, adding buoyancy and leaving out what is earth-bound. When it please God to slide us off easy as sleeping to a new sphere, it will be no transmigration as of summer-birds, but transmutation of life. Does not the soul conceive its capacity to live and act without these special organs, and paint in tints of glory the heaven to which it goes? "The Father's house" was no structure Jesus had seen; but, more solid than any edifice, it was a reality his imagination projected. With Infinite Personality every person is safe, from the elder above to each mite of humanity. You have not lost your child. The spirit that shone in its soft eyes, moved in its tender limbs, beat in its gentle heart, and spoke in its inarticulate voice, has title to unfold beyond any seed of the garden and the field. We called the negro an ape; and science avenges the insult by forcing us into the same relationship. They, whose bravery at Port Hudson and Fort Wagner no white ever surpassed, shamed millions of traitors or half-hearted patriots in the Free States. They were God's make-weight against the slavery they had suffered. They turned the tide of battle for the freedom by which alone the nation was saved. We owe the Commonwealth to a black skin. If there be no future for the black man, let there be none for me!

The impossibility of running a boundary-line between man and animal is hinted in the fact of their correspondence in every physical feature, which discovery of higher likeness with every close observation backs. It was thought the lower creatures have no conscience. But shame for misconduct, with susceptibility of correction and improvement in some of them, is plain. It was said they have no notion of God. What notion have we but in that sense of Being superior to ourselves, which the cow and ox show in *our* presence? It is said every day, the horse would not be so submissive if he knew his own strength. The lion, elephant, leopard, and tiger revere their keeper. We are told they have no language. But they communicate with each other. The sentinel-crow warns the flock. Many a bird calls its mate, with strophe and antistrophe of song. They understand much of our meaning in the natural language of expression. Whether they have or will ever reach arbitrary terms for abstract conceptions, or whether words are senseless in the parrot's mouth, let those who will presume to decide in the light of the training they are capable of and progress they make. But must we not admit they have no *ideas?* The term *idea* subtends an arc so wide, from Plato to the savage brain, it is not easy to settle their share. But some representation of the world, and of the creature in it who assumes to be lord of the creation, they clearly possess and are governed by in their course. The squirrel I stoned when I was a thoughtless boy, who stopped after much running in the centre of the ridge-pole of my father's barn, rose on his hind legs, and with his fore paws beat his breast, moved me with his prayer immediately to desist. Yet is any animal like man in proposing to himself an object in life? One kind of dog seems to choose for his profession the rescue of travellers from Alpine snows; and another kind seems to make it his business to save from drowning, though known sometimes to seize and bear from the water such involuntary subjects of compassion as only proposed to swim. The shepherd-dog's care of the flock shows more intelligence than some human sèrvants, and is daily engaged in what looks wonderfully like a regular occupation. Do we choose, or are we led and impressed into our vocations?

Surely there are things men do and animals cannot, such as architecture, legislation, astronomy, and finance. But the question is whether, in what they are competent to, they show signs of similar faculties and dispositions; so that students dispute, and are puzzled to know if man be an ascended brute, or the beast a descended man. The point of debate is whether an absolute demarcation can be run between them at any point, to make in Nature the vacuum she abhors. In our pride, we stand out for the godless gap. We inherit with our religion a traditional prejudice from the Jews, whose sacred superiority and antipathy to animals had to be withstood by the command not to muzzle the ox that treadeth out the corn. Paul bids, but I do not, "beware of dogs." But the just sympathy, in which man reaches out in our day to woman, may extend at last to lower tribes. What limits this fellow-feeling may have to observe we have not yet defined. I have a friend who declines to molest mosquitoes in their feast on himself. But the Society for the Prevention of Cruelty to Animals finds itself obliged to discriminate, and, according to the humorous proverb, "draw the line somewhere," — one of the Thirty-nine Articles of its creed being for the encouragement of "*insectivorous* birds;" while I have known a tender-hearted woman to bound her mercy the other way, with a wish that the mal-treater of a dray-horse might be removed by death!

But let us consider certain religious objections to this last view of human nature, which is now the main question under debate, not only in books of science, but in every newspaper of the secular and religious press, city parlor, sea-side piazza, and country town. To the first shock of the doctrine that the whole race did not arise from one couple, the cloud of Darwin adds the heavier clap that our ancestry runs back of all human creatures to the anthropoids, and behind even them to the first species and speck of organized being.

This endless series, of which humanity is but a link, is supposed first to reflect on the Creator, by doing away with creation in any proper sense, and substituting for cause and effect, for voluntary divine production, not special development, but general evolution, interminable sequence of existences and events needing no spirit, but only matter, for their substance and source; whereas the tale in Genesis presents a real Maker fashioning his child from the dust of the earth, and breathing into his nostrils the breath of life. But would God show more power, or man be clothed with greater honor, in this direct formation from the ground than by transformation of successive animal ranks? Did the earth lose worth, and was it soiled, by being shaped into a worm, a fish, a bird, before taking the upright figure? To the bishop denouncing such a transmission Mr. Huxley said, "Rather come from a monkey than be a block in the way of science!" The biblical theologian, and obsequious naturalist who defers to the popular creed and *explains* Genesis, offer no appeal to reason, but an argument to pride, in trying to persuade us man was made apart from every other creature; God stopping to draw a long breath and open a wide interval betwixt all that lives beside and him, that he might have the glory of a purely independent and isolated derivation. But attempt to conceive how this starting him all by himself took place. Did actual hands scoop the atoms from the soil, to mould, as an artist does the clay, into a perfect model of manhood? and did a mouth of flesh blow into the yet lifeless nostrils, to turn the stiff corse into a moving frame? Is that a credible mode of divine working? and is transmutation step by step from inferior to superior incredible? It is so only to the superstitious caviller, not exploring the contents of his own thought, or affirming a literal dogma instead of thinking at all.

The new hypothesis is not fully proven in any statement of it yet made. The record is imperfect. The trains of observation do not connect. But the objection holds not good. You have seen the conjurer's trick with his rings, now together and now apart, you could not tell how. Do distinguishable varieties of being suggest an Author more than an indissoluble chain? You suspect materialism in this unfolding of life from stage to stage, with no possibly perceptible boundary-line. But is Deity revealed by intervening rather than by propelling from the first? or is infinite power and wisdom required to project things one by one, as a sculptor does his statues, more than to fashion a mighty whole? It is thought the scientist would banish the Originator, and show the palace of Nature reared out of multiplied myriads of infinitesimal tiles. But it is absurd to fancy there ever was less or ever will be more universe, or that matter is a condition save as the consequence of mind. What is all existence but receptacle, prepared in the animal and enlarged in the human brain, while every instinct flows in, from what fountain who shall tell? It were as rational to say the granite reservoir makes the water it holds, as that the cerebral lobes create the thought and affection they are incarnate chambers of, and every nerve a service-pipe of the river of God. Shakspeare describes the ambitious man

> "Scorning the base degrees
> By which he did ascend."

Our disgust at the notion that we are graduates of this primary school of the animals into the university of souls proves like arrogance, acquired through sin, not natural to the simple, unsophisticated mind. They are somehow our fellows. Why are children so fond of them, begging to be taken to the circus and menagerie, eager to feed the elephant as he comes out to swing his trunk, to visit by turns the tenant of every cage, and run after every dog and kitten, lamb and calf, chicken and bug? Because, as George Herbert says of the healing plants, they "find their acquaintance there." "Do you think that fine infant boy came from a monkey?" asked one. "He is a monkey himself," was the reply; a speech the mother standing by did not seem to resent. "I always thought," said my friend, "the man was only something more than a monkey, and the monkey something less than a man."

But which way does the motion take? There is no law of progress by which every thing advances and nothing declines. If some angels are going up, others are coming down. The Maker is implicated in all. Were man to fall, God would go down with him! But particular men and tribes may sink to the brute and the worm. Some ethnologists see in the North American Indians the wreck and refuse of the ancient ten tribes of the Jews. A degraded race is harder to recover than an undeveloped one to ascend. Many a man is burying himself in some beast. I would be just and kind to every feeble member of a lowered humanity, Indian or African, for in every such member I see an undying soul; but I would not lift a finger to perpetuate the race. A distinguished Frenchman told me he thought the French type was going down. Surely, the German type more deserves to be and propagate than that which in the modern Gaul has lived so long not on duty, but glory. What was the Commune but the last struggle of a nation to preserve itself in the quality of self-worship? But, as

Goethe says, God will not see the once-loved features of the progenitors in the faces of a corrupted lineage. Without extinction, through long purgatory, by an ill-trained people must paradise be regained. All running down is for re-creation, as Tennyson's "Vision of Sin" ends with an awful "rose of dawn." Fallen races, like fallen leaves, manure another growth. Out of latent or suppressed germs better timber springs through the ashes of worthless woods. Would not a section of the creation show eternal equality of the æons in finer grades of quality than all the stuffs and goods of human art? The old mythology pictured the gods striding from hill to hill; but there is no mincing step so nice and short as their degrees. The geologist cannot see the glacier move through the Alpine gorge; but, as it must move unequally at the centre and the sides, he takes its measure by the relative position, after a certain period, of a series of stakes. What pins shall denote changing combinations of the smaller particles of magnetism, electricity, heat, and light, to build the living frame or inanimate things?

Yet, according to the Primer, this is not creation at all. Did not God make the world out of nothing? Try to imagine a time when was no universe. We can no more think away Nature than God. A naked Deity, or blank Unity with no diversity, One without many, is an unreal idea of impossible fact. The Trinity is a philosophic attempt to escape from a barren and bald monotheism. But no less preposterous an Infinite Parent from all eternity, with but one child. All that is must have for ever been. Like a changeable silk, the Almighty's robe, glimmering in the light of his countenance, makes the only alteration. Miracles — are there several, or but one impenetrable wonder through innumerable forms? Were the sea to ridge itself a dry-shod path, or the sun to rest on his axle, the green bush to burst into flame, or the water become wine, I should not be more amazed, however confounded and stupefied, than by every regular phenomenon and ordinary procession. My objection to miracles is not the scientist's, for he is incompetent to disprove them; nor the scholar's, of not evidence enough; but the child's, that a Father leading should turn round to confront his own method and take it all back. Whatever, like the marvellous healings, we have a gleam and inkling of in Nature, we can accept as going on from the least experience to the farthest reach. If species are distinct, every new one seems an added prodigy. But God is no theatrical scene-shifter, shoving aside his doors and curtains to let in new figures. Would dislocation more than gradual action show his might? He saw his way clear through! What characteristic of creation is wanting in the imperceptibly nice operation of his hand? A cataclysm, earthquake, eruption, thunderbolt, billow, startles us more. But is there greater ease or less mystery in the opening of a leaf, waxing of the dawn, or flow of the tide? The sublimity is not God's caldron of the volcano, or kettle of the waterspout, or sledge-hammer of the sea; but the *atom* he makes his tool. With that, too small for our sight, he rears the mountains from the depths or shaves the rocks to the plain, blends a few elements into potent substances thousand-fold and dissolves them again, strengthens every bone and swells every fibre, or wastes gigantic sinews away. Nothing can turn its edge. With that chisel too small to see he shall cut us down, lay us low in our coffin, and with that trowel build us up again. His finger it shall be to pick us out of our grave; and his vital sculpture, not by diminution but increase, for our resurrection into smooth, seraphic shapes. What are those strange powers Goethe writes of as "the mothers" but these agents out of sight? That man results from their inscrutable instrumentation is no disinheritance from his privilege of a heavenly birth.

But the theory of man's animal derivation is supposed to do away with his personal identity. If this means an absolutely separate self, so that your will or mine is an independent monad, like a monolith or monograph standing alone, undetermined by motives and unconnected with other wills, there is in such insulation no *personal* quality. Personality is the sounding through us of no private wish, but of universal truth, as his part does through the actor, or a tune through pipe or string. Personality unites us with our kind, and expresses the common interest. When, as I heard a host tell his guests at table to *fall to*, we set about satisfying carnal appetite, or parading in our peculiar set of jewels and silks, and being angry at imitators of our costume or turn-out, or seeking selfish aggrandizement, we may be individual, but we cease to be personal. We express or enhance the general welfare no more than a hawk stooping for its prey, a peacock lifting his tail, or pigs feeding at their trough.

Isolation is not the quality of a person, but rather of a brute. Even the lower creatures shame our by-ends in their flocks and herds, playing together as I lately saw two robins; and as dogs delight to, more than to bark and bite. I think Watts maligned them. Men and women commonly take more pleasure in a quarrel than they. Do not the wedges of emigrant fowl, that cleave the autumnal sky, show in such sociality of a general concern some degree of that personality our philosophy denies? Sympathetic service measures your personality. It is the overflow of affection from dateless tribes.

Woman, the flower of humanity, like the sweet crystal from the last refinement of the sugar-cane, seems oftener than man to scorn the notion of animal origin. Yet what more is her beautiful hair than a relic from the skin of some progenitor beyond Esau? Let the gay lady be ashamed rather of her velvet train sweeping across the parlor-floor, leaving no room for anybody's feet! I am not mortified at my trail stretching back over the floor of creation, in nobody's way. Is it less credit to have come vitally transmitted, or transmuted from lower but ever rising orders, than mechanically dredged out of the ground? Our personal identity consists in our intoning what inspires us from the past for the whole present and future good, through our particular gift; as a special melody is voiced by the entire atmosphere playing through trumpet or flute. But the individualism that would compass an exclusive benefit is a vice.

Yet no charge is more frequently false. We are accused of individualism for declining to join some particular sect. Some of us are marked as flagrant examples for not being members of an association or conference. Belong to what party you will; but plead "Not guilty" when you are flung at because you serve none in politics or religion. If you are unsocial and unkind, indifferent to philanthropic enterprise, an enemy to the freedom in others you enjoy yourself, a hoarder of advantage at the expense of the common stock, then you are individualistic; but not for failing to be an active zealot in any denomination. Is there not more individualism in ambition to be prominent on the platform, where some men and women not waiting to be invited procure their own opportunity to speak, or in travelling from Dan to Beersheba for small upshot of help to the community, and getting one's name clothed with flattering compliment in the newspapers, than in silence and absence for disinterested toils? Was Beethoven, Raphael, Milton, individual in the bad sense, for being each busy in composing, and each a composition of the breath of God, rather than running every day to some clique or club? Let truth and cheer come out of your closet, as Jesus sent them from mountain and desert to mankind; and, though never seen where men most do congregate, who shall question your personal claim? If he that says I AM be our Author, *persons* we are, whether we can tell how or not. Whence I came, I will not bother my head. Here I am alive, to love you and worship God. What if I cannot account for my genealogy, and map or photograph the family tree? Does the scientist say certain *phenomena* are all? But how of himself, the observer? How happens it he observes? Will he please to analyze his own curiosity to put things in a row, and have an hypothesis? *He* interests me more than the strata and coral-reefs, and fishes and beasts, in his discourse. Why leave himself, the man, out? He must pardon me, if I consider the experimenter more than the retort or oyster-shell in his hand. He is a person, offshoot of Person Infinite, in whatever bit of antediluvian cradle, too minute to see, he lay.

But many philosophers and Christians revolt from this unity of the animal with the man, because it does away with immortality. But what ground is weakened, on which you have credited a future life? Is the Lord's rising proof of yours? Is that rising disproved because man is older than the garden of Eden, has a chimpanzee for his far-off cousin, or a trilobite for his sire? The old burial-service implies a resurrection of the body. Can it not rise as easily if descended from any or every branch of the animal kingdom, as if composed, as the story tells, of the crude silt it shall dissolve into, or of the gravel dropping on its casket from the sexton's spade? But those animals in the one long lineage embracing us are not immortal: why should we be any more? What know we of their destiny, but from that Old Testament text about "the beasts that perish"? Some of them better deserve to live, are more faithful and patient, than some men; show more consideration and conscience than their masters. As Bacon says man is the dog's God, the dog is sometimes more worshipful than his owner. That beings in heaven will be all of one sort, nothing but angels, as we commonly conceive them, with crowns and palms and harps, is hard to think. It would be monotonous and tiresome! There must be not less, but more, diversity than here. The trouble in the argument is not any prejudice of our prospects from the new theory; but, like some people who have got on in the world, and cannot speak to their humbler kith and kin, we do not want to have these poor quadrupeds for our associates because we are ashamed of the connection. Two of their feet having in us been promoted into hands, so we have got the upper hand. But, in the birds, as if God would reprove our pride, are not two of the feet become wings, which we covet and expect by and by? I have a mighty fine notion of *my* flesh, and hesitate to think it bears a freight of saurian monsters, circulates megatherium blood, had a mastodon's bulk for its crib, is the bier on which myriad relics of vital antiquity are borne, and shall find its own grave and revival in who knows what coming animated forms! But why should I be made of finer stuff? God has no porcelain, but one clay; and all the vital fluid at bottom is the same. The materialist tells me he doubts immortality, not being able to credit the reassembling of his particles; and he says to the bereaved, "I have neither faith nor philosophy to comfort you." But we do not want the particles reassembled! When my body has dropped, let it go. It is mine no longer. I have no more use for it: let me be reclothed! The theory of human nature as part of a grand evolution, instead of a haughty pillar standing alone, and so more apt to tumble down, encourages my hope. If we survive, it is not by travel, but transformation, another step of development above ourselves, as we are above something else that went before. The problem of futurity is how to get one species into another, — the species man into the species angel; and, on the doctrine of strictly specific creation or inconvertibility of species, our expectation could not flourish, but suffers fatal blight. If man has got out of an immemorial infancy into his present altitude, what limits shall be put to his ascent? It is all dark and unseen. But humanity once was out of sight and reach as are the cherubim and seraphim now.

How shall we come to port across the sea? God, whom we launched and sailed from, cannot surprise us with the celestial more than the terrestrial shore. As, in the Pacific, some wave lifts the sailor's boat over the reef into the lagoon, we shall rise. Such faith is not damped, but kindled, by the idea that man was made not, according to the supposed Scripture chronology, by a sudden thought, six thousand years ago, — but was from measureless cycles looked forward to, with long-minded plan, in the least structure and faintest beginning of organized life. If I was thought of so early, contemplated before the morning-stars sang together, from the foundation of the world; if the great Architect had in view every room and column of my proportions in his original design, so that each joint of form and fit of faculty has an antiquity to which the Pyramids are but yesterday, and the globe itself but as a painter's easel; if the sky be the Artist's chamber, and time my Author's stepping-stone, — then may I not believe that the care for me, which was from everlasting, will be to everlasting; and sing with David, "Thou wilt not leave my soul in the grave;" and say with Jesus, "Now come I to thee"?

XII.

CORRELATION.

THE mind seeks unity. He has no genius for philosophy who is seduced and satisfied with any multiplicity, trinity, or duality. The heart, too, is content only with the One, mistake that One though it may. The dissipated man is he whose affection roves among a thousand objects, however he abstain from sensual indulgence. But the true soul loves one worth, delights in one beauty appearing in many forms. Also, the conscience discerns one right in manifold circumstances and cases of business, personal intercourse, and social reform: as Cicero said so long ago, sublimely, "There is not one law at Athens, and another at Rome." The soul, moreover, worships one Spirit. The sin of idolatry consists not simply in fastening veneration on an outward thing; but the moment it is diverted from the Infinite Unity, it will be distracted among "gods many and lords many," and catch up any fancy for its fetish. The objection to defining religion as "a recognition of the facts and laws of the universe" is not only that it misses the sense of Deity, — the trembling and peace of the breast, — but that, beside leaving out person, it divides thought.

Yet difference is not duplicity. All diversity is unity produced, as a million sunbeams continue the sun. It is the radiation of God. It is the graduation of essence into substance, and of substance into existence. It is extension of centre into circumference, and general into particular; there being no special providence of exception to eternal rule. Deuce is the devil. There are no *two* where the second is not part or repetition of the first and last — alpha and omega — to whom will go the homage which we must pay, if we do not pervert. He will idolize who does not adore. The materialist, who scorns the notion of prayer, adopts a huger idol fashioned to his hand than was ever set up in Mexican temple or savage hut.

In the modern doctrine of correlation of forces is a blazing illustration of this unitary quality. Correlation of truths and duties is as perfect as of the parallels and meridians of the globe. We sail on a great circle when we heed the smallest obligation. An eminent man, reproached with having been a drummer when he was a boy, asked, "Didn't I drum well?" When Mr. Bergh collects half a bushel of cunningly concealed spurs from beneath the horses' bits in Central Park, how distinguish his from any apostle's benevolent zeal?

There is, then, such a central unity in the human frame, we can let on our entire strength for any task, — as the Merrimac turns a spindle, or the Cochituate throws up a column, with the complete height and weight of its uppermost tide. We say of a man prompt in action, cordial in salutation, or zealous for any end, he is not double-minded or half-hearted, but whole-souled.

One power in diverse manifestation is the lesson of Nature. Light, heat, electricity, magnetism, and motion are the same essence, convertible into each other, displaying that single manifold Force we call God, in the physical universe.

The same fact is in our constitution. The senses — sight, hearing, taste, smell, touch — are different modes of perception, and meet in one sensorium.

Moreover, the faculties of the mind — memory, judgment, imagination, wit, and will — express the various activity of the one intellect, or inmost knowing instinct, which remembers, imagines, chooses, invents, or compares.

So with the character. Truth, justice, love, goodness, courage, mercy, are not contradictory or alien one from the other. An identical conscience is distributed to the need of the hour. All the virtues of behavior are offspring of one virtue in the breast; and if a man is guilty in one point, he is guilty of all. As, in the fountain on the Common, the same water is played through a number of jets into the likeness of a pillar, a flower, or a fan, — all that is requisite being to have a head of water to which to fit every mouthpiece, — so good affection streams into whatever conduct our relations determine, or the occasion demands. Outward integrity means this complete equipment from one holy purpose.

We are governed by circumstances, say some. Not we, only the lines of our activity. The power or quality of our purpose is not governed by circumstances. Is the lightning governed by the lightning-rod? The circumstances are only the conductors of the "centre-stances," in our motives and aims, be they low and selfish, or lofty and humane. Wind and wave are circumstances. Is the pilot victim of circumstances when the ship is cast away, or of his own ignorance and negligence? The same circumstances carried other vessels to port. The *Scotia* arrives and the *Cambria* goes down in the same gale. By the same temptations which some souls founder in others are sped.

We think one moral property higher or better than another. But each is of tantamount worth. Justice is as good as benevolence. Truth is never contrary to mercy. Courage does not withstand meekness. Self-respect is not opposed to humility. All these traits are but the methods one intent operates through by turns. To be master of the situation is to know which part of speech in the voice and word of God is in order, what temper to show, what stand with interlocutors or interactors to take. Doing with the sum total of our being what Providence in the premises calls for, that is perfection.

The judge dispenses equity on the bench. Stern we call him, or inexorable. But is it not kindness to the criminal to arrest him in his course? Were it not unkind to the community to let him go scot-free?

We protest against the enacting of hell on earth in this horrid business of war. A war of words is declared against Bismarck, and a woman's congress called for peace. But whether fighting is wrong depends on whether it is in place, — the thing in the

Divine plan at the time to be done. You see the refuse of the field, at certain seasons, raked together by the farmer, and the heap set on fire. What is war but the flame with which the great Husbandman burns up the refuse of sin and folly in the field of the world? Is it necessary, unavoidable, this Judgment-day? Then it is divine. The Prussian minister wishes to unify Germany, and out of a bundle of States like loosened rods to make a great nation. France is jealous that Germany will be too strong, as England was that America would; and war is the incident he has to encounter in his design, and must manage as he best may. It was the incident we had to encounter for the same purpose, — to preserve, bind together, and new-create our own land. At last, the French fight not for conquest but national self-preservation. Is the soldier, the volunteer, or drafted, instrument to this end, on either side a savage wild beast and mere brute? Should we allow anybody to say it in our case? No: the man who, when fighting alone was left the last resort and means of salvation for country, for liberty, for humanity, fought and fell in the trench or wilderness, on the plain, or bloody slippery deck when the *Cumberland* went down, not hating his enemy or the public enemy, whom yet he saw it was indispensable to overcome, — that man died as nobly as any passive sufferer persecuted to death, burnt or hung by religious or political foes. "I have no ill-will to the South," said Putnam: "I hope they will fight well."

The martyr is thought a grander character than the hero. Either is alike grand, as either is fit for the hour. When one said, "John Brown made the gallows glorious like the cross," some were shocked that should be said of the armed invader of Harper's Ferry. But his purpose, in the sublime bravery of attacking a sovereign State with a handful of men, and the patience as sublime of submitting to the sentence of the court, — remarking, as he went to the gibbet, on the beauty of the Virginia hills, — were the same temper that Master and apostle showed on Roman engines of torture. He bound up martyr and hero in his own person.

One soul moved by one Spirit maintains its level best in every exigency. We speak of cardinal virtues. But every virtue is cardinal that is seasonable. Only put the whole of yourself into the errand of the moment, as the ocean makes high tide successively at each point of the shore. The spider sits in the centre of its web of myriad strands. Whatever interferes with one of those gossamer lines draws the whole creature bodily, in watch and act, to that point. A many-sided man we style him whose talent applies at all quarters with equal ease. Cast your entire vitality and eternal redemption on a hair-breadth of instant responsibility, as our Chicago brothers did at the fire.

A woman is insulted, and the sphere of her sensibility invaded. She knows it, and the villain-invader knows. Her whole womanhood rises to resent and repel the hostile or disrespectful approach. The schoolmen said the whole of God is in every particle: the whole of her is at the point of menace. She is gentle and humble, charitable, a Lady Bountiful, gracious and sweet as summer to your courtesy. But your rude encroachment shall discover how much less terrible the wrath of the lion than the wrath of the lamb. The recoil from indecency, affront at insolent familiarity, rebuff of injury, is as lofty, becomes her as much, pleases God as truly, and is entered in as shining letters in the recording angel's book, as her most generous gifts and loving accents and winning looks, by which, with parallel closeness, some other position is matched. The soul has no *corps de réserve.* All is engaged. Run, without scruple, to the obligation now ringing at the door. It has been said, by a famous doctor of divinity, Jesus would not have driven the traders out of the temple at the close of his career. A scourge for others less became him whose crucifixion was his crown! But that Father's business he was about having many departments and details, — now a disputation with the doctors, and now a last supper with his friends, — whatever demonstration was timely, each diverse performance or endurance that embodied unqualified devotion proved the same worth; and he needs not the apology of some that the lash may have lighted only on the lazy oxen, unconscious of profaning the marble shrine, when it belonged so much more richly to the human chafferers that were switched out. It was the *same* whole and faithful soul, changing its operation as the conditions changed, that fell to the ground with the bloody sweat in the Garden. He was not in the despair which radical and conservative theologians suppose. But the burdens were so great, he had to summon all his strength, even that he ordinarily used to stand up with, to sustain them.

With economy, he accomplished every jot of the design before him there and then. At a hard question we drop the head, because we need the power it is held up by to think with. Some persons, when they wish to reflect expeditiously and with all their might, lie down at full length. Jesus prostrated himself, to concentrate his capacity for what Heaven bade, — not to give up!

This is the sum of morals. For what work strikes the clock? Meet the emergency, be it action or resignation, in zeal or self-control, with all the genius that lies in you, — now for speed, anon masterly inactivity, as the engine uses the same pressure of steam to go forward or back. Each is good, each is best alternately, according to the object in view. But each must have the whole power, whichever way it goes on the track. Do not try to move two ways at once, with your mind more than with your vehicle. The result is obliquity and overthrow, not rectitude in either. There is no such thing as "a divided duty:" 'tis always simple. The eye cannot look on two things, even separate panes of glass, with the same glance, but passes with lightning rapidity from the first to the second. Yet a covert purpose or by-end, instead of the ostensible one, is the great sin of mankind. We call it diplomacy, policy, expediency: "All which words," I heard my friend say, "I hate." We say of a man, who is always after something other than he professes or pretends, that he has two crowns in his head, making a type of the hair which in some heads is confused by curling to a point in two circles, and hard to comb out. The real man or woman is often so twisted as to be impossible to get at. There is no simplicity, or central and all-absorbing affection or aim. "There are two," is said of an inconsistent man. Sometimes there are twenty. How many a friend will assign false motives for his conduct! He has neglected us somehow, and wants to excuse himself. So he tells how much he wanted to be with us, but had to go elsewhere. "I wanted to be in your house, or at church." No: you did not. People do what they want to! You want to keep your friend, but not your vow. As easily serve God and Mammon; as soon pull opposite poles together. A fictitious reason for what we do or fail to do is the commonest lie, and the worst; for it is a lie we cannot prove upon anybody, or properly charge him with. It is lying in that interior sphere we cannot presume to inspect. The lie of circumstance, saying the thing that is not, is harmless in comparison. For *that* we can provide some antidote. If you have prevaricated in act, prevaricate not also in speech. Your apology is the dirty sponge, adding more uncleanness than it removes. We do not want a part or fraction. "Out upon this half-faced fellowship!" Neutrality, indifference, facing both ways, says Dante, is hateful to God and to the enemies of God.

Concentred energy is the miracle. The man in the lighthouse or observatory is all eye, and can see a glint of the tossing bark, far off in the storm, when you can see nothing. It is because the whole of him sees. You did not notice? Your inadvertence is your fault. Perception is integrity. Not to mind is not to obey. There is a correlation of the vices.

Do not cheating and lies, drunkenness and lust, the spendthrift and thief, go together? Take home one of Satan's relations, and the whole family will follow. Be profuse, and you will be mean: be ungenerous, and you will be unjust. "*Economy is revenue*," thundered the British orator. Frugality is the fund of charity. "Be just, before you are generous"? No: be just, and you will be generous. The politeness of the man that has just swindled me was part of his theft: it was the velvet over the claw. Does he see how he wrongs himself, like the mower striking at a harmless creature with the handle of his scythe, and cutting off his own head with the blade? Profanity in the street puts on another guise in the sanctuary. But does an honest oath break with God more than a formal prayer?

Excellencies cluster like grapes. In our version, "add to your faith, knowledge," with the rest of the list, the figure of a *chorus* in the Greek word is lost. *Three Graces*, *nine Muses*, *three Furies*, — always a choir! Every virtue, said the sage doctor, hangs round filial piety. In our cheap moralizing, we set the heart and head in opposition. But, when Napoleon's brother complained of the Emperor's want of affection, he answered, "My love has the dimensions of my mind," — not weak fondling of a kinsman, but legislation for Europe!

Thought is correlate of feeling, goes as deep in the mind of God or man. The preacher in doubting this is a sentimentalist, not a sage. We oppose the inward to the outward. They are not antagonist, but part and counterpart. The wind that bloweth where it listeth sometimes rises within and sometimes breezes from without. I have felt it in a Quaker meeting, and through the Lord's Supper, making every vessel, touched by departed saints, dear. Any way, every way, and always, let us turn to take it with our sails.

The vital point is that which the physicist overlooks. In the relations he loses the relationship. What is the correlating power but the Living Absolute, whose rest is all motion, whose abode is in every reference, and whose immutability ceaseless change? In vain to separate the spectacle into portions, make specialties of study, and affirm there are only phenomena. The countless drops run out of and into one. To that which renders it possible for a single energy or element to appear now as light and now as electricity, now as memory and now as judgment, now as rectitude and now as wisdom, now as vision and now as love, now a principle and now a rite, we must bend.

The correlation of human qualities arises from that of the Divine attributes. It is a false notion of both Orthodox and Liberal that God's equity was ever postponed or preferred to his pity. The laws of justice are not confounded in some mixture or after-thought called mercy, as forgiveness outright, or a composition for offenders by some innocent proxy suffering in their stead. There is no such misprision of treason, or compounding of felony, or partaking of crime. Leniency to a bad man may be the greatest cruelty. Indulgence is a morass of surrender where no virtue of kindness or sincerity can plant its foot, or a fellow-creature be reached with help. The Deity is no weakling to set us such an example. Let our demand of honor and infliction of discipline emulate his! His retribution is not revenge, but kindness suited to the case. Mercy does not so much, as Shakspeare says, *temper* justice, as express it; and law is the hand of love.

Human callings are correlative. What iniquity to set one honest trade against another, or make capitalists and artisans foes! The correlation of manual and mental labor is the core of political economy. The provoker of a duel betwixt them forgets their common bond. He is a superficial moralist to classify, as the old mineralogists did their stones, not by inward nature but external marks. Is not the body concerned in all labor? Yet labor is never a thing of mere muscle or nerve. Are not intelligence, will, fidelity, and the sweat of the brow alike in the student's and the digger's task? The mechanic often gets better wages for easier effort than the poet or the priest, who sometimes come near to starve. Some of the law-offices and one-half the pulpits are less remunerative than the master-carpenter's shop. The toil of the man that makes my road, lays out my grounds, turns my rock ravine into a stairway to the sea, and beneath boulders and rough fragments — the wreck of ages — discovers a beach, I rate as of more value than some sermons and prayers. Were all the mechanics employed in rearing the temple, or do some conduct the exercises within? Ceremonies may be more lifeless than any tools, trowel or axe. There are automatons in the professions; there are thinkers in the mill and field; and he may add less value to the Commonwealth who hammers at an argument or homily than he who beats on a lap-stone or a nail. How brainless or unfair not to heed the finer conscientious property which may appear in any avocation, and is absent from the unfaithful in every class, but should unite all! The agitator assumes a conflict of interests that does not exist. He is a fish so used to troubled waters, that he feels lost and not at home, unable to swim, in the smooth. In default of an angel, he descends himself to stir up the pool, in which none will be healed. With no mystic quality of worshipping God in history or sympathetic imagination of mankind, his mind has a cruel edge. Sincere and earnest he may be, but without wisdom or depth.

No pursuit is virtuous, only some man in every pursuit. Let us not be deceived by appearances. You are looking in the wrong place, we say to one who discerns not some object or resemblance we point out. How continually we do that! Before a picture of a dying soldier and of a sister of charity, a keen discerner of look and posture said, "I see the religion here in the face and figure of the wounded man more than of the woman who assumes to be its minister." Were the missionaries, who sent a tract about the impenitent thief to distribute in the army, themselves more honest than the brave troops that went down to the bloody plain?

We set the Past against the Future. They are friends. "Does he approve your view?" I was very recently asked, respecting a great scholar. "Not now," was my reply; "but when it becomes history he will." He that but conceives a thought finds in another's expression of it only a premature birth. But tradition and inspiration agree;

> And sage experience doth attain
> To something like prophetic strain."

If the critic denies only to define, restricts and excludes error to affirm truth, is he not conservative? Let me never write a line nor speak a word whose object is to pull down! I would only tear away to build, and blow up to arrest the fire, — as Jesus destroyed to fulfil. In a battery is the positive hostile to the negative pole? The organizer has no quarrel with the seer. Without vision every institution would decay, like a body unsupplied with fresh blood. The humblest members have no strife with the highest. When my head failed, I took to my feet. On the vessel's deck, amid burning sand, under the peak of Teneriffe, through the pine barrens of Florida, and along the Atlantic shore, I walked back into heart and brain some drop of feeling, some spark of thought. Society is a growth; and he is a public enemy who would interrupt its continuity, or thinks to cure its diseases by taking it apart. But it feeds on truth as new as last year's wheat. It is —

> "One army of the living God."

But does the host incur danger from the scouts it sends ahead, to be in Milton's phrase "all ear"? Abernethy detected disease at a glance. Let us honor the political physician who notes and treats the nation's ills.

In the vast system, let each, resigning selfish independence, act his part and receive his just income of love and peace. "Keep to the right as the law directs!" Ask only what belongs to you. The world is large. There is room for me and thee. Do friends drop off and favors cease? It is no accident. Do not regret or deprecate, do not wish or forebode. Let go what is not by eternal affinity yours. Your tax you cannot avoid, your property you will never lose. "I will not strain myself," said Daniel Webster, "to kill a fly." The bar that keeps you out you cannot break: the bolt admitting you turns with ease. This correlation is God's high chancellor to see that justice is done. Do you disparage my service, and drop out of the circle of my companions and friends; and do you justify your desertion with poor apologies, putting your disloyalty on false grounds? Waste not so your words, nor spend a thought or breath on the matter! I shall not suffer: take care of yourself, and have no alarm for me. Like the watchers in the judges' boat at the regatta on the river or the sea, God has his sentinels in the heart to secure fair play and punish foul. I shall make up in self-respect for your discountenance, just as, with my humility, I shall set limits to your praise. What are the scales on your court-house to Heaven's universal balance? Great evils to the black man were predicted from the abolition of slavery. But a right to his own earnings supplies motive better than came from the lash.

> "Nebber you fear, though nebber you hear
> The driver blow his horn."

Against all temptations to treachery one thought is an overweight, — that of being a pure instrument of truth. The idea of God's service, in that of his creatures, clean of all pride or vanity, or lust of gain or count of worldly success, stirs a joy with which no human favor can compare. Applause is a passing, pattering rain; popularity, the morning cloud and early dew: benefit is the well springing up unto everlasting life.

XIII.

CHARACTER.

WHAT reason the Oriental had to suppose divinity or divination in dreams I know not; only that I dreamed being in a great conference discussing Jesus Christ, till his name flew back and forth as between battle-door and shuttlecock, when at last he himself rose in the meeting to hush and astonish all with the words, "Touch me not!" What meant that repulse of Mary after the reported resurrection? Was he a ghost, such as Homer or Virgil tells of, whom the hand would pass through? Did he reserve his first greeting for another? Rather, saluting Mary and asking Thomas to test his flesh and blood reality, he yet declares to the fond woman, The time to dote on me is past: God whom I go to is as much your Father as mine. Let no critic call rude his rejection of whatever sign of regard she so naturally rushed to give! He threw cold water on her affectionate zeal to concentrate its flame for the shaping of all duty at the forge of her heart.

This was the topmost round of Christ's character. One step above self-sacrifice on the cross was the self-abnegation after the crucifixion. Not that he would disparage himself. He knew and asserted he was a showing of God; but, having shown him, he would retire. What appearance on the stage could match such self-withdrawal! Does any action transcend a graceful taking leave? He was a medium, whose virtue is to display the object, — like a window where nothing but the entry lamp is visible within. "You cannot see him: he is behind his Master," said Father Taylor, of a famous preacher. You see not the *Master* as he reveals the all-informing soul; as you do not the man who unveils a picture in some great cathedral, to be the valet of its beauty the business of his life. On the Wengern Alp I admired the spotless air that hid and denied itself, to draw the Jungfrau from its ten-miles distance almost to touch my eye. This temper of self-renunciation Jesus hinted not at the close only, but throughout his career. He resented being called good: he was willing anybody should speak against *him*, but not against the Holy Ghost. He insisted it was expedient for him to go away, to introduce the Comforter whom his longer stay would eclipse, but whose coming would lead beyond his lessons into all truth. What finer incident in history than that after the walk to Emmaus, when at the village table the old gesture in breaking bread betrayed and they knew him, and "he vanished out of their sight"! As the absence of his statue brought Brutus to mind, Christ was manifest less in his advent than his exit. It is a paradox of beauty. His arrest of us is his refusing to be stopped with. Did Cæsar or Cromwell or Washington decline the crown? *He* would be neither king nor idol. "Oh, that is *he!*" we say, when some man's quality is spoken of. We have Jesus only in being passed on by him. To worship him, if it be Orthodoxy, is infidelity and rejection of Christianity, and flat contradiction of his own bidding. To make him a finality is to make him a fetish. As an idol we lose him altogether. In the novel "Jane Eyre," Rochester says he could seize the woman he loves, but the essence he seeks would be gone. O fond believer! in your so tight grasp of your Lord, you miss him. Only your light touch of him, feeling after what he stood representative for, can appreciate him. *Let me alone*, he says to those who would still hang upon him. This is not his peculiarity. Of all true regard for friend or fellow-creature, the proof is not gross demonstration but delicacy, penetrating through the outward form and bearing to what they mean and are missionaries of. When Montaigne says, "I offer myself faintly and bluntly to him whose I most effectually am," he puts a good understanding before any kiss or caress. To every ecclesiastical sentimentalist Jesus gives this tonic: Live not for me, but the objects I live for; love not me as you do the righteous will. Did God, in a phrase lately controverted, take "an inferior man" for his instrument? This is supreme manhood. Pick a flaw, who will, in the diamond, to which those are dirt that have just been discovered in South Africa; find, if you can, cloud or stain in the pearl from the hand of the great Lapidary as he makes up his jewels. But this is indeed Milton's "human face divine." It is to reach the zenith, and touch the horizon of our utmost conception.

Do I tempt to a more refined idolatry? Not in

denoting a virtue whose beauty is a bond. It were a stride for a self-worshipper to adore such a character, or even an image, a bit of painted cloth, flag, or emblem; any thing but the gaudy butterfly or golden calf he is! When one expostulated with Mr. Thackeray for making young people talk so silly in his books, he said, "Nonsense! you can't make them talk half silly enough!" But, O flatterer of the Lord! Jesus is too busy for your adulation. He does not wait to smell this everlasting smoke of your incense. Do not keep me, he says: and I must not detain *you*. My business is to forward these goods I am trusted with. Have I introduced you to God? Let me stand aside. Engage in and enjoy the conversation.

With that sublime soul, to put one's end above one's self, then, is the method of character. Do your work, and divert attention from your hand in it. The fine actor is lost in the personage he represents, the orator in the theme of his discourse, the singer in the melody he chants, the poet in the verse he writes, and every artist, builder, agent, in the business Heaven sends him on. What does Michel Angelo know of bending his neck out of joint, painting the ceiling of the Sistine Chapel? What does John the Baptist resolve himself into but a voice in the wilderness? So Garrison did in the land slavery was making a worse desert. Why did John Brown think the sovereign State of Virginia and whole South no disproportionate antagonist, but that his cause was more than Union or nation? The best work everywhere is that of those absorbed in it,—like the silk-worm in the cocoon it weaves for its shroud; the bee lost in the heart of the flower it sucks; the coral insect, continent-builder, in the rocky reef. Self-oblivion is God's remembrance. The glass of admiring eyes is a fragile preserver. Service of God in your kind is a safe which the last fire will not crumble. That is a Raphael, we say of the picture on the wall. Is Raphael in it at full length? No: figures of others, — the Holy Family, angels that stoop, or cherubs that peep. That is Beethoven! It is an orchestra, playing his symphonies, till his bronze fades from your misty eyes. That is Shakspeare. Yes, most hid when most revealed; less apparent in the self-referring sonnets than in the disinterested plays: all the *dramatis personæ* but the metes of his personality, a dwarf in the incidents of his biography, a seraph that soars and sings in his immortal lines. The locomotive is splendid, speeding on its track; but modestly slipping aside, its task done, unseen, to let its living load roll into the station, has a peculiar charm. In all Dr. Channing's writings the sentence that always moved me most was that ending the Preface to his first volume. "In truth, I shall see with no emotion but joy these fugitive productions forgotten and lost in the superior brightness of writings consecrated to the work of awakening in the human soul a consciousness of its divine and immortal powers." So Jesus says, Not me, but my purpose, my method, my direction, my affection for God and man, — in these my mission is fulfilled; the new Jerusalem has many avenues; arrive at your station how you will!

But has not his character another side? What say of his conscious exaltation? his singular and unparalleled self-respect? We will say there is no self-interest! It is all instrumentality. He is illustrator, and his word illustration, of something deeper. He would have us follow him, as we follow a demonstration in geometry on the blackboard. Is it for the demonstrator's sake, or the truth's sake? It is what we follow to: as we follow a guide up the Alps or into the Adirondacks; as we prospect for gold mines in California, — not for the guide, but for the view or the treasure; as the Spaniards followed Cortez when he drew with his sword in the Mexican sands a line for the brave part of his army to cross, and cowards to go back. Such the only following Jesus asks, not to his honor, but the common weal. Follow him? We follow that in him which says, *Touch me not*, — and, like those men of Galilee, gazing up after him into heaven, find ourselves in the infinite unseen, with him somehow still. Well for the simple and unlearned then or now to follow him; but, when you follow truth and God, the personal following of him may cease. To those who knew not what to follow, he gave the command. "Have you experienced religion?" an unlettered woman of eighty was asked by the priest who would make a proselyte. "Yes, so far as I have practised it," was the reply. Such Jesus would have, not for followers, but peers; not servants, but friends.

But self-forgetfulness is not self-support. Jesus speaks of his glory he had before the world was. Is it not what we call the Ideal? He had an elevator. As the stream runs into your house from a head of water, as the wheat yonder at the Western Railway without stint flows down from a building raised high in air, so from what fathomless fund and storehouse of thought his disinterestedness was drawn! Why speculate so much? says the practical man. Why not go and *do* something, like the missionaries? But, after the missionaries have sailed a thousand leagues and sacrificed themselves with homesickness, exposure, and hard fare, what is it for the Sandwich Islanders, and heathen in Hindostan, they do, but proclaim certain views? The views, then, are of some importance: what is every act but the offspring of a sentiment? To the critic, wondering we should beat and puzzle our brains over the problems of the universe, we say, For every particle of pure truth, caught in pure vision or assayed from the crude ore of accepted creeds, our meeting or meditation is not in vain, more than the enterprise of diggers in the California mines. My friend admitted the correctness of my essay, but justified the current opinion on the ground of the necessity of some alloy to prevent wear and make the truth pass. But alloy we can pick up plenty in the street. How if the supply of virgin gold fail? Why has the world not drained the Jewish Master dry, and spent long ago the last farthing of the Christian faith, but because of the immense Bank he leaned on, that honored his drafts? O my busy brother, God speed your benevolent plans! But, to get along, we must have, not only the rolling stock, rails and driving wheels of some association or church order, but the locomotive power; and he that gives us only more and better vapor, — call it mere breath if you will, steam from human lips, — is in place, and his word as good as any deed! Has not what Jesus said, more than what he did, insured his longevity? What he said was no cut and dried scheme. He made it up, or it made itself, as he went along waiting upon God, holding Nature in solution in his mind, and putting character into every tone. In the conventional notion he is nothing but a Preceptor to his pupils, with the downward look. But what were his downward look without his upward one? He united his vision with sincerity, and was not double to different men, like those esoteric and exoteric clocks, on the outside and inside of railway stations, that never agree. He *grew*, says Luke: did he ever get his growth? That were the end of him; stoppage of soul or body is certain death. Call the sexton, then, to make a grave for both! Do you not deny for him the very immortality Paul says he brought to light, when you disown his progress, and say he had exhausted God, though having all of him his flesh could contain? Full of the element he floated in, how his capacity enlarged! Treading the line of beauty, where did his feet find the end, or what proof is there it was enough for him to tread it for us, and not we for ourselves? I should as soon think of the iron filings drawn to a magnet, or bits of down to an electric jar, emptying the fluid that pervades the world, as of his or any sayings or doings expressing the whole creation's life, or Creator's peace and joy, to illustrate not substantiate which he came and taught. His was the Ideal method; but are we bound to his Ideal, could we exactly find it out? No, but to our own. There is justly no more than one. It belongs not to him, but to all, availed of in whatever diverse degree. For a ship, to be of the fleet, need not take the same way to the same port or fight, in an exact mathematical line after the flag-ship. We are in Christ's convoy so far as we sympathize in his style. His style in character, as well as in chronology, affects us still.

Do not imitate him, we are told: deal at first hand with God. But God is no abstraction. We are part of him, and Jesus is part, in proportion to his worth. The society, State, church, household we live in, as well as stars that shine over us, are members of Deity, some hand or finger of God; and by the laws of life we reach him over every causeway that is portion of himself. "I put myself," says our friend, "squarely outside of Christianity." That, were it psychologically possible, were to be so far outside of God. We have a horror of examples; but the worst one is that which we often in our prejudice set ourselves. We are inside of all human life. There is no such thing as a come-outer. Everybody, as one said of himself, is a stay-inner, and Christian in some sense. As the eye searches in the sky for the Pointers to find the North Star, so we see his traits in line with that pole of truth we too must steer by. However clouded, is it not in our firmament as big and steady as in his?

"But an Ideal greater than he is, which we make for ourselves!" exclaimed a good doctor of divinity, in surprise. No, we never made it, more than we did Orion or the Pleiads. God makes it; he *is* it! Purely individual we cannot be. In every man is the Ideal, greater than any man and all men, or Jesus himself.

Such an Ideal had not Washington and Lincoln of a patriotism, which no details of service could expend, to make their names splendid myths of love of country when all the incidents and anecdotes shall be forgot? It is no accident. The human heart makes no mistake, more than God. The selfish, blustering, belligerent demagogue of the hour, with whom God seems not to exist when he mentions him, can reach no such fame. Of all excellence this Ideal property is the span, the last touch and first breath. There is nothing so small or low it does not bend to, or bend to itself. Which is the best picture, — that eked out every inch, as you have seen a cataract, mountain, iceberg, with a painstaking Chinese brush; or that conceived, swept and played upon with some humanizing design, finding in form and color but its language and silent tongue? William Hunt never took his brush but with such intent. Which is the best orchestra, — that which renders every piece like a great music-box, or that which turns pipe and string to such expression as to bear you like a wind to some heavenly shore? "It is too much sail to carry," said one at a pathetic performance. "It means," replied another, "you shall carry sail somewhere else." Who is the best speaker, — he that grinds or saws out with set teeth his sentences, or he that transpires what he is inspired with? Who accomplishes most anywise, — he that goes doggedly to work, as the Esquimaux make their dogs draw their sleds over ice and snow, or he that opens his faculties to be blown upon from above and plants them in the river of God, — as the miller makes breeze and water-fall turn his vans and wheels to more account than by any crank under his hands?

This vision is not for show, like gilt pipes on the old organs. In nothing is such use. The Indian had it when he praised a United States President, and pronounced him polite, for turning his back so as not to see how much his guest ate or drank. So in our war had the wounded soldier, with a bleeding mouth and burning thirst, refusing the officer's canteen lest with his blood he should hurt it for the other men. When Putnam, going to the Potomac, said, "Mother, it is easy to give life, terrible to take it," he bore the glory of Christ's lowly boast under his lieutenant's belt. The man had it who took me up on the windy road, and apologized for the little room in his chaise. Our friend had it when he said, not "go but come to the war." The Pilgrims had it when those staying behind wondered what such fools were thinking of; and they made us color-bearers of their idea, alive not to drop what will glorify us when we die. The savages in Central Africa, says a late traveller, still prick the image of the cross into their own skins, and weave it into their saddles. Do we not learn from our Fathers to abjure showy emblems for humane sufferings and deeds?

Action from spiritual perception, to form character, must complete the proof. When the English collier, in his bucket with the broken rope, cries, "*From under!*" to those at the bottom of the shaft; when the French soldier begs the surgeon to keep his ether for those worse wounded, and stuffs his bloody handkerchief into his mouth to bear without noise the unrelieved knife; when the fallen dying acrobat sings out, "Look after those girls on the trapeze;" when the conductor runs forward on the track to save a little child, and clears the stroke of the engine by a single foot; when the engineer sticks to his locomotive rushing to ruin like Cooper's boatswain going down with the *Ariel*, — of something more than mortal there is proof. Can you renounce the life you desire, turn your back on the heaven you conceive, — willing, as said Dr. Hopkins, to be damned for the glory of God, or like Paul to be a cast-away, accursed for your kind? Do you consent to be annihilated if that be best? You have what you give up! Relinquishment is possession, and death your mortgage on life. "I refuse not to die," said Paul to Festus. How kill what said that?

It is I, but not mine; it is you, but not yours. God can take care of his property! Calvin's God is Saturn over again devouring his own children. Love is executor of Law. These two have no mediator but whatever as momentary priest puts them in immediate relation, to pronounce them one. A Boston minister says, "What weight in the Sermon on the Mount from the authority of Him that said it!" Indeed, is the sermon true because he said it; or did he say it because it was true? Does authority or inspiration make truth; or does truth make authority and inspiration? "The mistake is," says the same minister, "to set truth before Christ." Then he made that mistake; for he set the truth he was but part of before himself. The worst sign of the times is this putting of what Webster, replying to Hayne, calls "mutual quotation and commendation," in place of free inquiry, in our religious press.

"Touch me not!" We cannot touch him till we

are transparent with goodness like him. Our Lord? He is the beggar whom the seeker of the Holy Grail shares his crust with, be he German or French; as he was the child Christopher bore over the stream. When one proposed in convention to resolve Christianity into love to God and man, it was objected, this is the end to which Christianity is the means. But as we learn to vote by voting, walk by walking, and to swim by swimming; as in the race or regatta the starting-point is to the rounding boat also the goal, — so I know no way to love God and man but by loving them.

We object to calling Christ a man, as if to be such were mean: "A poor thing," said the poet Daniels, "unless above himself he can erect himself." Christ's character is a flower human nature could not bloom into, and a fruit that never grew on the family tree! Which does this doctrine decry, mankind or its author? Have we ascertained the capacity of the soul, as we measure the cubic contents of a ship or puncheon? Do we know what is coming out of it before the time? Who predicted Homer, Shakespeare, Raphael! We are told of ghosts so substantial as to have their photographs taken; but no portraits of such as have never existed or been embodied. Those who maintain that Jesus, without human father, was begotten of the Holy Ghost, do not deny he had all the parts and properties of a man. Had any organ, faculty, affection, been wanting, he would have been a monster, and every moment of his life, each breath he drew, a new miracle. Had he shown any virtue beyond others' reach to practise, it would equally defy their ability to admire or understand. Your praise is your potential possession of any excellence, in intellect or morals, in science or art, music, painting, poetry, or eloquent speech. Were it not latent in us as a susceptibility which culture might unfold into accomplishment, we could not have the glow of one heart-beat of delight in it. We could not shout at the oration, clap in the concert-room, or say Amen to the prayer. Do I know what it was for Jesus to hang on the cross, or drop the bloody sweat in the garden? Then I could have agonized and hung there. The stupid crowd that throw up their caps with one genuine throb of gratitude or cordial cheer of applause, as the hero or deliverer passes by, could every one have dared or suffered as much as Grant at Richmond, or Washington at Valley Forge. Did twenty millions of men compose the funeral procession when Lincoln's body was borne across the States to the tomb? Every sincere mourner had in him the germ of the great President's martyrdom. Not a trait of the master but is a copy of the disciple's latent worth. Nothing actual in Jesus that is not possible in you and in the feeblest babe in the crib.

It is not only incorrect, but injurious, to shut off from the common soul any merit, or say it can only be imputed or imparted, never indigenous; as if goodness were not native to the mind, but only immigrant or an import. Superhuman is it? Then certainly I shall not try for it! Why should a man strain after something beyond his manhood? "*Stop!* STOP!" cried a lad with his carpet-bag to a railway train gliding from the station. I might as well try to arrest qualities I cannot emulate. "What is the use of his running?" said a fellow-passenger to me of a person who expected to overtake the cars getting full under-way. We do not want an unattainable standard held up before us. It would be insult to our will, mockery of our weakness, discouragement of our hope. Arch-angelic displays, by a being different in kind from us, would but tantalize and torment.

But I challenge this peculiar superiority of traditional and historic virtue. The preacher describes the transcendent truth, love, meekness, conscience, self-sacrifice, and says it is no use to attempt: you cannot be as good as that. It can be passed over to your credit if you believe in the atonement; but cannot, save by favor of the pleading and dying Advocate, be really your own. Every honest drop of blood resents this fiction of the court, which theologians fancy for their forensic God, and tingles with the assertion that *it* too can flow with sincerity or flow out an offering to any worthy cause; as it did ten years ago, to drench the land it saved,—not boastful blood, though claiming the right to give itself, and running so freely! What strikes us in these empty-sleeved, scarred men, is their making so little of what they did or endured in *their* wilderness on the Potomac, or Gethsemane of the Mississippi; their silence, abstinence from profession, having to be drawn out to speak of the scenes they passed through, and using the lowest terms in their description, the farthest from travellers' tales, and regarding all as within the line of simple duty. What sin mixed with their holocaust? Always so in tasks and trials that are sublime.

I do not disparage past example, or dishonor the holy biography, in saying it is matched by present worth. Why do I declare what I have sometimes the privilege to see, in living and dying men and women, is equal to any sacred tale? Because I can conceive nothing better than I behold. A woman, listening many years ago to a famous sermon, said, "That is as good as Christ." "Oh no! rather good as anti-Christ," said her friend. But what is indeed Christian is as good as Christ; for it is the same thing of divine inspiration. He would have said he was not a Christian himself! If you question the supreme worth of that patience, resignation, fearless departure, or self-consuming devotion, which you witness to-day, you confound with doubt the very glory and identical element in the Saviour of the world. To be shocked at its appearance in or ascription to another, is to suspect it in him, and disbelieve it altogether. It is infidelity! Was the light, air, water, in Judæa better than ours? Had love, truth, purity, superior preciousness then? Wonderful, Jesus forgave his foes! Cannot you? If I feel I cannot afford to have an enemy, if strife is no luxury to me, if I must love and help my adversary, why tell me to find a better disposition in Canaan two thousand years ago? The earth may be between me and Jesus; I tread the ashes of fifty generations fallen on his grave; but there is no thought betwixt us, no misunderstanding; the ideas are common; we occupy the same celestial globe.

But do you not make a *mere man* of him? Not at all; there is no such thing as a mere man! I never knew one any way or where. *You* are not a mere man, but fashioned in the Maker's image. If species are diverse, none absolutely distinct; all kinds in God's creation run into each other without boundary or bar. Mere man? There is no mere animal, without something human. There is no mere vegetable. The sponge drinks, the fly-catcher is a flower that catches insects, the orchids grotesquely mimic our fancies, the sensitive plant has nerves. There is no mere mineral. The rock is not solid nor at rest, but appears a whirl of atoms ready for transformation into regularity of higher rhythm which is life. The rock in me is resolution: I got my will out of the cliffs that overhung my father's house. God is my Rock, higher than I. Your companion deceased, you see in heaven. Was he a mere man on earth? Then how did he get up there, without ladder or wings, or Tower of Babel, to climb by? My dear friend Ephraim Peabody appeared to me in a dream at the top of a hill lofty and steep as that peculiar one I clambered up two thousand feet at Dixville Notch; and he said, "Come up." "I cannot!" "Yes, you can;" and, buoyed by some strange force that seized me, I rose to him as in a balloon. But our rising to the seraph is no airy ascent. It is getting out of one sort of nature, the human, into another sort, the seraphic. It is not travelling, going so many miles into space; but transmutation, impossible if we were mere men. You say of your dear partner, She is an angel. You see half-open the spiritual pinions she will soar on. In every hour of aspiration, we are conscious of forces not yet in use, ready to uplift.

So when you talk of the simple humanity of Jesus, my Unitarian brother or Humanitarian believer, I must tell you, You cannot part man from God, and keep the man. He would bleed to death; his manhood would perish. Jesus is of no other order nor a class all by himself, but the supreme instance thus far, in the verdict of history, of this common life with Deity.

But, if we classify him with all the rest, where is his honor, and what accounts for his place, pre-eminence, and unrivalled influence? I answer, The idea he stands for, of the Divine Humanity. This is the signal he hoists. No signal-tender on the long road of our race ever lifted one so high. Before him God was outside, in the sky, among the elements, on a throne. He was the Thunderer at Sinai, the Dropper of manna in the desert, the Divider of the Red Sea. Men did not dare to bring him down and domesticate him in their own breasts. He was in some pew, easier to get at in Jerusalem or Gerizim, till Jesus showed him universal Spirit, whom neither Jew nor Samaritan could own, but every gentile and barbarian shared. He delivered God from keepers, and made the connection of trains we are all passengers in. He is God-man; and I hold it as unjust as ungrateful to dispute this claim. It is no individual assumption. He is our conductor; but will not follow us round the streets after we arrive! He is the representative man. He no more wishes to have dignity to himself than monopolize bread or heaven. "A white man's government!" said Frederic Douglass; "as well talk of a white man's sun or moon!" Sonship of Christ alone with God were a worse exclusiveness. In whatever he said of himself, he published the common privilege. Son of God was he as well as Son of man? Who is not? There are no two natures: the human is divine.

But the Word became flesh! In that single instance wholly and only? Is the Divinity an absentee from your frame? Is Satan inmate of your flesh, and every ill demon a birthright tenant of your babe? Then, O Orthodox brother! if anybody is totally depraved, it is you in having the babe. You have no business with it! Wedlock is sin, the marriage vow is blasphemy, love is shame, the infant you hail the advent of is your dumb accuser, and the nest of the cockatrice or serpent's den is a harmless thing, to be spared till you have broken up your cradle. Else we are all partakers of the incarnation. Something of the reason of the All-wise, love of the All-good, sanctity of the All-pure, is embodied as inspired in us and our offspring.

But he is the *Mediator* between God and man! Yet he was a man. So this is a function not confined to any, but belonging in some measure to every man. The mediation between God and man goes on in every bosom. In the electrical toy, called Dives and Lazarus, a pendulum plays betwixt the full and empty jar, and the fluid passes all the time. What is that agent you are all acquainted with, ever going to and fro between the Divinity and the humanity, to move and check, guide and warn, cleanse and correct, remove the dry rot of folly and vice, build and rebuild of the sound timber of righteousness the inner fane? It is the mediator between God and man in the human soul. Everybody that knows himself knows this other self, — third party or person of the inward Trinity, day's man between us and God, operator whose telegraph cannot be bought up and never lies, ambassador that will take no bribe, plenipotentiary whose business is not to dissolve the personality, which it makes ever more divine. This incorruptible GO-BETWEEN reproves my coming short, will not let me prevaricate, has a lash for my vice sharper than the whip of scorpions, and imprisons me for staining my brother's name or sister's honor in a dungeon darker than that to which criminals against the State are sent. There are those who can distinguish this agent in them, as they discriminate between their body and soul. They feel something not dependent on clay, but adequate to finer form or organization. Such as reach not, or distrust, this spirituality, Jesus serves as the apparition of God, a visible Holy Ghost. This is the secret of his hold; the millions he has performed this function for, and will still for whoever finds not that heavenly factor he calls the Comforter, the something better than himself he promised. To be his, and sit at his table, is to partake his vision of God and immortality. Eating and drinking a little bread and wine cannot make you one with him, unless you eat his flesh and drink his blood, fed and stimulated with his sense of eternal life.

This is the question of the world's unbelieving wisdom: Was Jesus aught but a credulous enthusiast, in declaring an endless career? Show just where the credulity lies! The Christian believes man is not an ephemeral creature, that his soul is older than and will outlast his flesh; and you, O sceptic! believe it is but a transient property of his material composition, which his birth lighted, and to which Death will say, "*Out*, brief candle!" You believe all these thoughts and hopes and plans and feelings can but, with the ashes they crumble into, line the tomb whose marble letters will be a longer decoration; and, after the funeral procession and the sexton's spade, not an idea or sentiment, that once illumined and inflamed the mortal shape, shall dare to "mutter or peep." Once dead, you think you "will not be able to pick yourself up," and there will be nobody to pick you out of the dust. Well, in this comparison between the man of Nazareth and yourself, his critic, the credulity is not his but yours! You bring the strain on faith. You are believing a great deal, what is unbelievable, that death is annihilation, extinction of love, and disappointment of hope. You believe that God deceives the expectations he inspires, breaks his word, plays false with his child, and is a person wanting veracity, on whom we cannot rely. You believe the claim of the heart on its objects, though it is constituted never to give them up, is less valid than that to a farm or beach, or piece of goods, or wild land in Kansas or Oregon, or field or mine in Australia or California. That is a *claim;* but the soul has none, no title. There is no deed drawn up for it. Its talk about other mansions and plains is mere pretence, delusion, impotent attempt at usurpation. As between you and him you reject my mind is made up. I go with the Galilean! My faith compasses more with him; but it would be stretched more with you. When report came of a painless operation in mesmeric sleep, a doctor said he would swallow no such camel as that. "Well," replied the surgeon, "in believing we were all mistaken, and the poor sailor here, whose limb I cut off, is a false witness, you take down a dromedary, a camel with two humps, with perfect ease."

Is the joy of Christ's faith no proof? He did not argue the matter. Much argument confounds the instinct. "The more I reason about it," said one to me, "the less I believe." The silent dropping by friends of flowers and tears together on the coffin hinted immediately more than the loud voice of the priest proclaiming the resurrection of the body. Surely as fell the blossoms and the holy water they shook from their eyes to keep them alive a little longer, the soul had risen to Him who turns all blooming into the language of his love to us, as of ours to each other. He can make his chariot of these delicate leaves of the opening buds as well as of the mighty clouds that go sounding through the sky with their rattling wheels; and of the same soft vehicle that takes him to us a vessel, on the return journey, to bear us back. Meantime we weep. But, with upward-looking eye, —

"The tear, that to the earth descends,
Belongs of right to the earth;
To its home above the soul ascends,
Where it had its heavenly birth."

This is no calculation; it is testimony. The act or word that sets the world forward is always inspired. Calculation is unbelief. "He looks like a fox," said one of the portrait of a man. "That is what he is," was the artist's reply. Luther's *Here I stand, I cannot otherwise*, shows the God-driven man, as the

Spirit drove Jesus into the wilderness. Let such a man have credit, whatever he says! Let him say *I* as he will: it is no egotism, but God in the world. Avoid the personal pronoun as the self-seeker may, he has no humility nor faith. What I think, believe, hope, love, and sacrifice my lower self to, differs from what I covet, lust after, indulge in, am proud of, sell or forswear myself for. The self-allusion of the man who carries a mirror of vanity to pulpit or platform, to look at himself in his discourse, is not the same with that of him who makes it the emphasis of truth and duty and the presence of the Deity. This selfhood was Christ's crown. M. Renan intimates a sentimental relation between Jesus and the women. But his repulse of the one with whom he was on the most tender terms, when she rushed to salute him, saying, "Hands off; touch me not; go to the disciples, and worship the common Father," shows a deeper secret in his character than the French biographer found. While we are so fond of him as to fall short of his centre, we continue the offence he rebuked. We are not *with* him till we have gone beyond.

XIV.

GENIUS: FATHER TAYLOR.

IN the year 1833, being a student in the Divinity School in Cambridge, and learning that a Bethel for Seamen was to be dedicated in Boston, withal catching a rumor in the air of some peculiar gift in the preacher, I walked in to North Square. As soon as I entered the new brick building, so famous as a sailors' harbor to all the world, and the master of ceremonies appeared, I felt he was such a one as I had never seen before in the shape of minister or man. It was no decorous individual sitting silent and solemn in the pulpit-corner till the people were all assembled, and it was time for the services to begin; but a figure of restless and uncontainable life, which no box of a pulpit seemed able to hold. The chafing in such close quarters, the glance that reached every point and seemed to fall on every body, the swift step from side to side of the desk, the radiant look, the voice strong and mellow as thunder or a breaking wave, the gesture (whose lively expression could not have been bettered by Kemble or Booth), with which, saying, "My pulpit has no doors," he beckoned up such as could not find seats below, and the white heat of enthusiasm which seemed no excitement, but a normal state, — proved that no pompous ecclesiastic, droning parson, or strait-laced bigot was to discourse that day and be primate and bishop of that establishment. Last summer I was again in the same place. The human form, so long aflame with zeal at its busy task, lay quiet enough at last. The contrast between life and death was never so great. My friend had fallen into the sleep to which the sweetest slumber known before is uneasiness.

This new hand indeed at the bellows, forging human welfare, ought not to vanish without some memorial. In all praise is a certain disrespect; yet such a duty lies in the desire to speak, the presumption may have pardon. No American citizen, lawyer, scholar, or statesman made an impression so unique, or left reputation more solid. Webster, Clay, Lincoln, Calhoun, by no advantage of stormy debate or political prominence, printed their names deeper on their time than this Methodist, whose method transcending limits of sect was all his own. How did a poor clergyman, never leaving his own little spot, haunting with comfort and rebuke of love the vilest part of the city, — beside his boys, as were those on every quarter-deck or before the mast, — draw all men unto him? In the hall of memory, what service puts his spiritual statue for ever in its own niche? Let us try to learn, lest without record of biography or autobiography the name of Taylor be scarce more than a tradition.

He belonged to no class. He was not, for any system of theology or philosophy, either leader or led. He will be identified with no dogma or reform other or less than of the way of regarding and treating those whom he served. He is the sailor's representative. Those other great ones were landsmen. He stands for the sea. He is the great delegate from the waves to the congress of intellect. In thousands of ships, by almost millions of mariners, to whom by baptism of the Holy Ghost he was father who christened their babes, his fame was borne to every port. The sailor says he has been where the United States had not been heard of, but never where Father Taylor had not. How did a man, — no discoverer in the kingdom of ideas, no martyr of principle, nor marshal of opinion, — so touch the common mind? The answer is that word about whose application we are always in quarrel or doubt, — *genius*. It is a large word. It signifies a universal quality. It is an office and warrant to speak to or act on people of every sort, to span every social gulf, and bring all who differ or are opposed into one mind. Such was his gift. As the people say, he was a gifted man, perhaps the only one of his generation among us to whom the term *genius* absolutely belongs. May I show this by some enumeration of marks?

First, genius *possesses* a man. Others have been as intuitive as he, with perceptions as clear and judgment more harmonious, holding the glass steadier to spiritual things, weighing values of thought more coolly, analyzing subjects more keenly as in a mental spectroscope, detecting correspondences more exactly with the wide-open eye of imagination, and with more masterly combining of old elements into new maxims or ideas. But who has been with the truth so taken and carried away? His vision was passion. It made a train of his faculties. His insight was enactment. It was said of one, "In company he leaves the scholar behind: in his study he is a different man." Taylor never left nor lost himself, nor seemed made up of parts and pieces. He moved altogether if he moved at all. His casual talk was better than any preparation; his impromptu, his finest performance. A gown would have "wrapped his talent in a napkin." He put on no dress nor garland. He was as inspired at the street-corner as addressing a throng. There was grandeur in his trivial converse, and humor in his grave discourse. He provoked laughter in the congregation, and wet your eyes with his private greeting; put you in church with his grace at table, made an April day of smiles and tears at his evening vestry, or overcame you with solemnity in your house, so that you were inclined to say it thundered, or an angel spake to him. One said he was like a cannon, better on the Common than in a parlor. But in your sitting-room he could be a flute. He was a man-of-war, or tender and soft as a maid. In accidental encounters he melted hard-faced persons with his pathos, or surprised the despondent into good cheer with consolations effectual because before undreamed. In all this was no calculation. As the Spiritualists say, he was under control. He was an Italian improvisator in America, an extemporaneous speaker condensed beyond example, with combustion and no dilution. In many a wit we see the diamond shining: he was the diamond burning. "Do not get worn out," a friend said to him. "I tear out," was his reply. He served some strange power, having its way with him, and which he could not resist. The spirit of this prophet was not subject to the prophet.

After possession the second mark of genius is *facility*. There was in Taylor infinite ease. His display of power cost him no more effort than for the sea to roll or the wind to blow. It would but have been hard to resist his influx and inspiration. Never aught violent or rough. To storm or scream is the false note, — counterfeit that passes current with many. When a speaker raises his voice, and aggravates to fury his manner, we say, It is all true, and I agree with you; but do not cave in my head! Some orators and readers collar us like a sheriff, or worry us like a terrier-dog. They are ruffians with our minds. But this man's persuasive magnetism drew us without interference of our will or his own. He had at his mercy alike our pocket and our heart. Yet this gracious respect had in it no weak gushing, nor the smallest leak. If he ever boiled, he never slopped over; like George Washington, whose temper was a caldron, if not an awkwardly lifted pail. He carried no looking-glass of self-admiration or mutual admiration. His extravagance was elevation. His glowing commendation of the men and women, his fellow-laborers, was like the lustre with which the sun flatters the mountain-tops. His approach was no defiance or assault; but he always accepted a challenge with courage that was courtesy in the duel from which he never ran. He was nothing if not spontaneous. His originality was never insolence, like that of Mr. Brownson, who told his audience their resentment of his doctrine proved its truth.

The third mark of genius is *communication.* In Taylor this was perfect. "Her very foot speaks," says Shakespeare. But in most persons not a tithe of the frame bears witness. His marvellous suppleness of fibre and organ made his whole body a tongue. When the ballet-girls came out in the theatre and commenced their astounding pirouettes, he, sitting on the front row, turned round to the spectators with a look that diverted the house from the spectacle and outdid all the mimicries of the stage. He was as ingrained an actor as Garrick or Kean. He did not believe in preaching from notes; and, making a speech at a meeting of his brethren, he took off a clergyman confined to his manuscript, looking from his page to his hearers, gazing one way and gesticulating another, to the convulsive laughter of the victims he scored. I remember his impersonating a dervish in his spinning raptures, so that to see that Oriental character one had no need to travel. There was in his word a primitive force none could withstand. "Move a little: accommodation is a part of religion," he said to some who took up too much room in a crowded seat; and, as though his request were a favor, and in such quaint phrase they had received a present, they moved. Every *subject* was to him such an *object*, he marvelled at our philosophic self-fingering. "Height of the sky!" said William Blake; "nonsense! see, I touch it with my stick." Taylor's thought touched heaven. At eight years old he went through all the motions of the minister's service, not stopping with sermon and prayer. He must also have funerals. But how get the bodies? By shying stones at chickens, and having obsequies over their remains. When the supply failed, or perhaps, for the cruelty, his heart misgave him, the little resurrectionist dug up the bodies for a second performance. Mourners, too, were necessary; and that office he required the negro children on the place to fill. If words would not move the lazy things, he whipped them into the traces of his machine of grief. His acting was no illusion or trick, but perfect nature, and so perfect art. He could not, like Delsarte, have picked out the muscle to express heaven or hell. How he did it he knew not. Great orators have studied their motions in a glass. But, if he ever saw his own face for a moment, he must have straightway forgotten what manner of man he was. Never was a less self-conscious countenance, — more ignorant of its own looks. The Cape-Ann farmer said Rufus Choate could cant his countenance so as to fetch tears out of you in two minutes. But there was no canting in Taylor.

Of true genius *sympathy* is a mark. In him it was raised to the highest power. He not only saw into people, but out of them, or saw as they did from their centre; and for his eye-glasses put on their eyes. His word grew out of the occasion: his feeling was generated on the spot. His thought fell like an aerolite, and did not crystallize like a gem. Dr. Channing had *views: he* had *visions.* He preached as the birds sang. He could not help it or help himself. Where he stood was a drama, not a desk. He was the character in "Midsummer-Night's Dream:" it mattered not what part he took. Riches dropped from him unawares, like pearls from Prince Esterhazy's dress. His concern was wide as his race. Genius is love. Was Byron misanthrope? So far no poet. Taylor was no cold peak. His mountain stood on fire. His was a southern heart married to a northern brain. He went back to Virginia, and asked to see Johnny, the little boy he had played with at school fifty years before, and they brought in a white-haired old man; and Taylor came home and represented lad and gray-beard with his marvellous transformations, needing no stage-dress. He entered into every nature; with the Dutch painter could have become a sheep, and seemed only a larger one among the pigeons that swarmed round him in his back-yard to be fed. As he walked in the Public Garden, a sparrow flew startled from its bush. He stretched his hand after it, saying, "I will not squeeze you." For a moment I thought the bird might come.

In his illustration of genius, *liberality* was a mark. A Methodist, Methodism was not his gaol or goal. Like the Indian on the prairie, he said he *walked large*. He knocked at every door, Orthodox, Episcopal, Romish, Radical; and, as in the Arabian Nights' tale, every door opened. He had the freedom of the city. Thirty years ago he attended a meeting of the Transcendental Club. There were in the company, as he entered, doubtful looks! He was asked to speak, and began in his chair; but soon saying, "I must get up," he rose, rubbed the rumples out of his trowsers with a laugh, and pictured our climbing like spiders with such vivacity that when, as he concluded, another ventured to speak, our leader said, "When the spirit has orbed itself in a man, there is nothing more to offer." Who shall come after the king? Pentecost was repeated, and we were full of new wine. He was not humorous, but humor. He compared polemics to two bands of turtles he had seen march on a ship's deck, stretching out their necks to each other, till from those that got their heads uppermost the other party beat a retreat. The turtles would have been content with their representative. To some Liberals, denouncing the notion of hell-fire, he lifted thumb and finger to his nostrils, and said, "We all have a sentimentality of that sulphur." No close communion for him! He appraised others beyond their merits. His liberality was worth something, making him ready to do battle with intolerance. In his large toleration he was a Radical, in his own order born before the time. "Are you cheating the Unitarians, or are the Unitarians cheating you?" asked Dr. Beecher. "Doctor, a third party has come in that wants to have all the cheating to itself," answered the edge-tool the veteran attempted to handle. He, that had been in the Spanish cruiser from New Orleans, and the American privateer *Curlew* from Boston, was a born soldier, and knew how to carry arms.

Boldness is a mark of genius. He hated Spiritualism, and claimed to be an exorciser. "The spirits never can do any thing after I come," he said: "they all run away." His deck was always cleared for action. When the clergy of the Methodist circuit were disparaged by a Unitarian as worth no more than the small salary they were paid, how his battery blazed! "I will set them foot to foot against any of you, with a Bible in one hand and a wilderness of human souls before them!" He bade a boastful British officer remember we had whipped England. "What credit to whip your mother?" growled the commodore. "Not much," answered Taylor; "and I promise you we will never whip the old lady again unless she gives us very particular occasion." His repartees were droll enough for harlequin with their grotesque style, but always had earnest meaning. A young man having upset the Bible, and stooping for it in his desk, "Never mind," says Taylor; "I can put it up next Sunday." How he strode up and down, patting the book he loved, as if it were alive! "How long shall we compass this Jericho?" he cried at a revival meeting in the vestry of the West Church. I suggested our conversion was not finished, and we needed still food of humility more than the mince-pie of praise. He left us hurt and hot. The next time I met him, he embraced and kissed me in the street. He was a placable enthusiast, charitable devotee, fanatic but for his love. Entering a Boston church, one said, "This seems so entirely dedicated to God as to leave no room for man." There was always room for man where Taylor was. How audacious to explode conventionalities! Arguing with him about perfection, I asked if anybody had been as good as Jesus. "Millions," he replied; an answer which, against my testimony, Unitarians and Methodists discredit and try to explain away. Of a great Rationalist he said, "There is a screw loose somewhere; but I have laid my ear close to his heart, and have never been able to detect any jar in the machinery. He must go to heaven; for Satan would not know what to do with him if he got him. Give the devil his rations, it will change the climate, and the emigration will be that way!" Of Transcendentalism he said, "It is like a gull: long wings, lean body, poor feathers, and miserable meat." "Too far off: the King's business requires haste," he would tell the dull speaker at his conference. His speech was seldom bitter or biting, however sometimes wounding, it being to him sacrilege to keep it back. His censure was a frigate's broadside or a lion's roar; his praise was a medal, a badge, or the freedom of the city in a gold box, the terms were so solid and precious in which it was put. He named the sailor-talkers,—one, "pure Hebrew;" another, "North of Europe;" a third, "Salvation set to music." But for the iron in his blood, and the gauntlet on his hand, he would have been a spiritual glue, a mere sympathy, a dissipated mind.

Beauty is a mark of genius. Of the poor old ministers he said, "They should be fed on preserved diamonds. They are camels in the desert, bearing precious treasures and browsing on bitter herbs." The charm of his manners who, this side the Orient, could match? At a distance, seeing you afar off, he would touch his heart, his forehead, and his lips with a salute that seemed too much for aught below angels or less than the universe. His love was as the sea; but never billow lapped the beach more softly than his affection touched its object. His untaught courtesy, the delicacy of demonstrativeness, was conspicuous in his treatment of the other sex. The show was a drop to the gulf behind. He felt the truth, that no man is indebted to any other so much as to some woman. His purity was not ice, but flame. His bearing was royal, and made every woman a queen. No calamity could extinguish his cheer in the church or by the way. At the funeral of the woman whom he said he should claim and could not spare in heaven, he leaned his shining face out of the carriage, and astonished the conventional gloom by greeting people on the way. "You do not know that old Irishwoman," one of the family said, trying to put on him some decent restraint. "Why shouldn't she have her share?" was his retort. He and Miss Sedgwick once met suddenly in the middle of the room. "Did you mean to kiss me?" she cried, starting back. "I only know," he answered, "I got mine."

Veracity is a mark of genius; and that is a false notion which makes it consist in any exaggeration, which Dr. Johnson said all eloquence is. There is in it no distortion or high color. It is true to Nature, low and neutral when she is; and Taylor was a piece of Nature hewn out of her rock. He was autochthon as well as, and before he was, seraph. It was said of Daniel Webster he gravitated to the truth, and could not argue a bad case comparatively well, — as we had melancholy proof. Was it southern blood or sensitiveness to the agitators' faults that hindered his rank on the roll of any reform, save of the common opinion and treatment of his dear sailors? One trait of genius we might say he lacked, — *foresight*. He was no prophet of freedom, of unacknowledged rights, or the fine arts. It was wonderful how a man, in zeal and expression so extreme, kept the middle path. *Prohibition* he opposed; said, people arriving tired and late ought to be allowed some refreshment; and, being asked his views of the unexecuted prohibitory law, keenly replied, "I did not know there was in Massachusetts any such law!" For examiners and lawyers he was a terrible man to have in the witness-box. Yet warmer friend of temperance nobody could be. He said he would have "all the alcohol buried in a cave, and a planet rolled to the door." What a Peter the Hermit he would have been, enlisted in any cause! But he thought reformers overstated, and were dangerous and unjust. He was too sympathetic for the work of those who have to disown society, to put on John the Baptist's leathern girdle, and war against base organic ways. To be a crusader, he must have been made of sterner stuff. Well that he did not leave his own stint. The commonweal is a factory, in which each operative must be held mainly to his special task. The good genius, that made him in general at once so brilliant and just, and wrought mightily through him like the demon of Socrates, was not always present. Sometimes he failed and floundered; and the friends or strangers, that had come to be transported, hung their heads. The engine was detached, and the train halted, though he was often dextrous to recover himself and escape. "I have lost my nominative case," he said once, "but I am on the way to glory." A ship entangled in its manœuvres is worse off than a skiff. All the movements of his mind were radical, and could suffer no mortgage. "What are you going to preach about next Sunday?" he was asked. "I do not know: I shall not forestall God!" His quickness could not be anticipated or outsped. "I never let a carriage go before me," he said. His foot was the type of his thought. Beside the canonical Scriptures I know not what he read but the old English divines; and perhaps no man of note ever *wrote* so little, in the modern world. "Why do you go round so, muttering to yourself?" he was asked. "Because I like to talk to a sensible man." But he had the broadest sight and the deepest heart. He was charged with inconsistency for sympathizing with both sides in a quarrel. But he saw truth and right on both sides. "Disinterested!" he said; "I like not the word: I am interested." If religion consists in fearing God, he was not a religious man. "Do you see the black speck?" he said, lifting a child to baptize. On no bed-plate of a creed did his machinery move. His tenets were shrouds, only better to help him spread his sails. Any resentment in him of a new opinion was not ignorance, but forecast of the mischief into which he supposed it would lead. He was a loyal Christian; nor from his moorings could be torn. Yet he fed with his face, and wanted to feed on all others' faces. His artist nature froze, and the shadow of an infinite grief fell on him when he was misunderstood; and he could be overheard sobbing and groaning in his room. It is the lot of genius! God taxes us on the amount of our property; and to be driven to appeal to him is the condition of excellence. Yet he said he had never seen an unhappy day. Boston was his crown. How dear to him the Port Society! "Laugh till I get back," was one of his farewells. He said of a gloomy theologian, "He seems to have killed somebody, and wants me to help bury the body." The reconciling is the highest mind. It was the glory of Jesus. Taylor was an atonement for us. He said the Good Samaritan did not "maul the wounded traveller with texts." "O Lord! we are a widow," was his prayer for a bereaved wife. He threw a little fish he had caught back into the sea, saying, "There, go tell your grandmother you have seen a ghost!" The chaise he once owned was always so full of ragged children, his own family could not get seats. But all his sentiment was the soaring of common sense. It was the weight not of a sparrow, but an eagle. In the noble Methodist no jot of Methodist cant. The little girl, who explained her kneeling at his coffin by saying, "He was my friend," and the orange-woman who walked up the aisle of the crowded church with her basket on her arm, were his witnesses.

Newness is a mark of genius. Taylor was full of surprises and novelties. He astonished a minister, who had refused to enter his pulpit because a Unitarian had been in it, by falling on his knees on the pulpit-stairs and crying out, "O Lord! deliver us in Boston from two things, bad rum and bigotry: thou knowest which is worst, for I don't!" When Lincoln succeeded Buchanan, he gave Father Abraham an outfit of benediction and gracious prophecy. "But, O Lord! as for this stuff that is going out, we won't say much about that!" Reading a proclamation after an election, and pronouncing the words, "*God save the Commonwealth*," he added, "He did that last Tuesday!" He also prayed that the "creatures about the President would not bore a hole through the sheathing of his integrity." After some trivial talk was over, at a conference, he informed the speakers he was glad to see the "light stuff floating off." "Won't you make a prayer before you go?" said a woman to him in her house. "What do you want?" he asked; "I can't *make* a prayer." He said of metaphysicians, "They are like lightning-bugs in a cedar-swamp in Carolina: snap, snap, and there seems a little light; then all dark as ever." Mr. Webster ridiculed the Higher Law, comparing it to the Blue Ridge and other things above all practical concern. Taylor said, "Higher Law! a meteoric stone: stand from under!" It killed Mr. Webster. His opposition to it was the unpardonable sin. He knew better. Taylor said to some stolid worshippers, "I would as lief have so many canes and umbrellas in the pews! I see some fat people, corpulent. That is swine's flesh." How the obesity shrank from his eyes peering round! As a visitor concluded his patronizing survey of the Mariner's House, Taylor said, "Now we will hear any other up-town sinner who wants to confess." He explained the verdict of the governor on the "good wine, kept until now," by saying it was the best of water in the jars, of which "that old soaker knew not the taste." He said to a minister, some of whose young folk a new pulpit celebrity had taken away, "I understand he has had his shovel under your garden-flowers." Leaving home, this was his picture of Providence: "He, that gives the whale a cartload of herrings every morning for breakfast, will take care of my babes." Called upon by an impatient throng, waiting for Webster to speak, he hushed them by saying, "I never saw such a crowd of good-nature." The wonder of his pathos was, that when you cried, and he was crying more, tears rolling down to bathe his face, he kept on swift and even as the ten-feet diameter wheels in an express train. He described Channing dying, with the setting sun making its way into the chamber through the clambering vines; and melted his hearers with the charge, "Walk in the light, walk in the light!" His wife gave him fifty dollars to pay a bill. He brought the bill with no receipt. "What have you done with the money?" she asked. "Why, I met a superannuated brother, and how could I ask him to change fifty dollars?" Describing some sot, he exclaimed, "I will pursue that man, and never give him up!" His little child thought it was his face made the flower open, and said, "It is sunshine, father; isn't it?" He loved like God.

But his genius had *authority* too for its mark. He denounced a troublesome shiftless character as an "expensive machine." His brain was camera and battery too. "Can a Calvinist be a Christian?" he asked Dr. Bushnell. "Certainly!" was the reply. "Don't be too quick! Suppose God should say to the elect in heaven, Now I will turn this stick, and give the other end a chance: would they be content?" One, who had given information secretly about his conduct in the sick-room, asked him to say grace at table. He found her out; and, stirring his coffee, and not shutting his eyes, but looking straight at her, said, "Lord, deliver us from deceit, conceit, and tattling!"

The boy that ran away from home when nine years old was, as Mr. Webster said of himself, rather hard to coax, and harder to drive. The reformers, he thought, tried to drive him, and his back was up. He could not be second, being first. He was called commodore, and felt he was in command. He curried not the favor he got. When fashionable folk took the sailors' seats in the Bethel, he told them *they* must stand, and not Jack. He was superbly polite and deferential, but in no company subordinate or abashed. No culture could exceed the polish his substance took; but he was at the head. This guest was equal to any host. He was a chief in his black cravat; and, when he had been combed, how handsome he sat while the wisest hung on his lips, from which every word was an artist's piece in color! "The sea, majestic!" he said; and his face was "the wrinkled sea," with all its grandeur, and the incalculable laughter of which Æschylus writes. For him there must be "more sea!" He had the dignity of one on the quarter-deck. "If my employers are not content, they shall see the back seams of my stockings." He would have been like Adoniram Judson, of whom the captain he took passage with told me that, when the ship was attacked by pirates, he loaded and fired faster than any man he ever saw. Taylor was not mealy-mouthed. A Unitarian preacher having descanted on the ever-lingering misery of sinful memory after repentance, he compared him to a beetle-bug rolling over the sand his ball of dirt. Something supreme and final was always in the sentence he pronounced. He was lowly and lordly too. The belt of no man or woman was adorned with his scalp. "He will have his hide on the fence to-morrow," said a coarse man, of the way a certain master would proceed with his opponent. Easy to be entreated as Taylor was, he was ready for whoever wanted to contend, and meant there should be no drawn battle. Seeing a man in the pulpit whom he did not like, he turned rapidly to leave the house. His genius was no wandering impulse: he was borne on as a billow, but with a mighty design. There is an inspiration to the will from the perception of truth which gives the right to decide and direct. The doctrine of Infallibility is true, though not of the pope as such. Sixtus said the truth had been committed to him, though he sometimes thought he had lost the key! It is committed to every man who knows that truth is truth, knows it when he sees it. Human fallibility is a mean phrase. Uncertainty is atheism and despair. My beholding warrants my affirming. Intuition justifies assumption; and Taylor, because he transmitted, swayed.

A sure mark of genius is its clothing of *grace.* Nature, says Goethe, is pledged to the protection of genius; and she protects not only its life, but its action and speech from all deformity and bad taste. Taylor's most unforeseeable flights kept the line of order; and accomplished philosophers were awkward and angular before the flexile motions of his body and mind. In his oddest figures we had to own a charm. When he said of a famous soprano singer, "She screams like a pea-hen," or of the two or three, that came to the meeting, out of a great body, "These are the absorbents;" he showed himself a detective of correspondences Swedenborg might admire.

Another note of genius is *presence of mind*, or the whole man at the occasion, in what he says and does; though we call its inattention and deafness to our irrelevant trifles of talk and procedure *absence* of mind. It knows where it is! "I feel," said Ole Bull, after an improvisation on the violin, "as if I had been in other worlds." "The light that never was on land or sea" is sometimes in a human face. Female vanity hides little jets of gas-light under the hair to make a halo round the head. But Taylor was like Moses: he wist not that his face shone. Presence of mind in him was sometimes absence of body as well as self-oblivion. He forgot his wedding-day, and was out on Telegraph Hill, in Hull, with a spy-glass, talking of his dear Deborah, when she was waiting for him to keep his appointment as a bridegroom in Marblehead. Nature was strong in his character. This convert had no change of heart; though listening to Mr. Hedding's sermon he said, "I cried for quarters soon."

One more trait of genius is *continuity*. He did not, like oratorical experts, hoard his good things to say over again, so that following him round we had the same old fund of commonplaces and store of jokes; but went on, his word a marvel to everybody and not less to himself, fresh as the morning or a new-blown rose; because his was not Everett's art or Phillips's genius for elocution, but his own of eloquence. He was fearless of death, but stoutly said he would not give up till he was dead. Being told he was going to the angels: "Folks better than angels!" he said. He was grieved because the last time a friend visited him he could not wait upon her to the door. Shortly before his death he went several times to the glass and addressed himself as another man needing salvation, saying, "I guess you are not ready; you, old man and infidel, have not made up your mind:" then looked at himself with silent scorn, as if comparing his reduced estate with former glory. His last audible prayer was: "Lord, what am I here for? What am I doing here? I'm no use to anybody. The love my friends have for me will soon be gone. The love I have for my friends will soon be gone. Now, Lord, some morning suddenly snatch me to thyself!" The Lord heard; the Lord did! He went, as a sailor would, just at the turn of the tide. It was ebb-tide here: it was flood-tide somewhere. The death below was a mighty birth above. Such a soul, beyond miracle or prophecy, is proof of immortality. A brother once said to him, "Give me a subject." "It would be too hot for you to hold," he answered. Marvellous such a flame burnt so long! The fire has not gone out, but the fuel. Must there not be more fuel for such a fire? I ask leave to see it burn again! He was restless the last nights; and his nurse, a man that slept by him, tried to keep him in bed, as if with an unconscious hand. "Do you know," Taylor said to him, "how smoothly you are sinning? You are trying to cheat the Devil; but he will find you out!" Happy continuation now is not that unrest?

Shall we not say he was one of the universal men? He resists all sectarian claim or classification. He drew every furrow with a subsoil plough. He was not a local celebrity, but an honor to mankind. Unknown to literature, he will be a tradition in the common mind. Across the line of party he stood a colossus guarding the harbor for humanity. He was a Radical, not born late, out of due time, as Paul said, but before the time. Yet he was no heretic, but a uniter, reaching the *man* in all men. He spoke not to one set or sort of persons, but was understood with equal delight by every class. Fine lady and scholar — Miss Bremer and Jenny Lind and Charles Dickens — mixed, in the Bethel, with the tars that had anchors in India ink on the back of their hands, or clumsy rings in their ears, or vertebræ of sharks to hold the kerchiefs round their necks. Two hundred millions of miles measure the diameter of the earth's orbit for the yard-stick of astronomy. The circuit of his revolution was a parallax for the race.

Faith is a mark of genius. Systems of doubt or pessimism have been built by able logicians, but never by intuitive men. For every truth of the spirit is a lie in the understanding; and the head, informed but by the senses, is an infidel and atheist. The finer intellect of love and imagination discerns truth and being. This intelligence in Taylor was so perfect, — his thought was in such contact with the ideal thing, — that he never talked of *faith*. That seems to interpose a process between the faculty and its object. He *knew*, and had a lofty scorn for anybody's refusal of the term knowledge to spiritual matters. He owned the One God in some Trinitarian way, as the Athanasian Trinity hints the infinite mystery better than that bald Hebrew and Unitarian monotheism in which God is an individual; although a three-fold Deity be not so good as a manifold.

Once more, a mark of genius is *joy*. It denies the reality of wickedness or woe, and affirms the prevalence of the Good. It chants the rhythm of the river of God. The test of the soundness of any scheme is, Can it be sung? Is the essence of harmony and poetry in it? We are told there is a wedding of misery and music in some famous compositions, as Bach's St. Matthew passion-music, Dante's "Inferno," and Milton's "Paradise Lost." But the wretched tenets never inspired the tune. The wondrous score of the Prince of harmonists means from his choral soul more and other than the Calvinism attached to it. The old dogmas hang as a weight on the wings of the English bard, and make his poem, which Dr. Channing called "perhaps the noblest monument of human genius," in parts heavy reading. It is the justice, not the curse, that gives such lurid glory to the Italian's lines. Yet both these mighty works are of the past, — Songs, as David says, of degrees, diminishing, — hardly of the present, not at all of the future, and sure to feel the tooth of time as the conceptions they grew out of are outgrown by the advancing human mind. "Faust," for eschewing their fatality, may outlast them, till itself yield to some deeper discovery of the gladness of creation's root. Wigglesworth's "Day of Doom" and Pollok's "Course of Time" are just expressions of the gloomy theology in its discord of untruth, — the harmonies of Orthodoxy being to those of the coming faith as Chinese gongs to Beethoven's symphonies. Taylor was the happy nature. He was a day of jubilee. The Sun of Righteousness was always rising on him, and the vapors could not stay. The burden of sin, he declared, could be dropped in a moment. He admitted no essential evil; and, though he said *devil*, he despised and routed that adversary as Luther did. With his irresistible cheer, he practised the apostolic gift of absolution to sad and despairing men, as well as Peter or John. He was not tolerant on the surface and a bigot at the core, like some Radicals, as sour when they are ripe as when they are green. No dogmatism sailed under the flag of his liberality, and no Indifferentism stretched his charity so wide. He was no eclectic, with a patch-work of opinions picked from every quarter; and no syncretist, in whose mind contradictory notions throve together. He professed not that large swallow for all sorts of belief, which is called catholicity, and means crudity. Nor had he any scrupulosity to thrust on others, by which to square their conduct to his judgment, and sacrifice God and man on the shrine of a morbid conscience. He never flew in your face with ill-advised interference, nor crowded you with that self-pronouncing and intruding individuality which by dint of present honesty and absent sympathy becomes the worst tyranny. His weight was not oppression. He was no cynic, taking exceptions; and, if he could roar, he did not know how to bark. He was in no covert, conceiving suspicions, pregnant with plots, or hatching any hate. If he was ever for a moment angry, he never nursed his spite. His presence was a lifting of the curtains and letting in the sun. He was a medium, and God not a scientific conclusion he waited for, or a metaphysical abstraction constructed of arguments, like a child's doll of rags, but a living spring, not to be cut from the stream; appearing best not in the earth or the sky, but that image of himself in which he made man.

Whence came this prodigy of power? What blood of England or Italy flowed in his veins? Neither he nor his seem to have known. He is our King Melchisedec, without father or mother, every thing hid but his divine descent. We must claim for an American one whose patriotism would have made him equally ready with Franklin to argue in a foreign court, or with Farragut to lash himself to the mast in the harbor of New Orleans. He hated secession as Satan; and, while at home with foreigners of every nation, was proud of his native land as the crown of the globe. He was a case of Nature's bounty in her most royal mood, and, himself a true sovereign, the head of every board at which he sat. Doubtless in him was something presiding that could not take the inferior part. When his little daughter, being chid for ill-reading, took it to heart, he said: "Don't be a fool. Why don't you go on?" — "Because, father, I am a fool." — "Yes," he rejoined, "that is a capital thing to find out!" quenching in drollery his severity, with that interplay of faculties always at his command. Is not this *genius*, to blend all powers in one? We knew not what he would do next; only it would be some happy turn; for he was not of that order of mind that sees the dark side and flies to the sore spot, the critic that spoils conversation and shuts out those whom he is intent on convicting from enriching himself. It was Taylor's generosity to be open and receptive, — to give and take as a child.

How account for this phenomenon of genius? It is easier to assign its characteristics than its conditions. We shall trace its origin, when we can give the genesis of God. There is nothing a metaphysician will not attempt; but no manufactory has yet been set up to deliver such articles as I have described, run smoothly as the barren machine of a theory will. "Who shall tell his generation?" Even the Christ Christendom worships is no pure historic person, but in part a creation of the human mind. Glory of Greek myth through John's Gospel flows in to fill out the synoptic figure of the other evangelists into sublimity; and Paul is so entranced with the ideal Saviour of inward revelation, he does not want to see the actual one of flesh and blood; while we never hear of Thomas as inspired to do aught with his proof of fingers in the print of the nails, and hand thrust into the side! Plato translates into poetry the Socratic prose. But Jesus was the poet of God. What he showed and acted he melodiously spoke. It was a near and intimate fact. In something like the same solution was Nature in this loyal disciple's mind. He used no telescope of philosophic thought. Nothing was far from him. Such manifestations as came from the untaught mariner's minister escape analysis. The breathing they articulate who can measure or understand?

XV.

EXPERIENCE.

WHEN Paul spoke of himself, he said he spoke as a fool. Yet how glad we are he spoke! In the assizes, answering to the apostle's confession, held for a minister on his anniversary days, he seems to have an unfair advantage. He is judge, jury, advocate, witness on the stand, sheriff, and prisoner in the box, which the pulpit is. He is all but the spectators in court. Yet they are the silent bench with which lies the decision of his competency. I plead guilty, after protracted illness, of which I gave no speech or voluntary sign. To all concerned, let me say, the confession could have come earlier only as a groan. Now it is detached from experience into a thought, I feel that any suspicion of my wrongly remaining a minister tallies with my own judgment.

"Superfluous lags a veteran on the stage."

I have lingered, hoping to be a helper still, haunted by some dream of being more useful because of what I have endured. But I would especially give a lesson of sympathy for that class of patients I have belonged to, called *nervous*, always numerous in a community under high pressure, and with many cases arising from the tremendous strain of our civil war. Is this sort of sickness hard to bear with? It is harder to bear! What are its symptoms? Loss of appetite, loathing of exercise, and greater disgust of quiet, discontent alike with motion or rest, irritability of fibre, magnifying of trifles of dispute, indecision, and dissatisfaction with either alternative, preference of the thing we did not choose or was not chosen for us, impotent thought, fugitive sleep. Sleep He gives to his beloved: does he hate those from whom it is withheld? Sleep, God's sub-creator of the human body and soul, his æon or emanation needful to plants and animals, preserver of reason, fender-off of death, more to us than food; sleep, which we must have, even at the cost of a poisonous drug, else expire or become insane; sleep, for which God made poppy, opium, and ether, and chloral,—*that* is the banished friend, vainly implored visitor of the weak or disordered brain that needs it most.

> "O gentle sleep, how have I frighted thee?"
>
> "Macbeth hath murdered sleep."

It was the worst of all capital crimes. Young man or woman, do no evil or excess to kill your sleep!

> "When restless on my bed I lie,
> Still courting sleep, which still will fly:"

How often, as the midnight hours rolled slowly on, and my bed became not a refuge, but a rack, have I repeated and thanked that good bishop Noel for the lines his own necessity must have inspired! How often have I lain, and noted the signs of the city's waking: the scream of an early train near the station, — an affront to the sick that ought to be put away by some substitute of noiseless signals, — the tread of some preposterous walker before peep of dawn, the rattle of a milk-cart getting the start of any coach; at last, the street official putting out the gas-light, without — let us be thankful for so much — his noisy ladder now; and, all through, alternating with fits and snatches of uneasy slumber, the clang of the neighboring town-clock, telling the hours or tolling them for whom, — man or woman, — in the glare of some night-lamp drawing the last breath! Putting the head in a particular position, counting mathematical figures, walking like Franklin round the chamber, and many other specifics against sleeplessness, have been prescribed. I have found tranquil prayer for sleep the best. He who does not sleep is never truly awake. The calenture of the night succeeds comatose dozing in the day. Capacity for comfort fails: the charm of life is gone.

The sufferer endures a curious divorce of eye and heart. He sees clearly what he cannot enjoy. "Beautiful!" cried those who rode with me through woods and flowers, along the Connecticut banks, round Sunday Mountain, in New Hampshire, or curving in and out of the beaches and tide-lapped indentations of Cape Ann. "I perceive it," I answered, "but do not feel. Strange! I who have felt such things so much." "Sublime!" sang my fellow-voyagers of the sea, roofing its calm floor with the eternal vault, or rolling its surface into floating crests that mocked the fixed ones of the everlasting hills. *Yes:* I could give it an understanding, but no heart or tongue! The great Atlantic, shouldering with the weight of a thousand leagues of billows against the harborless Azores, the ship-devouring rocks, like tusks, the light froth on which I could distinguish three miles off; Fayal, with its lovely gardens to match almost those of Kew or Versailles; Madeira, frequented by English invalids, a huge emerald, with color more enchanting for the mist that laced its sides, and curled through every rugged gorge; Teneriffe, like which, Milton says, Satan stood, but which seemed to me not defiant, rather as one that bore a smoking censer, and worshipped before God; Oritava, a town creeping safe into the hollows betwixt its spurs of brown volcanic tufa and the boundless surge, — these are pictures I gaze at now, with my mind's eye, with tenfold more pleasure than when I saw them indeed. As I leaned, and would scarce have resented or resisted being thrown over the gunwale, the floating sea-weed on the blue water seemed less adrift and more at home than I. The pine barrens of that big sand-bank, and last bit of the continent which the Gulf slipped off from, — Florida, — delight me in reflection as they did not when I wandered through them, and picked from the rugged waste, in February, as delicate blossoms as New England field or garden can show in June.

It is a question, through which we get most, the eye or ear. The deaf and blind would not agree! I should say the eye; yet, in some conditions of debility, more from the ear, partly that it is a more passive organ. There never was a time when a hymn sweetly sung by a human voice, or the piano struck by a friendly hand, or the church-organ making the pews tremble, or gushing through the windows, as I wandered outside, too weak to go in, could not soothe a little the agitated soul. But Jesus was right, as he always is: the Spirit is the Comforter. When I could not enjoy conversation, or write a letter, or without reluctance sign my name, or visit a friend, or do the terrible business of shaving my beard, or read a book or column of a newspaper, save sentence by sentence, and nobody wrote to me, because I wrote to nobody; when my nature recoiled from a familiar face, like the hand of a boy first touching a galvanic battery; when the Diary I took abroad with me to make notes in came back blank as it went, without one record; when I could not think or love or pray, save as in lucid intervals the pall lifted to shut me in again, — then, the sun being gone, some One, as in the English Hunt's picture, came with a lantern. The blaze of ideas, whence I knew not, visited my wintry season; as the earth's procession through the shower of countless stars comes at the dismal November section of its annual round. Talk of poor Joseph cast into an empty pit! This mental depression is a pit of deeper vacuity, harder than solitary confinement in jail. When a noble woman, living companionless with her disease, was admonished for saying God's dealing with her had been rather hard, she answered, smiling: "Oh, I tell him worse things than that when I am with him alone!" Have you never been tempted to remonstrate like Job, or cry, with Luther, "God, art thou dead?" The medicines in his chest, like the arrows in his quiver, exceed computation. Yet "how long, O Lord?" Why wonder what Christ meant by being abandoned? Has not everybody been in Gethsemane? Travelling does not take you there. 'Tis not by steam or rail you arrive. I want no commentator to tell me what particular Psalm he quoted from. I have been down with him, unable to cope with Nature or struggle with the crowd, — "the world too many for me," as said poor dying Tulliver, in the story. The earth rejected me, too weary to stand or walk; the air rejected me, chilled with its slightest east or northern flaw; the sea rejected me, sick of its easiest motion. I was the man overboard, with head under and hand uplifted, whom no rope is thrown to. What shall I do? Whither can I go? "Why hast thou forsaken me?"

When the substance of anguish had passed, a long comet's tail, such as you have seen athwart the heavens, of thinness and inefficiency, drew after. But "in a hundred and fifty days," we read, the deluge abated, "and the tops of the mountains were seen." Every cloud is fugitive: the sun remains, holds his station, and is bigger than any cloud. By imperceptible degrees, strength returns, grain by grain, too small for a month of them to be weighed; atoms from the ground through a million foot-falls, particles from the atmosphere to the convalescing invalid the very breath and Spirit of God, undulations from the light the sick man lies and suns himself in, as beams of His countenance. He seems conscious of invisible increments from the jar and jolt of every ship or carriage that drags or tosses him across the hobbly land, or over the shifting, uneven deep; most of all from looks of that unaltered human love, best witness of the Divine. I was in need, and found help. After breaking the bread, I was famished myself. Then I fed on friends' faces. Others' death and sorrow, which I had grappled with, got me in their grip. Why did I not give up my Church? I was too selfish. I was so identified with it, in a common circulation, I felt I was gone if I gave it up; I should have died. I clung to it as my life-boat. I hung to it as a sailor to a spar aloft in a hurricane, or half-drowned in the boiling gulf. If I could not keep hold of some support, I was lost. My office was my support. The line of good-will which I grasped, I was buoyed up by. If others' patience gave out, they never told me, and I knew it not. If God be as considerate as man and woman, there is nothing to fear.

In my enforced vacation, I wrote a dozen discourses, as an anxious squirrel lays up nuts for winter in his nest. I have scarce looked at them since. Thank God not for ease, but for work! Complaint of labor, in mill, shop, trench, or dock? The privilege is to toil. If I can do it any way, — at desk or tackle, with hammer or pen, — my neighbors may have all the play. I had envied the dogs in Jacksonville that, as I sat tired on some door-stone, licked the sores not of my flesh, but my heart. I thank those dogs! My pain is mine, my property. I have been rich in it, made a large investment I cannot part with, and nobody can rob me of. I suppose it would be accounted no charity to give it away. But it pays well. It has cancelled self-love, quenched worldly ambition, signed and sealed me to sincerity, offset undue love of life, made the grave attractive, assayed the worth of many a friendship, wiped out worthless securities; reckoned up, among various obligations, the bad debts, like notes all have held, — the sums not worth the paper they are written on, — and left a great remainder on the credit side. Be sick or sad, and who is cruel or kind you will find out fast enough!

But, partially competent again in body, am I so in mind? Have I got softening of the brain? Are my views infidel and unsound? I have refused to swear by any words or symbols of sect. Ecclesiastical independence, absolute freedom of thought, — have I by these wasted my Lord's goods? Long accounted a poor sort of believer, sometimes denied entrance to Unitarian or Universalist pulpits, given to understand that religious organs would not welcome contributions from my pen, — if I am now invited to write, and find myself unexpectedly no outcast from either wing, in full communion of good-will with Radical and Conservative schools, I take it as a sign of the advance of ideas in Theology. I would help both sides with what is true in either, but commit myself to none. The trifling touch of martyrdom, the little taste of excommunication, has been to me no injury, but a real treat. I early discovered that reputation, popularity for actor or preacher, so far from being a thing to be seized or coveted, is the chief danger, and almost inevitable harm. When David said, "I am small and despised," did he reflect but for that he would never have written his psalm? It is a great blessing to be obscure and unnoticed, not run after or asked to speak on platforms, to pray on great occasions, or say grace at public tables. "I am nobody," said a good woman, after telling me what she thought. — "Is it," I answered, "because you are all spirit?" It is very good to be no *body*, and go down into this cavern of nothingness, where no human favor follows, and love of approbation cannot breathe. Does not the miner get his treasure out of the rayless bowels of the earth, as the diver fetches up pearls, and ingots of sunken ships, from airless depths where no lungs but his could hold their own? So spiritual riches are drawn out of the humiliations where mortal vanity dies, and nought but irrepressible persuasion can survive. Thus we learn the Spirit is more and greater than any form of religion, superior to and including Christianity, using it as prime minister.

Of this teaching, the test is the opposition it waxes through, like the day-star. Its seal is the sickness and grief it suffices for. Its demonstration is in souls content with information from that secret tongue all scriptures are but sentences of, dropped by the way, and, like your conversation of yesterday, forgot in new calls! From everlasting to everlasting its speech of instruction and consolation. God's accessibility to man and man's to God is all. The explosion of the old dogma of verbal inspiration, falling before geology like Metz and Strasbourg at the tread of the German hosts, drives us from the letter that killeth, to refuge in the pavilion of Real Presence. The miracle to which study turns all creation dwarfs special wonders. The proof of one God appears not in the first verse of Genesis, but in the style of Nature graven on pages of rock and in tables of the heart. It is not made of metaphysic star-dust, like the solar system of nebulæ, but inborn. The depth saith, It is not in me; and the sea saith, It is not with me; but God knoweth the place of wisdom. The evidence of immortality rises in our consciousness of qualities that cannot perish, of whose endurance no resurrection is more than a sign. Can *science*, groping among things ponderable or imponderable in its scales, grub up any demonstration apart from that *con*-science which is its own head and king? The Church I rejoice in is aloof from strife, — a stepping-stone between contending sects, and across the wildly running stream of controversy.

But these themes may be dwelt upon too much, to the sacrifice of health! To this judgment I demur. Whatever injury may arise from imprudent habit or undue sensibility, honed like a razor by social duties, I impute none to an over-wrought intellect, least of all to the particular line of investigation pursued, or the conclusions reached. Free-thinking has odium enough to bear, without being made the scapegoat of private infirmities. When I have had to contrive all sorts of ways, — gazing into shop-windows, perusing the panorama of faces unrolling on the high-way, riding in cars, lifting in gymnasiums, rowing in boats, looking at pictures, doing mechanical jobs about the house, and falling so low as to play backgammon, to get along and make the day pass; when time became the pillory I stood in, not the chariot I was borne by, and an hour was a heavy thing for me to carry; — how amusing to be told, "Don't work too hard, but rest! These ingenious investigations are doing you or anybody no good." As Horatio said to Hamlet, it was hinted to me,

> "'Twere to consider too curiously,
> To consider so."

Alas! not work, but to be forced to strike work, is what kills. I was dying in the Sahara of a barren brain, starving for want of bread from the mouth of God. Duty is restoration. It makes the desert in us blossom as the rose. Is this but a fond fancy of returning faculty, when the actual power is gone? As Nature hides ruins with moss, she may conceal the inward ruin of men growing in years with an illusion of freshness and wonted strength. The hunter leaves the hollow tree he has rifled of its honey: people will not resort to us for knowledge, when no more sweetness is left in this hive of the brain, or only some whimsical, solitary bee, in the shape of an odd notion, buzzes in the bonnet of one's head. There is not much more music in him: he is getting old, and rides his hobby! Is that hobby an eternal idea, deserving a better name? Has the minister any thing more to say? Affection, however tender, will not draw people to the failing voice, on whose resources of vital vigor they once hung. *I* have nothing to say to gather a throng. What the multitude follow, I cannot furnish; for I do not follow it myself. Where it is afforded, I could not, save as a task, go to meeting. When I see by what cheap gifts the masses of men are summoned; how even the Liberal Church is led not by its wisest, but some of its shallowest men; when, in what is vulgarly considered eloquence, I note the violence, as of a deafening gun, while those whose accents thrill me have no wide hearing, — then I ponder the truth of Christ's text of the broad and narrow way. The multitude ran after him not for doctrine or miracle, but for the loaves. Said a magazine editor: "I could improve my articles fifty per cent, and diminish my subscription list at the same rate." You can fill your pews, as you can your pockets, with what would never fill or feed, but only make lean, your souls. Do I cheapen others' gifts to chant my own wares? I value captivating qualities, if solidity go along with show. Be fascinated, if you can be saved! But take some organ of principle, not a compromiser who can play well, using an audience as the instrument to accompany the tones with which he voices his own love of influence or ambition of fame! A minister no more than any other man can thrive without fellowship. Self-sustaining as we may be, doubtless they keep us alive who persuade us we are of some importance, and that there is reason for us to stay yet for a time in the world. So Jesus was encouraged by Martha and Mary, by Lazarus and John, and all those common people who heard him gladly, because they had more sense than the deaf Pharisee or Scribe.

Sickness is a thing to be ashamed of. Somebody has blundered! The ignominious egotism, to which no reader will suppose vanity could tempt, may have value of testimony, especially as regards health. "My child is prostrate," said one: "what has cured *you?*" The answer is, perpetual open air, with its slow uplifting of the body, like the Spirit's of the soul. Nature, and no man, is the resurrection doctor. The roof and the furnace are our foes. Embrace Nature, and she will befriend you. The *earth* is the Lord's.

We must respect it in us and out of us, or it will take its revenge, and resolve us from this sensitive frame into itself.

But the moral relief is not less signal. Have you suffered any grief, calamity, disappointment, or treachery, through whose wound from a falsely trusted hand your life threatens to bleed away? Take it with you to the temple, the house of God, which he makes of beauty and strength, without hands; and you will soon find you have left it behind. My Judas did not go with me into the woods, and I could not discover my sorrow on the sea. The dust of the ground stanched my stabs; the rippling air cooled the fever of my mind, and the chasing waves bore off every trouble faster than the sailing ships. What power, without intruding, entered so deep?

The elements are the nurses, too, of faith. When my life was fading away, I took my companion with me to the beach; and, as the billows rolled and retired, and the sandy channels creased themselves every moment anew, I said to him what I here repeat, that no miracle or prophecy, no ancient promise or written text, but the trust in God coming to the heart in a whisper from his work, is my token of immortality.

XVI.

HOPE.

A PERFECT human spirit would have no argument about a future lot. Evidences of immortality could be no more sought by it than by an angel. When we project our thought to the place in the ground where our flesh shall lie, or query what is for us beyond, we have fallen from grace and lost the everlasting present of duty and joy. God might as well doubt his continuance as we ours, when in communion with him. But this height is so rare and momentary in the best souls, the question of destiny cannot be escaped. The boy I met, crying because he did not know where his father was, expressed an anxiety wide as the world about vanished friends. No question but something, every thing some way, must last. The knowledge and love that light and kindle these chambers of the breast will blaze on. But will it be *our* light and knowledge when the walls are taken down? or will the occupant be crushed, like those islanders of St. Thomas under the ruins the hurricane made of their abodes? We are tenants at will, liable any moment to be served with a notice to quit; living some of us in old mansions which, as Mr.

Jefferson said of himself, the owner refuses to repair. What a spectacle! mankind marching up, rank after rank; each generation, as it crosses the stage, taking a look at the magnificent picture, then passing on to give place to the next; the world a great inn, and every soul a guest at the table, well fed and waited on, but resigning his chair to the coming traveller; as the Northman said, like a bird flying in at one window, and out at the other, — from darkness to darkness. As a visitor of Titian's paintings said, it seems as if we were the shadows. Is matter solid, and spirit the reflection it casts? That is an absurdity to thought.

But what proof of immortality? None, we must confess, but the *hope*. Elijah's ascension in the chariot of fire, if such a spectacle astonished Elisha; Enoch's translation, if God took him, sending no angel of death; Christ's raising of Lazarus, or his own resurrection, — were no assurance. I see many persons counted worthy of things I do not attain; and some of the ancients held to the immortality of great souls, but not of common people. The ghosts, which my friends the Spiritualists tell me of, do not show themselves to me; and, if they did, they might cross where I should slip.

I fall back on my Hope. No demonstration, — only a hope? That is all; but what is that? By whom is that candle lit that sends its beams so far? Who put it into my head that I am going to outlive my body, outshine the stars with my eyes, and be when the heavens are no more? No mortal did it. I did it not myself. What hand dropped in the human bosom the seed of this blossom of faith, fairer than from the sod of any sepulchre? My Hope is my argument. It is a note of hand which needs no indorser, which the drawer will pay though the name of never a prophet were written on the back. My constitution to aspire to endless being is evidence which no miracle can strengthen. It is a prophecy Job or Jesus cannot add to, though their lamp carried through the inward crypts help me to read the Maker's record. Make out hope as part of your nature, — no accident or whim, but an angel He despatched, — and the case is won. A man is indicted at the law for exciting expectations he did not fulfil. That is a crime God does not commit. I saw the remains of a dear mother borne to their rest. Silently the coffin was lowered. No gravel from sexton's spade rattled on the lid. No burial-service was said at the grave. Heaps of flowers from hands of mourning friends dropped after, with showers of tears to keep them alive a little longer above the more precious human flower fading away. Hope soared over-head to say, only the broken vase where it had bloomed was there, like that which, when you transplant, you cast away. The real flower was in another garden. A deceiver, a lying spirit is it, sent only to tantalize, torment, and disappoint? Then talk no longer of the God of hope, but let Deity and immortality go together, and introduce a new worship of the demon of despair.

Hope is the parent of faith. I believe in the Heaven I am made to forecast, whose horoscope no human hand constructed. Marius the Roman general meditates among the ruins of Carthage. Amid what wrecks human hope will sit! The soul, distressed and afflicted, impoverished and bereaved, yet never surrenders, but yearns and longs and anticipates still. God cannot shake it off, smite and buffet it as he will. It takes sides with him against itself. David from his depths cries out, "It is good that I have been afflicted;" and in an old Bible I have read the pencilling of one in sore grief against his text: "With my whole heart I acknowledge this." What is it that accepts misery from the Most High, defends the Providence that inflicts its woes, espouses its chastiser's cause, purges itself in the pit of its misery of all contempt of his commands, and makes its agonies the beams and rafters of the triumph it builds? It is an immortal principle. It is an indestructible essence. It is part and parcel of the Divinity it adores. It can no more die than he can. It needs no more insurance of life than its author does. Prove its title? It is proof itself of all things else. It is substantive, and every thing adjective beside. It is the kingdom all things will be added to. "My mind a kingdom is," pass popedoms and empires and temporalities as they will.

But this is not argument: it is ecstasy. What is ecstasy? An uplifting to some position above our usual stand. We always see more, as we get up higher on a tower or hill. On yonder cape, whose name of *Ann* some love of woman gave, I have been amazed at revelations of beauty, from rising forty or fifty feet into the air: forests in the dim horizon, intervales stretching along the banks of streams, and the far-off Atlantic swell and roll girdling with foam the isles. It is an ecstasy to be on Mount Washington or Mont Blanc: it extends the view. Some years ago, I sailed with some friends to pick up that little pin on the floor of the deep, — the island of Fayal. As we surmised from observations of the sun that we were nearing the latitude where it is laid down, there was debate whether a vague cloudy line we saw in the distance was land or mist. But a great surge tossing the vessel brought out plainly the hump of vineyards washed with breakers and laced with streams, to our exclamation of unanimous joy. So from the surge of feeling we may descry the heavenly shore, hid from the level survey of common-place life. It is no halcyon, but a stormy, sea that lifts us to the vision. Not on the bright glassy surface of our prosperity, but on the sullen, heaving tide of sorrow, shall we behold the port we would make. Gray weather softens the landscape, and assists the sight. It was said of England, she imagines she sees further on a cloudy, threatening day than with all clear. So through gloom we discern glory. The storm throws up the sea-weed to enrich the land. Foul weather is needed to make the fair fruitful. The bolt that shatters your roof directs your eye upward. The Almighty blesses us with menace as with promise. When our children, the heirs we hoped to leave our lodging to, are carried dead from its door, we seek a city that hath foundations; for we, too, on our own thresholds must turn our back, and, able to walk no more, be led and lowered through the same low gateway.

No argument, but the operation of the human mind,

the divine order of mortal life and the anticipation our Creator stands sponsor for, — of immortality.

But the trial is to dissociate the spirit from the body; which we keep unburied long as we can, and but for the offence would keep for ever. Does the objection to incremation arise from an apprehension that from the deeper hurt of fire the mortal figure may not be restored? We cannot separate our idea of spirit, in God or man, from form. We understand, the form must pass. But it has been the tabernacle of the mind. Some celestial form corresponds to it, the faintest earthly likeness to which our piety would cherish, till Nature, in whose lap we lay it, resolve it into mother dust. Something of the familiar appearance and expression of our beloved must go up, for us to know them by, when our turn comes. Father Taylor said, when told he was going among the angels: "*Folks* better than angels." But angels are folks. An aged woman objected to dying, and going where she was not acquainted. Shall we not find our acquaintance there?

Beauty and power reside not in the grosser masses, but the finer elements, — the atoms and rays, the undulations and electric streams. Whoever credits God as being can trust his provision of fit frame for the picture and living image of his creation, when the coarse setting of clay cracks and falls. There is in death, as the Psalmist says, a shadow; but through that alone the vista shines. Darkness is the condition of lustre. It is the great Painter's background. Sadness has brightness which no hilarity can show. There is a flower, though growing in gloomy places, the most brilliant that blossoms in our woods, which is yet not gay, — not for merry-making. No maiden would wear it in her hair at the party for a dance, or use it for a wedding-favor, or put it, like a rose or lily, in her breast. In its scarlet or crimson leaf is a purple tinge, which as we gaze may draw a tear. But its shape and color outgrace in the damp pool all the bloom of the garden. It is the Cardinal Flower, deserving its princely name, as an emblem of that hope which springs so splendid in the shady spots of our fortune and dim recesses of the heart.

To build immortality on any bodily resurrection is a mistake. The ascension of Christ's mortal flesh to eternal glory, what a monstrous conception which Unitarian and Trinitarian still hold, with the logical inference that the flesh of all his followers out of corruption shall rise! In Indiana, an aeronaut, missing his seat, but clinging to the cords of his balloon, rose a mile into the air, and then, exhausted, fell to the ground. All bodily rising must end in fall. Not so the good father, not so the dear child, will rise. Risen they have, and gone forth; leaving, like Jesus, the linen garments, as the roused sleeper does his bed-clothes behind.

Meantime how fruitless the quarrel about dialectic names! Intuition, consciousness, demonstration and revelation, are the correlation of one proof, and end in one sense of continuance. Science bids us wait for it to decide if the future life be a fact. But that "fell serjeant, death," will not wait. We cannot postpone the coffin and the grave. Shall the question of destiny lie on the table to give posterity a monopoly of solace?

Immortality as an external conclusion were but a mortal affair. Its definition is knowledge inherent in the soul. What does it consist in but our community with God? Were our nature an island, or planet rolling outside, no space could be certified in his eternity. But if he is our Common, we can be conscious of him as the lower animals are of us. When the birds altered the style of their nests to accommodate themselves to the settlement of New England, were they not conscious of the immigrants? "My horse understands me. If I do not pat him, as usual, when I go into the barn, he is mortified, and hangs his head." The *centaur* was no monster, but a cordial figure of man and horse in sympathy. There is no such thing as boundary. Man is a bridge. What is the angel that stood one foot on the sea and one on the land, but our nature arching the stream of time, and uniting the cherub with the beast; finding that not its degradation, but dignity, is in its mighty span. Our family tree has its roots in the ground and boughs in the heavens; and our journey is no declivity from paradise, but up from the savage that grovels to the seraph that sings. Not alone, as Wordsworth tells, in childhood are we

> "Moving about in worlds unrealized."

Evermore, as grown men, we converse with things that pass understanding.

But, if conscious of divinity, is it not absurd to say *conscious* of immortality, — that is, of some thing yet to come? I answer: we are conscious of durability as a quality, if not of future duration as a fact. The date of a century-old structure is implied in the solidity of the work. Why is a gem so precious? See the greedy diggers rush to South Africa for diamonds! What makes for a diamond the rate of valuation? Not only the splendor and the brilliant polish the stone will take, but the property of hardness, to hold for ages the glittering angles unworn. How without stain or fracture it goes from one crown and tiara and empire to another, while king and queen and lord and pope pass! It is drawn sparkling as ever from the thousandth finger, where love and fealty put it, and triumphs over the ashes of corse and shroud, ages without end. Shall its composition and not the mind's endure? Is our perception or affection, in identity with its supernal object, of texture less tough? In my boyhood I bought a silver pencil; and, looking at the screw, asked the Swedenborgian jeweller if it would wear out. "Every thing," he said, "material will." But will ideas and principles? or the soul they are espoused by? or any one that dies for them? "Lasting" the maker calls a certain kind of cloth: what is everlasting? Do we call God so because we have applied any measure to him? No; but because the absoluteness of his being defies time. Sounding it, we lose our sinker in the sea.

What gracious human sentiment can be gauged? The Danube, forcing its way through the hills, hints the flowing charity that overcomes and wears away our flinty creeds. Mr. Huxley says, it is not the land that is solid, but the sea holding its level, while that of the earth shifts every year. So generous feeling outlives the hardest dogma. Chronology of world or mind follows reality like a waiter or shadow. The French name a man's constitutional limit his *viability*, as Mr. Weston's is the time he can keep on his legs. What is the viability of the spirit? Can it be dead? It were a contradiction! The noble mind believes in destiny, and admits no doom. David says, God will not suffer his holy one to see corruption. Goethe thinks his fidelity entitles him to another body. Vaughan feels, —

> "Through all this fleshly dress,
> Bright shoots of everlastingness."

Jesus declares, "He that will lose his life shall save it;" and tells his Father, "Now come I to thee." Friends, taken from flood or fire, are found locked in each other's arms: was that quenched or burnt which prompted the last embrace? The scholar's manuscripts lie like white thunder round him, — a concentric battery against old forts of error and sin: shall the moral cannoneer perish? The spotless boy could remember nothing to repent of, but that he had once whistled on the stairs when his grandmother was sick: is that tender conscience extinct? The heart will bleed. As we say of a flesh wound, let it bleed, and so not fester! But its love abides.

My friend says he cannot credit immortality: it is too wonderful. I tell him I am wonder-struck here! Once in, nothing can amaze me. I never expect to be so much astonished again, though all the hierarchies of heaven deploy in my sight. You do not believe? Then you do not. It is a sad fact. So much the worse for you! Drawing the hand over the skin or hair in some persons fetches the electric spark. Will some wiseacre doubt the statement, because it is not noticed or verified in other persons? Faith is worth somewhat as a characteristic, and it is an attribute of the noblest natures, — of Plato and Socrates, Newton and Milton, Jesus and Paul, — and to be respected as of so much value, just as to be ductile or volatile is an attribute of price in any mineral or metal.

But people have believed all sorts of things: witches, fairies, apparitions, demons, possessions and obsessions; visions of heaven and hell and distant transactions on earth, like the Swedish seer's; presentiments, premonitions, and spiritual communications. Belief is nothing! But, I ask, from no beauty did all these shadows fall? Justify your domestic love, and I will vindicate my divine confidence. Science is substantial. But the soul's apprehension of rectitude is as exact as of arithmetical numbers or geometrical lines.

We must, say some Free Religionists, be willing to sacrifice the belief in God and Immortality on the altar of truth. What is truth, but the very thing you are thus ready, if required, to sacrifice on its shrine! If God or the soul be not truth, we have lost the definition; and, in default of worship of the Spirit, we make an idol of our lexicon, as if verity and Divinity were two things. There are, indeed, inveterate or congenital deniers. So there are deaf-mutes, persons born blind, and men with no music in their souls. But they are wanting in themselves who think they have measured the realm of reality with their individual rod and chain. Unbelief is lack of character. We hear how noble unbelievers are. A sceptic may be honest and kind in exchanges and tokens of friendship and trade. If that be all, let one cloth cover body and soul! But if aspiration for excellence opens and dawns into a perfection, whose standard dwarfs every example and shames all biography, faith in opportunity to realize our ideal is part of virtue. I have heard persons profess no repugnance to annihilation. They could hardly have had such an ideal. They lacked the fiery spark in Jesus which said, "I have power to lay down my life, and power to take it again."

Faith seems, in the best men, no permanent state, but a temporary exaltation or shifting mood. But, though the clouds close in, one perception of the celestial land is, for evidence, enough. At Rhigi or Mount Washington, travellers wait for weeks for a good ascent. Hundreds toil to the top, in the rack and haze, to miss the panorama from the peak. But against all failures, holds the view of those whose eyesight reaches from the summit to the shining lake or the rolling sea. So, when a friend, going, leaves a track of light across the dark valley and an open door into upper rest, the impossibility, in your vision, of doubt is a recollection for faith to live on for ever.

The use of prophets is to make the assurance of such beholding accepted by the unbelieving world. "I am the resurrection and the life:" of every burial-service, from the Charles to the Rhone, such words are the balm. One shaft of darkness in Gethsemane across the blazing sun proves Jesus to be a man and our model. "Father, forgive them; for they know not what they do:" was this a piece of sentimental acting, from a deluded tongue, that found no hospitable ear? I can entertain your scholarly doubts about manuscripts and versions, and your scientific balking at a blasted fig-tree or multiplied fishes and loaves. But experience was mother of that record! Virtue composed that story. That language was uttered and heard. In some blind alley or Ishmaelite pit, it may prove our register.

Life has been called a tragedy; but triumph is the close. No dirge, but a jubilee, for that new beginning out of the seeming end! Such faith is born of that sympathetic imagination which is the kindler of love, solvent of pride, secret door of inspiration, crown of beauty, consummation of excellence, common benediction and boon. When Jesus or his disciple gives up life, is it the same life which he saves? No: sacrifice of the meaner feeds the grander self. That is no accident for death to sweep away. We have all some acquaintance with that glorious stranger, which has warrant in us to survive every earthly show.

Is this a purely human property, no spark of which glimmers in the beast? Although the parallelism of the human and animal brain hints rudimentary correspondence of mind, vast difference of degree seems tantamount to diversity of kind. Yet what likenesses exist! A dog defends his master's property with his own life; yet who thinks it deserves the name of devotion? Would you be safe from the mastiff at the gate? let him see you speak on good terms with the owner, and the understanding is quick as light. The walrus intervenes with her body between her offspring and the hunter's spear. If the *human* reaches the three hundred and sixtieth, the animal act touches, at least, the first degree of the same round. If there are bestial hints of displays like Peter's in the dungeon, Christ's on the cross, and Brown's on the scaffold, of what inconceivable glories are these latter the germs? Nor need we search for them afar. Do we not see, in daily experience, what nothing in history can surpass? "Two things," says Kant, "are sublime, — conscience and the stars." I lately beheld a soul pass with majesty before which the heavens shrink; when dying was the thing to do, laying down earthly things with a smile so sunny, death was a flying shadow, till the chamber became a place for tabernacles. There was a babe that must go to heaven to know its mother, and the mother was only concerned nobody should think her babe the cause of her disease, and could serenely say, *Beautiful!* to the phantom from the tomb, and declare, *God makes no mistake.* Why wonder how Stephen's face shone as it were an angel! This is to be sick and die to some purpose. Many flowers on the coffin: I could but see the one in it.

We ask for evidences of faith. Faith *is* the evidence. It shows how the habit of God's presence heals and lifts the soul, as perpetual atmosphere does the body. He is our native air. Whatever thing or person beneath him we rest in is our fetish. In the noblest mortals, beauty comes and goes. Be any man's devotee, and your fondness will be the cloak of self-seeking. Our idolatry of Jesus makes him the frame in which our own portrait is set! The only escape from selfish conceit is spiritual worship.

Faith is moral. Character is the office where it is insured. It is not possible to think of any one as dead who has shown great qualities. Will it be an interpolation to tell of a nobleman by nature, who was for thirty years United States consul at Fayal? How vivid the picture to me still of his coming off in his boat, on the rough waters of the harborless Azores, to take to his hospitable house a sea-worn sick man, and treat him with the double bounty of his ample board and of his sympathy with free thought in religion! How the proper fruit of the tree of liberty appeared in his goodness to many an invalid; in his open purse to the poor of the island; in his equal courtesy to humble Portuguese or proud Englishman; in his lavished resources in time of famine; in his creation for the natives of a profitable trade at his own risk; and in the beauty his art added to Nature in his almost matchless garden, set over volcanic ground in the azure sea! In what other soil must there not be food and blossom for him now? Is nothing immortal in mortal person and name? or has Dabney found King, who once found him, over-sea? Are the believers and lovers a joint-stock company that have failed? and is all our confidence in sacred story frail as the printed verse that fades or is blown away? No: the soul but rests on some brave prophetic sentence, as a sea-bird for a moment on the ground-swell, till ready for its instinctive flight.

Only what is pure is immortal. Love lives, and vengeance dies. Yonder Somerville hill shows how Romanist and Rationalist agree at last that fine houses, better than charred and mouldering walls, adorn the summit where the Catholic convent was burnt by a Protestant mob. I shall live while I can grow. Progress is the law. Why reproach me for not saying still what I said thirty years ago? Is my anchorage and mortgage in the past? There is no such idolater as memory. Paul is anxious *especially* that Timothy should fetch his parchments; but we never hear of them afterwards. He must have forgot his notes, after all! I write and preach my sermons with heart-beats and tears; and, after a few years, send them by the thousand, without compunction, to the paper-mill. Our brother, with admirable and instructive industry, expounds the great systems that have prevailed of religious belief. A step forward beyond them all must we not take? What the age is with child of, who in words shall tell? But the Jews had no monopoly of messiahs: we, too, ever expect a Saviour's birth. We cannot abide in any letter or rite. Does the Grand Army of the Republic worship the flag, or the liberty and reunion it means?

But the executive department must not be overlooked. We cannot stop with vision. Not only the discoverer, the organizer too of principles deserves our honor; and the seer waits on the reformer. How secure unity without compromise, and co-action without coercion? We would get the flock along, and keep the flock together. This is the problem for the church, as it was to Abraham Lincoln, shepherd of States. No Radicalism alone can solve it. It requires consummate wisdom combined with clear sight. On ethics of concession we subsist. We would not use what a statesman called his *foolometer*. Yet a compensation pendulum keeps the best time; and truth for us is not absolute, but a relation. It is an atonement of opposites. It is a reduction of discords to harmony. It is fulfilment of those conditions of social solidarity by which men cohere and move on. Yet the honest word is a main factor, — a term that in the sum of human welfare never disappears. It is *everlasting*, — finished in no book.

Utterance, as unreserved as any Indian eloquence, is among the grounds of that hope which regards not only individual persistence, but the prospects of mankind. Our definition of immortality runs on the line of earthly fortunes, and is not restricted to a heavenly bliss. Whatever notions cannot be converted to practical benefit, with a smile let us leave. The brain in some brings forth empty wind. It is a bank that passes its dividend, or declares one not of sterling value, but worthless stock. Yet let us be slow to pronounce any speculation barren! In a ship-yard the straight timber is good for masts and yards; but the crooked serves for knees and joints, and many a stick lies for years before it comes into play. Thought, fresh as it is free, is not only building material, but motive power. How many factories buzz and spin in Great Britain to contribute tools for every useful art wider than her drum-beat round the globe! But the realm fears the giving out of her coal-beds. Then how mill and maker, pilot and steamer, would be at a loss! The master with sailing directions for the ship of Union, which Longfellow sings, and the stoker at the moral furnace, would find their occupation gone, should the mines of wisdom fail, or cease to be wrought with new yield for the need of every year.

The assumption that our precedents suffice, — that all truth is laid down, and we have but to go to the huge cellar of past revelation for food and fuel to feed and warm all generations "to the last syllable of recorded time," — the exigencies of society perpetually refute. The Bible is a mighty bin; but it gives out, and we are forced to resort to new growth. I recited to a reverent church Paul's chapter to the Corinthians on the relations of men and women. In a quite different way from Christ's hearers, they were astonished at the doctrine. Some admired my courage; some suspected irony; and some said the minister might have made a better selection. But the apostle meant well enough! Corinth, with all its Greek polish, was a loose place. Men kept their hats on in meeting, and got drunk at the Lord's Supper; while women took off their bonnets, and let down their hair. Paul acted as police. The absurdity is, on the ground of verbal inspiration, to make his text an everlasting canon, when the reasons are so shallow; his major premise being but the old fable of woman's formation from the man, whom anatomy finds never to have missed the rib out of which she was made! What shall we say of his not suffering a woman to teach, when women are the best teachers in all the Sunday schools in Christendom? Would not some very orthodox and conservative folk be discomposed, if his decrees about *long hair* in men, and plaited hair, pearls, gold, and costly array in women, were enforced by beadles on the spot in a religious company, like a prohibitory law, or Louis Napoleon's orders, by his instruments in the *coup d'état?* The executives would have their hands full, and find themselves in business, so shearing either Episcopal or Methodist flocks!

Modern science, scholarship, and common sense command that the Bible be criticised as well as explained. Does it hold so many rations, one for every day, — as the frontier-woman seemed to think, when she told the colporteur she did not know she was so near out of it, bringing to the door a torn leaf. No: there must be more Bible, and better than some of that we have! The Romanists, wiser than the Protestants, affirm that the truth within sacred lids needs the supplement of the living voice of the Church, from which it came.

The worst of bibliolatry is its strain on clerical candor; for no man or minister, however he pretend, can practise as he preaches any theory of the omniscience of the written word. The case is kept on foot by the old policy, of one doctrine of the philosopher for the people, and another for his peers, — one view in the study, and a different in the desk; on epistolary authority, meat for men, and milk for babes. How condescending, in educated men, to say, "You must give according to men's capacity to receive!" So we might, were men and women infants in these days. But many of them, reading and reflecting, know more than the priests. The minister has not before him so many narrow-necked bottles, into which to pour a little of his wondrous information with care. He will not find his best thoughts so premature as he fears! The plate is prepared for his finest photography. His locomotive is not so much ahead of the train. We will excuse him from the benevolent conceit that he has convictions about the nature of God or origin of man, for which the community of intelligence, that bears him up as a crest-wave on a groundswell, is not ready.

The teacher's is a threefold qualification, — of intelligence, sincerity, and love. But how is it possible to hold as final the holy writ that allows slavery, polygamy, retaliatory capital punishment, fighting because God is a man of war, or deep draughts of miraculous wine at a wedding; and decrees subjection of woman to man, because of his being as superior to her, as Christ to a common person, or God to Christ? The letter is a block, drawback, and drag to the most needful reforms. How much wire-drawn subtilty is used to prove that it confines and exhausts the spirit nevertheless! We lie for our sect, for our party, despite the prophetic warning not to speak deceitfully for God or what we account his word. Woman's rights men and women, with disingenuous ingenuity, try to argue the hard texts of the Old and New Testament into consistency with their views. So the Northern pulpit labored to prove that Hebrew slavery did not justify American or any other. The advocates of abstinence will have it that *the* wine made at Cana was not intoxicating; while those who consider the extreme penalty of the law as *legal murder* explain away the text in Genesis from a statute to a circumstance; and the non-resistants balk at Psalms and Chronicles, and have to make a piece of rhetoric, in Christ's mouth, of the two swords unsheathed and shining in his eyes! When a woman undertook to speak in a late Prohibitory Convention, in Boston, the Baptist Boanerges of the cause resisted her as an infidel. Who would have thought Paul's verse about not suffering a woman to teach would, like a bomb-shell of long range over land and sea, fall and explode in Tremont Temple? How much of the blood in our Civil War flowed from a Southern superstitious ministry's sincere defence of the system of bondage on Scriptural grounds! Ten thousand teachers were not pure hypocrites. Do not half the human race likewise suffer prejudice of their claims to the use of their own persons and property and the exercise of social and civil rights?

Doubtless some act on the Jesuit principle of *reserve*. Many clergymen, too well instructed to accept the old letter as decisive of the new questions, and fearing to make trouble with their creeds and congregations, take up other themes, let the *moot points* go. They are guilty, if not of false witness, yet of the crime called *suppression of the truth*. "I am very careful," said a preacher, "not to tell any lies." So he avoided the offence of being a Radical. But was he settled simply not to tell lies? Did he keep his ordination oath of telling the whole truth? How many cowards there are in the priest's order of Melchisedec, be they called orthodox or liberal, it is no satisfaction, but a grief and shame to think.

Only one position is tenable. All these matters of reform which stir the public mind at the present day, however illustrated from profane or sacred history, must be argued on their own merits at the tribunal of reason, not of Moses or Paul. I am not of those who think alcohol, under all circumstances, a poison, and never a medicine; but I would not have the extremists in Temperance embarrassed with an ancient miracle and a text. Debate the sumptuary law in the modern light, and God defend the right! What hypocrisy is generated otherwise! At a great meeting of a society of doctors, many years ago, the leader and president got a unanimous vote that every drop of ardent spirits was in the human system a bane: whereupon one member rose and asked if they, all preparing medicines with alcohol, were not, in the extravagance of their statement, presenting themselves as a pack of fools and knaves. Water is put for wine on some communion-boards. May not the element as well be dispensed with, when it comes to that? A *form* is destroyed when it is changed. How else can this momentous cause of Temperance be promoted than with Truth, from which no enterprise of philanthropy will bear to be divorced? But all Scripture is not truth. So from such as find no deeper basis, and cannot themselves build on the same foundation with apostles and prophets, instead of building on them, we have abundance of double-dealing and special pleas. The Devil, in the old proverb, can quote Scripture: is it not because he has tried his hand in making some? Surely, cruelty to the Canaanites and oppression of the children of Ham were among his texts! Had our construction of the Book but antiquarian interest, we might let men sleep in their prejudice. But it touches every imminent issue and live question of the day. The pulpit's sin of reservation is a projectile of pure insult to the people. The prince of the virtues is the noble apostle's own, — to speak with all boldness as we ought.

The old theology does not atone for its gloom by moral effect. Whatever reason it had for being, it has for now ceasing to be. Under its existing frame its heart is eaten out. It is what Sherman called the South, — a shell. No Genevan or Florentine or Swedenborgian or Miltonic genius can keep hell distinct from heaven, or the Devil as a rival of God. It has been said by liberal critics that a grain of Calvinism does not hurt the flavor of the bread, and that it has under its ugly look a musical soul. It sang once of civil freedom, which has nobler minstrels now; but not a note any longer of spiritual truth. It has lost its voice! In a rude age it made God felt as an iron power; and out of its shadow a glory came like the sunrise from the storm-cloud whose spent fury settles in the East; but the Orient for the coming day is a more generous faith that absorbs its lurid lustre, as I saw the ascending sun take all the grim and ruddy pomp out of the vaporous horizon to itself. Nursed on the unadulterated diet of the New-England creed fifty years ago, may one not be a better witness than an observer whose cradle lay inside the liberal fold? Imagination is quick to make of the present writer a boy, not suffered to leave the close parlor on the Sabbath, though sunshine and green field so invited him as to make it a sore prison, — save to walk straight to the church, whose clamor of denouncement, without one gentle strain of nature, still rings in his ear. Those who fainted in the ill-ventilated building, he thought, were borne out to be judged. In his solitary walks, in his seventh year, he had begun to hang his head; and remembers how for hours he would repeat the one sentence, "*God be merciful to me a sinner;*" though he wondered what the guilt was that should forbid him to lift his eyes to heaven, and had eclipsed the beauty of the world.

Too much has been put between the soul and its Author. Comfort is too far to seek in Judæa. We want our own Immanuel, God with us. No imported can equal an indigenous faith. The soul in its extremity must have immediate help. No circumlocution avails like the direct whisper. Our hope beyond the dead-line is no letter, promise, miracle, or bodily rising, but trust in the Power that made us. If my life is of no consequence to him, it is of none to me. What is best, he will do, and I accept. No ticket of vicarious redeeming in my hand, no self-salvation, no insurance against accidents on the road; but such acceptance is all my immortality, present and to come. The property is his to reinvest or throw away. This is the rising faith with Internationals of the Spirit! The ecclesiastic bar loses its terror. Conscience is a tribunal that dispenses better justice. The assizes are no longer remote, beyond the sound of trumpets and the quickening of a million generations' dust. The Judge standeth at the door. God's bench is the human mind. When the consul said to the Portuguese priest, "Why do you, knowing better, still apply the Romish scheme?" the priest answered, "C'est mon métier,"—it is my trade! But religion, as a business and function, must yield to vision of the fact.

Every thinker has his prospect of improvement for the human race. We make our prophetic sketch. So it will be, we say, in politics, society, worship, or affairs; "but we shall not live to see the day!" Dr. Franklin wished to come back, after some ages, and look on the renovated world. Perhaps he does, and we shall, in a way unlike his fancy. This anticipation of earthly progress is token of divine destiny. Meantime how pleasant to contemplate the renewing force! After the bitter week, that had brought the earth near to zero, I went to Gale's Point, on the coast. The broad harbor between the headlands was frozen to the channel, and resisted the tide that crunched against the encroaching ice. Down the slope of the land flowed the image of an arrested cataract of water, hard as the congealed masses in which the northern whalers met their fate. But where this stiffened torrent started was a living spring, lifting its sandy columns as it bubbled noiseless from the earth, to keep its surface soft and smooth as a summer breath. It told the gentle, resistless persistence of a higher life than its own. Death is before us. But what an advantage for them who have it behind! Their position we shall find no marvel, but natural as the dawn when it shall become ours.

Meantime let us discuss radical problems without fear. Religion depends not on the institutions she forms. Were all bibles and churches swept away, she would spring immortal; as out of the burnt forests of Wisconsin time is bringing other trees, perhaps ot nobler growth. Orthodoxy must show us better fruit, in our neighbors and their children, before the demoralization charged on Liberality will stir any alarm. Looking back at the long line in my own Church, how the names of Hooper, Mayhew, Howard, and Lowell shine to signify no novelty in free thought and independent speech! But to make an idol even of liberty is as narrow as it is profane. Let our inspiration be wrought into the social body, which is our incarnate nature and common flesh. Every talent and human element we need. Great expectations should they have, who number scholars like Martineau and Hedge, organizers like Bellows and Hale, and mediators like Collyer and Clarke. There may be room for whatever thoughts are here repeated, because men and ideas are alike dear.

All powers, in all ways, however diverse or contrary, compose the resultant harmony. The ground of fellowship is reverence. Fun or humor to make light of things has its place; but a mere entertainer is a low character. I thought it great praise when my friend called Jared Sparks a *serious* man. The child in Willis's poem is "tired of play;" and how weary we get of those who spoil conversation and insult our convictions with their untimely wit, turn on our talk the jet of water instead of flame, or would make fireworks for amusement of all the light and heat of the soul; and, when the dove of the Holy Ghost is just hovering to light, shoot it with a jest! They must worship, who would commune. Why cannot those two persons abide each other? They belong to the same church, neighborhood, and social circle; they dress with equal elegance; they sit side by side at the concert or play; they drive hard after each other over the fashionable road, but cannot set their horses together. What is the foil to a hundred sympathies of interest, pursuit, and taste? What these human pith-balls are mutually repelled by is the same electricity of self-conceit! They keep each other at such a respectful distance, because they have no meeting-place in God. Swift said Addison was very "civil," after his famous satire on him under the title of *Atticus*. What can have alienated your old friend? Your vanity or his! Self-pronunciation is secession: ambition to lead is disunion. Cæsar and Antony, Octavia and Cleopatra, could not inhabit one sphere. How many seek to king or queen it, to set the fashion, captain the troop, or champion the ring, like the as finely dressed and feathered cock of the walk! They grind each other to pieces with identical sharp corners, that can find no counterpart, and are walking figures of irony on their own several pretence! Chanticleer wishes his note to resound without reply. O friends, love and serve together the Infinite Being and Beauty; and, in what smooth gear, soft as a psalm, you would run! "Behold, he prayeth," was reason enough for Ananias to visit Saul, or Channing to honor Rammohan Roy, or Dean Stanley to embrace Chunder Sen. When we learn that Christ's ascension was a daily habit, and no bodily act, we shall understand that his board is not spread for a private entertainment; and none, revering his character, can by any master of ceremonies be driven from his feast. The Ideal, that floated over him, can lift us out of sight of all outward rising. The line of beauty, once discovered, is discovered for ever; and how he kept that faultless curve! He held Nature in solution as a sea of love, and was full of the element in which he moved. It is enough if we be among the snowy-winged comrades in his convoy, though we follow in graceful freedom, and no rigid lines, the flag-ship.

Our political union has for its condition some honest reverence and loyalty, not any uniform faith. Let Christians cease their unchristian clamor to name their religion in the Constitution! God and Christ will be in it, unmentioned, when the government is just to black and white, to copper Indian and yellow Chinese. Equity to Jew and Mormon shall be our Book of Common Prayer. Protection of atheist and infidel is the best petition. More than thirty years ago, I was blamed for signing a request that Abner Kneeland should not be punished for blasphemy. A venerable parishioner said it was the first mistake his young minister had made; and the remark came to me for an admonition on the lips of a distinguished counsellor, afterwards judge, still living, but not disposed to move or consider such a bill of indictment now.

Shall you *fellowship* the Radicals? If you find in them that reverence which is the root of sympathy! "I did not go to Theodore Parker's meeting," said one; "but I never knew one that did, who was not zealous for good works." Over the coffin of a reputed sceptic that heresiarch said: "O God! if he doubted thy being, he lived thy law." "We must have larger contribution-boxes in our great society," I heard a man inform the sexton; and must we not, of our communion-board, make an extension-table? "I am a wide liker," said Allston, when somebody disparaged pictures of a style different from his own. "I prefer Mozart and Beethoven to Schubert," remarked one to Perabo: "they come down upon us with such an elephantine tread." The pianist replied: "This elephant is just as big, only a little further off!" A French writer tells us: "Not to praise warmly is a sure sign of intellectual mediocrity." It is a proof of irreligion, too. Contumely to man is disrespect for God. Adoration inspires magnanimity. An English hunter, in Omaha, coming suddenly upon a violet peeping out of the snow, could not pluck the flower, it so overcame him with thoughts of home. Remembering the homestead we all belong to, we shall be tender to our kind.

XVII.

IDEALITY.

THE idealist we count impotent, only impressible as a photograph-plate; prey of wandering fancy. But ideas are active powers to revolutionize and reform. God is the great visionary, enacting his thought in every stage of his work. A late French writer holds that freedom to think and to speak implies freedom to act with no let of law. In a perfect mind it does. But God, says one, is the only being who is thoroughly awake. All men are somnambulists. Their murder and theft, lying and lust, are a sort of sleep-walking. In a fine sense, Mr. Choate's defence of the famous Tirrell was true. But we share with the Creator as we open our eyes.

First, as partners in making the world. What is the earth? Not so much crude bulk, finished when God rested on the seventh day. Is not the line of steamers, Pacific railway, telegraph wire, storm signal, mill on the stream, and Mont Cenis or Hoosac tunnel, part of the universe as much as Niagara, the Merrimac, a hill in Switzerland, or the morning star? Is a picture less solid, a symphony more transient, than tree or rock? "The works of God are great," said an admirer of art, "but the works of man are wonderful!" The Supreme Artist left his sketch for his children and pupils to complete; and their orderly continuation is as good as his beginning. "Is your lecture done?" I asked my friend. "Never," he said. So with Nature.

But in a deeper sense we co-act with Deity. Nothing is what it is in itself, but in its relation to every thing else; and that relation is ideal. What a false notion, that, with none to behold it, the planet would be just the same! It is nought, separate from sight. Could all that lives lie down in one mighty sepulchre, no constellation would shine on that grave. Without perception, no light. God — infinite mind — said, "Let it be;" but human intelligence was part of the fiat.

This is no hypothesis, but a truth in which imagination and science meet. Has matter a single independent property? It looks, feels, smells, tastes, sounds, so we say; but it could do no such thing without reason and the sensitive nerve. The secondary qualities — form, color, odor, audibleness, and touch — we all allow to be a spiritual addition to the outward scene. The primary ones too, weight and extension, supposed inherent in external things, are but part; the intellect, counterpart and constituent; space and time, modes of understanding.

If the elements have intrinsic, why such shifting worth? The dog looks on the same prospect with his master; the lynx and vulture have a keener than the hunter's glance; the eagle is said to gaze undazzled on the sun; beasts and birds of night discern and find their way through what we call pitch dark. What but some new chamber in the brain or joint in the spy-glass reveals to us, in the common house, a size and store hid from their view? To our ideality it expands into many mansions. To their sensuosity it contracts to a den under ground, a nest in the tree, so much air to sail through, or so many holes to worry their game in. How low Hamlet, in his melancholy, reduced the sphere he so grandly described! But to the hawk, what but a barn-yard is the land, or fish-pond the sea? Schopenhauer makes the world a mental projection; and Wordsworth says the glories Nature lures us with are not hers, but born of a luminous cloud that issues from our own soul. To the Bible-seers she waxes old like a garment to be folded up, and flees before her King to find no place; and how modern philosophy verifies ancient poetry, resolving masses and particles, heaven and earth, into pure force! But that such conceptions ever entered the head of any animal we want proof. I noticed a setter looking through a car-window, and seeming to take some pleasure in surveying the landscape; but his ear played active as his eye, and I queried whether he observed that integrity which is beauty, or was looking after his natural enemy, and watching if aught appeared he could serve his master's sport by beating the field to start. Without spectator were no spectacle fair and sublime. The mind is busy to make what it beholds. What signifies calling such doctrine the peculiarity of some moon-struck man? Nobody so practical or gross, so bent on his crop, grist, or hoard; no hewer of wood or drawer of water; no smelter of ore or digger in the trench; no cunning politician or Tammany thief, — but, because he is a man, and of his human nature cannot be rid, must scan and construe the world differently from the brute. We all idealize, and only so realize; for of no marriage but of the actual with the ideal is reality born. Mind is term, as it is source of matter; and our thought a factor of every thing.

Our idea is a needful factor of the people too. "What do you *make* of *him?*" To the pure all things are pure, because they generate purity in whatever they touch. Mephistopheles comes at the call of Faust; but it is an ill-principled will that creates him, —not, in Shakspeare's phrase, "the heat-oppressed brain." Edmund Burke holds man a wise unwise animal, and Thomas Carlyle calls the population of a country forty millions "mostly fools." The difference of judgment shows how much higher on the scale of genius the sober statesman reached, than the wilful though splendid pamphleteer. He that considers his race a knavish set betrays lack of that insight which produces their goodness. He is the Alfonso who could have counselled God! To like your kind is your virtue and theirs. Sympathy is the hand to renew and eye to behold. In a smoking-car, amid cards and tobacco juice, and coarse words and peanut-shells, from horny-fisted lumbermen and brawny-necked sailors with brass rings in their ears, I have witnessed a politeness to give up their place to one less tired than they which few Boston parlors could match; while well-dressed women of fashion in the train behind were covering the seats with their spreading skirts and selfish bags. One woman told two lies, saying the seat was engaged. My thanks are not more for gentlemen and ladies than for civil conductors, courteous brakemen, and grimy but smiling engineers. On what slight provocation of your fellowship the love and good works will come! It was the *making* of him, we say of some small furtherance of a young man. A country bachelor's objection to the fair sex was their *liking to be made of.* O strong and resolute husband, do you know how much you can *make* of that tender and malleable nature you name your wife? The woman lifts the man into her circle: the man sinks the woman to his; but either can turn the other into a vessel of beauty or sharpened steel. In Eugene Sue's story the words *heart and honor* open to the vile *Chourineur* a new career. We, like God, create in our own image, and as he made every creature, "after his kind." I shall be to you what you ask, with your character as well as your tongue.

A nation in its need regenerates its children. When some old friend of Jefferson Davis and political sympathizer with the South was startled from that leaning by the gun at Sumter into a war-democrat, why charge with being insincere one who is but patriotically new-born so to help the land, that the Confederate president becomes not a martyr, but a cipher? The fouler the corruption, the purgation more sure! If dirty water must fetch the pump, there is clean in the well. You cannot kill conscience more than oxygen. The thunderbolt forms and lurks in the heavy sky of municipal robbery and intrigue; and the crashing of base authority in the metropolis of the land proves public virtue, in its excessive reserve, yet an overmatch to annihilate official guilt, though more hands than appeared bore the stain of the enormous bribe. "I would rather," said one, "be a door-keeper to the Committee of Seventy than dwell in the marble halls of Tweed." But how different a tune the moral sense has set for Tweed now to sing!

"I *dreamt* I dwelt in marble halls."

When thieves refuse bail to their head, we see honesty rising as a power to break every wicked Ring. It is ideal holiness certain to conquer iniquity, and triumph over all shame.

So we make the Christ of our faith. Christians are disturbed by any hint that their Saviour cannot be certainly drawn, with every word and prodigy, out of the historic details. What if we cannot circumstantially verify the image of the God-man? Is that image therefore a vapor that passeth away? Fact is never the ground of principle; but principle the womb of fact. All the texts and wonders illustrate, but do not procreate spirit. We are grieved at discrepancies in the Gospel tales, and the impossibility of proving the miracles even if they occurred. But though, in the mouth of many witnesses, every word could be established, or the portents rewrought before our eyes, we could get from them no saving belief. Faith is a principle, not a conclusion. The test of a man is what he builds on, an incident or an idea. The letter that killeth is not only a written sentence, but every outward appearance. Sun and moon, sea and star, are but an alphabet. The world is God's metaphor! All cognitions of sense are signs and counters of conception. We do not want a factitious redeemer.

A purely historic creed is the house Jesus spoke of, reared on the sand, and sure to go before the storm. None but the ideal underpinning will stand. A miracle over the greed of the multitude was noble; but a multiplication of baked bread and fish that never grew as wheat or swam in the sea, what a lie of God or Nature! The ideal foundation is so firm, every man's constitution forces him to fashion his Lord according to his light after his own heart. To the Jew Jesus was a stumbling-block, and to the Greek foolishness; but to whoever believed, God's power and wisdom. To such as could receive him, he became righteousness and sanctification and redemption. Paul saw him, and Thomas did not! To Mary angels were in the sepulchre, to Peter a linen roll. John the Baptist was a reed shaken in the wind, a figure in soft raiment, or a prophet in the van of the whole line, as the vision of one or another varied in the wilderness. Jesus was a Jew: the Christ was born of the wedded Greek and Jewish mind. I doubt not the depth of that immense personality would justify more than all we can say. But the personality is not constructible from any particulars of the story without imaginative help. I should not believe the narratives so heartily, did they all four agree, or if Paul had nothing more to tell us than Mark. Eye-witnesses, every lawyer knows, always differ. Sir Walter Raleigh, noticing what diverse accounts several relators, with equal opportunity, gave of the same events, wondered at his own undertaking to write annals, as if any thing could be exactly reported or found out. We say Genesis is a fable. Is Moses, or whoever wrote it, less trustworthy than

Gibbon or Hume? We dispute about what was done by John Adams or General Greene. In a few years how many myths there will be respecting Abraham Lincoln and John Brown, and the power gone to distinguish between fiction and fact; but, as to the devotion to country and humanity, what doubt?

If a man or clergyman is incapable of this spiritual idea of a divine humanity latent in every breast, preeminent in the Nazarene, he will not be at home in the Unitarian, Liberal, or Radical fold. Like a tired soldier, he will drop out of line: he will join some larger army for an easier march. Why have Spurgeon and Beecher more following than Martineau and Hedge? Because the ideal faculty is so feebly developed; and the popular preachers are with the animal crowd, who must be met on their own level to be usefully served. Lament not the departure of whoever can act with more power elsewhere! Doubtless men and ministers are sometimes misplaced. Had I any voice in the Church, I would recommend the custom in war, of an exchange of prisoners.

Christ is the increment of Jesus,—the individual expanding to an ideal. He is spiritual formation, not literal fact. He is a creation of the human mind, not a deduction from particulars. He is a development, like his Church. But does not this view undermine his permanence? How can he *so* be "the same yesterday, to-day, and for ever"? I answer his spirituality is his durability. The interior is a citadel for him no hostility can shake. Were it but demonstrable facts he rested on, Christianity, like yonder sea-wall, would be washing away with every wave of time. Is the solidity of the material world sapped by the science that proves its dependence on the mind? No: this ideal quality is the reason it cannot, by God himself, be unmade.

> "He can create, and he destroy,"

writes the poet. The latter part of the proposition let me doubt! He cannot shake off this great-coat of Nature he wears. It is alive like himself. We piously say, He can do as he pleases. Can he contradict himself, commit suicide, break his own laws, annihilate a soul? We are not independent of him: is he independent of us? Not if I and my Father are one; for the Father's unity is constituted by the childhood, which is no accident or growth of time.

I know the Trinitarian theory assumes a peculiar and limited sonship of Jesus, generated solitary and eternal. But the divine personality *de*generates thus into individuality. Two individuals were from everlasting, one Almighty, the other co-equal as co-eval! Unitarian people and priests backslide into this heresy from incapacity of that inward vision which comprehends in unity the Parent and all his house. Jesus effected the passage from the human to the divine for the common-sense of mankind, like a man throwing the line across Niagara or Menai for the suspension-bridge. But on the firm structure once laid all men are as free to walk as himself, — nay, he but shows the way over an old road already made, though blocked up or overgrown. These sporadic cases of reaction to an orthodox or semi-orthodox faith only show who is weak and imperceptive enough to be diverted by a false scent from the narrow way of that true direction which intelligence and character are bound in fine to take, however the fondness of multitudinous sympathy seduce into the broad one, to mistake *large* following for *great;* while the votes that are to be weighed and not counted are cast by genius and science against the evangelical clamor of numerical superiority in disciples however zealous, and superficial preachers of whatever notable fame. This method of the ancient religion, spite of sceptics, will vindicate itself. *Deism* was the doctrine of God excluding, but *theism* including, Christianity,—a singular aggrandizement of an identical term. The theist fulfils Paul's prophecy of the Son's subjection that God may be all in all; for how absurd to make that a matter of chronology, instead of widening inward sight!

This divine humanity, being the soul's essence, dates or derives not wholly from Christ. An American bishop told me, when, being weary in his journey, he dragged himself in a lonely by-way of India into a deserted hut, perhaps to die, one, of the most despised sect, rescued him and lent money to the stranger, trusting his remittance from Europe. What more could Hebrew Rothschild or Christian Baring do? Not long since, in New Zealand, an Englishman, on some local charge, was ready by the savage executioners to be cut down, when a woman whose husband the British had killed rose from the gloating dusky crowd, slowly walked across the space to the centre where the victim stood and the knives were half unsheathed, and sat down at his feet. At once fell paralyzed the hand of revenge! The reprieved prisoner rose, mounted his horse and rode away. Can Christendom show aught more fine? The glory of the gospel is its education of mercy in the normal school of mankind. *In this sign, we conquer:* the old Latin motto hints better victories than of arms. Walking along the Western avenue last winter, on the lowest edge of the marsh I encountered a throng gazing curiously where the sluggish tide crept to and fro through the flats. Day after day I met them. They gathered month after month. A poor Irish girl had there been violated and murdered by a yet undiscovered man, to liken whom to any four-footed creature that crawls on its belly or honestly walks were insult to the beast. But that continual presence at the spot was human nature, — to pity the unfortunate and disown the shameful deed. I asked one wet-eyed lad if he knew her. No, he replied. But the Christian touch, to reach the lowest ignorance, was shown in rude carvings on the fence of the cross, beside the name of the doubly-slain, *K. Leehan*, from whose dreadful struggles the compassion of God released the soul, while the Christian compunction in fellow-creatures would do more than any execution on the gibbet to prevent repeated crime.

The test of Christianity is not any substitute or mediation, but closer introduction of Deity. The Chinaman in San Francisco, lazy at his work of dusting the church, hearing the shout of the concealed sexton, cried out, *God, is that you?* — his own conscience becoming the God of the temple to rebuke his sloth. The Israelites made them gods of gold. We, too, have a hand to make our God after our mind. God made man in his own image; and man, it has been said, returns the compliment by making God in *his*. How else can he make him? Making God a person is objected to as confining him to human measure. What measure have we else? Can we get beyond our own thought? A God foreign to human nature is none. If He be not implicated in us, and we in Him, He is not, and we were not! Your God will be no better than you,—your inmost self. "Like master, like man," runs the old proverb. *Like owner, like dog*, we might add; for I have noticed how the mastiff at the gate represented the occupant of the house, and they would be surly or sweet together,—the man a commentary on the dog, the dog on the man. Perhaps natural selection of the animal, or careful cultivation, or the dog's keeping good or bad company, accounts for the remarkable fact!

We must retain or do away with God and Christ and man all together. A Spiritualist correspondent insists that the Christian Deity must go. The castle of faith will stand not by any literal, but an ideal, defence. Based on any text, with any miracle for its corner-stone, or special pre-existence for its cement, its architecture will crumble under the blows of criticism, or yield to the tooth of time. As an existence and entity in the human soul, suggested, illustrated, and confirmed by recorded words and events, it will survive. The assailant of true Christianity will not have the easy victory he beforehand so loudly boasts. He is fighting not a doubtful register, but an Ideal of the human mind, formed from many an age and race, with solidarity of communion through a hundred generations and what woven fellowship of manifold tongues! He defies an inward standard, with a metaphysical phrase. Whatever new dispensation may arrive, the old banner will not be hauled down before any ambitious individual flag. No private notion or interpretation can prevail over the force of the common life, the general incarnation of truth, and embodiment of the Holy Ghost.

We, like Paul, may claim to work with God forming others and ourselves. Character is creation, his and ours. But what God? No dogma of the Bible, or abstraction of the mind, no internal particle peculiar to an individual, but the atmosphere of souls! God makes man, but not any one man, in his image. Each of us has but a share in his likeness. It takes us all to make it. "I must," said one, "act my own ideal." Nobody owns one! It is common, and owns him: not possessed or originated by any person, — Jesus more than Judas; but an admitted law claiming all for its inspiration and property, repudiated by come-outers and seceders from that faith and instinct of their kind by which every renovator from Luther to Bismarck is stirred; and cutting off from which, to be agitator and destructive is all one can attain. No greatness or goodness stands alone. Teneriffe and Katahdin seem solitary, — unlike Mont Blanc, which is the last uprise of a thousand, or Mount Washington amid its cabinet of hills; but the granite of the Maine mountain joins it to the New Hampshire range, and the volcanic tufa near the African shore reaches to Madeira and Fayal. So the monuments of human genius and virtue tower from some general base. The triumphs of literature and art, in Homer and Æschylus, Shakspeare and Milton, Michel Angelo and Raphael, grew from a soil, fed on a stream, flourished in an air of congenial circumstances and favoring events, in Britain and Italy and Greece; to make such delegates to all countries of their own land, and spokesmen for the age of Elizabeth, Pericles, or the Pope. A great naturalist thinks the universe of life sprang from no single vesicle or monad, but an ocean of germs; and the human community has put forth all nobilities of private worth as leaves. O complainer of the multiplication of your kind, which samples will you reject? Your own is a specimen to be saved! *Little sinner*, we say to the babe: what *ne'er-do-well* has blossomed at last into your virtue? England, New England, Virginia, New York, shrinks from the sight of its own cradle.

Have we a natural right to vote ourselves immortal? No, we must earn our heaven, laboring with God! Continuance is the incident of immortality, truth the essence, love the assurance; and this a contribution to our conviction from our kind. The separate soul could never credit an endless life! My faith is a flower out of the stem on the stock of my race; and, without these encouraging affections, I were a helpless infidel. They teach me identity with my Source; that the world is not a whim which the Almighty after a past eternity took it into his head to make, but an expression inextricable from that being his goodness names. Love informs, when it rests in its object and does not cat-like rub round it to come back again, resembling the devotion that beats and breaks the idol which does not in danger deliver the devotee. Of that love which is the acquisition of sacrifice, time cannot rob us, nor God will. This natural communism of spiritual worth, this concrete trust in God and destiny, the Power will justify which instigated and ordained. The Fashioner forsakes not the work of his own hands. No metaphysic sponge can wipe off from the black-board of history fact or wonder which the miraculous soul begets. From my balloon, staging, or ladder, I may have to come down; but not from the elevation to which the rising spiritual continent lifts; and from that the perfect whole is the view! Youth may rejoice without the vision; but old age is dismal if it lay not hold of eternal life. "*Five minutes to the cataract*," shouted a German to an Englishman abroad, gliding down a river in his canoe. How near are we to the final plunge? We want the beaver's sense to double-line his dam against unwonted cold! By no theory or ceremony can we be guided and sustained. To know Christ's rank will be nought to breathing his love. The stained windows that make corpses of the congregation will throw no light on the last darkness. Only One, revealed within, whom we partake of, can be our Sun and Shield. To call God an Idea, some think, makes him unreal. But the Ideal is the Real. To speak of an ideal, is to speak of an imagined but not imaginary Christ. "Is not this the son of Mary?" the gaping wonderers asked. It was, and something more! Which was true, — the girl Beatrice, Dante saw in the street, or the glory in Paradise? His fancy exaggerated not, but fell short. Why did the cross I gazed at, cut with a jackknife on the unplaned board, enlarge to my eye, outshining those on cathedral spires? It was an Inner Light mixing with the beams of the sun! What makes immortality? No selfish wish. I shall be immortal if anybody wants me to be. If I am not wanted in heaven, I will not go! But God, who is my Cause, is my Causeway. Prayer is his inhalation and exhalation in my breast.

Because Jesus felt this, he is representative between both parties, and joins man with God. To call him ideal is not to deny he is personal; for ideal, real, and personal are all the same. Wind and sound, spirit and person, how he, whose life is a divine sonnet, identifies in his talk with Nicodemus! He was the *sounding* forth of the mind of Him whose own personality is the meaning of all the motion of the world; but whose word and image the whole humanity is, more than any one member, though with title of Christ; and the date of whose road and right of way to the soul what man or angel can tell? When, in some famous biography, the literal Jesus is put for the infinite God, in childish ignorance of all scholarship and science, we must needs have a new spiritual departure in religion, lest, in the yawning gulf between ecclesiasticism and common sense, the Church as a school of honesty and wisdom be swallowed up. That Ideal, insulated in no individual, is not all above, but stoops to our side. "You may," one said, "idealize your wife; but you cannot *kiss* the portrait you make." Nay, nothing *but* the portrait can you kiss! The ideal is the real woman:

the flesh and blood are but the painting or pigments with which, by the Artist, the picture is ever improved. When you put her into any act of sense she is gone! In your definition of her she dies. Only as representative of spirit is she yours. "In thee," said the expiring Bunsen to his wife, "I have loved the Eternal." That is not love for any mortal which stops short of the unseen.

Cambridge: Printed by John Wilson & Son.

www.ingramcontent.com/pod-product-compliance
Lightning Source LLC
Chambersburg PA
CBHW032317280326
41932CB00009B/844

* 9 7 8 3 7 4 4 6 5 2 8 0 3 *